MW00885981

Easy

Mediterranean

2024 Diet Cookbook for Beginners

2000+ Days Quick, Delicious & Nutritious Recipes to Help You Build Better Habits for Living and Eating Well | No-Stress 28-Day Meal Plan

Gayle M. Beveridge

Copyright© 2024 By Gayle M. Beveridge

All rights reserved worldwide.

No part of this book may be reproduced or transmitted in any form or by any means, electronic or mechanical, including photo- copying, recording or by any information storage and retrieval system, without written permission from the publisher, except for the inclusion of brief quotations in a review.

Warning-Disclaimer

The purpose of this book is to educate and entertain. The author or publisher does not guarantee that anyone following the techniques, suggestions, tips, ideas, or strategies will become successful. The author and publisher shall have neither liability or responsibility to anyone with respect to any loss or damage caused, or alleged to be caused, directly or indirectly by the information contained in this book.

Table of Contents

INTRODUCTION

Welcome to the 2024 Easy Mediterranean Diet Cookbook for Beginners, where you'll discover the vibrant and delicious flavors of the Mediterranean region. This cookbook is not just a collection of recipes, but a journey through the history, culture, and traditions of the Mediterranean.

The Mediterranean diet has been recognized as one of the healthiest in the world, with its emphasis on fresh, whole foods and an abundance of fruits, vegetables, and healthy fats. But beyond its health benefits, the Mediterranean diet is also a celebration of life. It's about gathering around a table with family and friends, sharing meals, and savoring every bite.

In this cookbook, you'll find a wide range of recipes that capture the essence of the Mediterranean. From hearty soups and stews to fresh salads and grilled seafood, each dish is bursting with flavor and nutrition. You'll also learn about the traditional cooking techniques used in the Mediterranean, such as slow-cooking, roasting, and grilling, which help to preserve the natural flavors of the ingredients.

But this cookbook is more than just a collection of recipes. It's a guide to living a healthier, more fulfilling life. By incorporating the Mediterranean diet into your daily routine, you'll not only improve your physical health but also your mental well-being. The Mediterranean way of eating is all about balance, moderation, and enjoying the simple pleasures in life.

So come join us on this culinary journey and discover the magic of the Mediterranean diet. Your taste buds (and your body) will thank you!

Explanation of the Mediterranean Diet

The Mediterranean diet is a dietary pattern that emphasizes the consumption of fresh, seasonal fruits and vegetables, whole grains, legumes, nuts, seeds, and olive oil. It also includes moderate amounts of fish, poultry, and dairy products, as well as limited amounts of red meat and processed foods. The diet is characterized by its high intake of antioxidants, fiber, and monounsaturated fats, which are believed to have a positive impact on overall health.

The Mediterranean diet is associated with a number of health benefits, including:

1. Reduced risk of chronic diseases: The diet is linked to a reduced risk of heart disease, stroke, and type 2 diabetes.

2. Lower body mass index (BMI): The diet is associated with a lower BMI, which can help prevent obesity and related health problems.

3. Improved cognitive function: The diet is linked to improved cognitive function and a lower risk of Alzheimer's disease and other forms of dementia.

4. Lower risk of certain types of cancer: The diet is associated with a lower risk of certain types of cancer, including breast, colorectal, and prostate cancer.

5. Improved mental health: The diet is linked to improved mental health, including lower rates of depression and anxiety.

6. Lower risk of age-related eye diseases: The diet is associated with a lower risk of age-related eye diseases, including macular degeneration and cataracts.

7. Lower risk of age-related cognitive decline: The diet is linked to a lower risk of age-related cognitive decline and dementia.

8. Lower risk of Parkinson's disease: The diet is associated with a lower risk of Parkinson's disease.

9. Improved gut health: The diet is associated with improved gut health, including a lower risk of inflammatory bowel disease and a higher abundance of beneficial bacteria in the gut.

10. Lower risk of chronic inflammation: The diet is associated with a lower risk of chronic inflammation, which can contribute to the development of various health conditions.

Chapter 1 History and Origins of the Mediterranean Diet

Brief History of the Mediterranean Region and Its Traditional Cuisine

The Mediterranean region has a long and rich history that dates back thousands of years. It is believed to have been inhabited by various civilizations,including the Phoenicians, Greeks, Romans, Byzantines, Arabs, and Ottomans. Each of these cultures has left their mark on the region's cuisine, which has evolved over time to become what it is today.

One of the key features of Mediterranean cuisine is its emphasis on fresh, seasonal ingredients. This is due in part to the region's climate, which allows for year-round growing conditions. The cuisine also places a strong emphasis on olive oil as a primary source of fat, as well as on legumes, nuts, and seeds for protein.

Some traditional Mediterranean dishes include:

1. Pasta alla carbonara - A pasta dish made with eggs, cheese (typically Pecorino Romano), and pancetta or guanciale.

2. Tabbouleh - A salad made with parsley, tomatoes, onions, and bulgur wheat dressed with lemon juice and olive oil.

3. Hummus - A dip made from chickpeas, tahini (sesame paste), garlic, and olive oil.

4. Moussaka - A layered casserole made with eggplant, ground meat (usually beef or lamb), tomato sauce, and béchamel sauce.

5. Baba ganoush - A roasted eggplant dip made with tahini, garlic, lemon juice, and olive oil.

6. **Couscous** - A grain dish made with couscous (semolina) and typically served with vegetables and/or meat.

7. **Falafel** - A fried ball made from ground chickpeas, herbs, and spices.

8. **Shawarma** - A sandwich made with shaved meat (usually lamb or chicken) that is marinated in a blend of spices and then grilled or roasted.

9. **Gyro** - A sandwich made with sliced meat (usually lamb) that is marinated in a blend of spices and then cooked on a vertical rotisserie.

10. **Baklava** - A sweet pastry made with layers of phyllo dough, chopped nuts (usually pistachios or walnuts), and honey syrup.

Cultural Influences on the Mediterranean Diet

The Mediterranean diet is influenced by the cultural traditions and culinary practices of the countries surrounding the Mediterranean Sea. Each country has its own unique cuisine, which reflects its history, geography, and climate.

For example, in Greece, the Mediterranean diet includes olives, feta cheese, and seafood, which are all staples of Greek cuisine. In Italy, the Mediterranean diet includes pasta, tomatoes, and olive oil, which are all integral parts of Italian cooking. In Spain, the Mediterranean diet includes paella, chorizo, and saffron, which are all traditional Spanish dishes.

In addition to these national cuisines, there are also regional variations within each country. For example, in Italy, the cuisine of the northern regions is different from that of the southern regions. Similarly, in Spain, the cuisine of Catalonia is distinct from that of Andalusia.

Furthermore, the Mediterranean diet has been influenced by the Islamic world, particularly in the Balkans and North Africa. The use of spices such as cumin, cinnamon, and turmeric is common in these regions' cuisines.

Overall, the Mediterranean diet is a reflection of the diverse cultures and culinary traditions of the countries surrounding the Mediterranean Sea.

Chapter 2 Key Principles of the Mediterranean Diet

The key principles of the Mediterranean diet are:

1. Emphasis on whole, unprocessed foods: The Mediterranean diet focuses on consuming fresh, whole foods that are minimally processed. This includes fruits, vegetables, whole grains, legumes, nuts, and seeds.

2. Use of olive oil as the primary source of fat: Olive oil is a staple in the Mediterranean diet and is used in place of other unhealthy fats like butter or vegetable oil. It is believed to have numerous health benefits due to its high concentration of monounsaturated fatty acids.

3. Incorporation of fruits, vegetables, whole grains, legumes, nuts, and seeds into meals: These foods are consumed in large quantities throughout the day and are the foundation of the Mediterranean diet. They provide essential nutrients, fiber, and antioxidants that promote good health.

4. Moderate consumption of dairy products and fish: Dairy products like cheese, yogurt, and milk are consumed in moderation, while fish is a regular part of the diet. Fish is an excellent source of protein and omega-3 fatty acids, which are important for heart health.

5. Occasional consumption of red wine in moderation: Red wine is considered a healthy beverage option in the Mediterranean diet when consumed in moderation (usually one glass per day for women and two glasses per day for men). It contains antioxidants that may reduce the risk of heart disease and certain types of cancer.

6. Reduction of red meat and processed foods: While red meat is not completely eliminated from the Mediterranean diet, it is consumed in moderation. Processed foods are generally avoided in favor of whole, unprocessed foods. This helps to reduce the intake of unhealthy fats, salt, and sugar that can contribute to chronic diseases like obesity, diabetes, and heart disease.

Why Following Mediterranean Diet

The Mediterranean diet has been shown to lower the risk of heart disease, stroke, certain types of cancer, improve brain function and reduce the risk of cognitive decline, reduce inflammation and improve gut health, manage weight and improve blood sugar.

1. Heart disease and stroke: The Mediterranean diet is high in healthy fats like omega-3 fatty acids, which help to lower blood pressure and reduce the risk of heart disease and stroke. It is also low in saturated and trans fats, which can increase cholesterol levels and contribute to heart disease.

2. Certain types of cancer: The Mediterranean diet is rich in antioxidants, which help to protect cells from damage and reduce the risk of certain types of cancer, including breast, prostate, and colon cancer.

3. Brain function and cognitive decline: The Mediterranean diet is high in omega-3 fatty acids, which are important for brain health and may help to improve cognitive function and reduce the risk of cognitive decline.

4. Inflammation: The Mediterranean diet is low in inflammatory foods like processed meats and sugary drinks, which can contribute to inflammation in the body. It is high in anti-inflammatory foods like fruits, vegetables, whole grains, and olive oil.

5. Gut health: The Mediterranean diet is high in prebiotics and probiotics, which help to improve gut health and reduce the risk of digestive disorders like irritable bowel syndrome (IBS) and diverticulitis.

6. Weight management: The Mediterranean diet is high in fiber and low in calories, which can help to manage weight and prevent obesity. It is also associated with a lower risk of type 2 diabetes, which is often linked to weight gain.

7. Blood sugar: The Mediterranean diet is high in whole grains, which are rich in complex carbohydrates that release energy slowly and help to maintain stable blood sugar levels. It is also low in simple carbohydrates like sugar and refined grains, which can cause blood sugar spikes and contribute to diabetes.

Tips for Incorporating the Mediterranean Diet into Daily Routine

The Mediterranean diet is a healthy and delicious way of eating that can be incorporated into your daily routine. Here are some tips for getting started:

1. Eat plenty of fruits and vegetables: Aim to fill half your plate with colorful, nutrient-rich produce at every meal.

2. Choose whole grains: Incorporate whole grains like brown rice, quinoa, and whole wheat bread into your meals instead of refined grains.

3. Include lean protein sources: Choose lean proteins like fish, chicken, beans, and legumes in your meals.

4. Use healthy fats: Incorporate healthy fats like olive oil, nuts, seeds, and avocado into your meals.

5. Limit red meat and processed foods: Try to limit red meat to a few times a week and avoid processed foods as much as possible.

6. Snack on nuts and seeds: Nuts and seeds are a great snack option that provide healthy fats and protein.

7. Drink plenty of water: Staying hydrated is important for overall health, so make sure to drink plenty of water throughout the day.

8. Cook at home: Cooking at home allows you to control the ingredients in your meals and ensures that you are eating a balanced diet.

9. Enjoy wine in moderation: If you choose to drink alcohol, stick to moderate amounts of red wine, which has been shown to have health benefits when consumed in moderation.

10. Practice mindful eating: Take the time to savor your food and enjoy the flavors and textures of the Mediterranean diet.

What Else Can You Do

The Mediterranean diet is not just about eating certain foods, but also about an overall healthy lifestyle. This includes regular physical activity and exercise. Here are some exercises that can be incorporated into a Mediterranean diet routine:

1. Walking: Walking is a low-impact exercise that can be done anywhere and at any time. It is a great way to incorporate physical activity into your daily routine.

2. Swimming: Swimming is a full-body workout that is easy on the joints. It is a great way to stay cool during hot summer months.

3. Cycling: Cycling is a low-impact exercise that can be done outdoors or on a stationary bike. It is a great way to explore new places while getting some exercise.

4. Yoga: Yoga is a low-impact exercise that focuses on strength, flexibility, and balance. It is a great way to reduce stress and improve overall well-being.

5. Hiking: Hiking is a great way to get some fresh air and exercise while enjoying nature. It is a low-impact exercise that can be done at any fitness level.

6. Dancing: Dancing is a fun way to get some exercise while listening to music. It is a great way to socialize and meet new people.

7. Group sports: Joining a group sport like soccer, basketball, or tennis is a great way to stay active and meet new people.

Remember, it's important to find an exercise routine that you enjoy and can stick to in the long term. The key is to make physical activity a part of your daily routine, rather than something you only do occasionally.

28-Day Meal Plan

DAYS	BREAKFAST	LUNCH	DINNER	SNACK/DESSERT
1	Smoky Sausage Patties 10	Herbed Polenta 31	Tortellini in Red Pepper Sauce 59	Eggplant Fries 90
2	Spinach Pie 10	Tomato Rice 27	Stuffed Pepper Stew 60	Garlic Edamame 86
3	Berry Warming Smoothie 11	Garlicky Split Chickpea Curry 28	Crustless Spinach Cheese Pie 62	Sweet Potato Fries 91
4	Mashed Chickpea, Feta, and Avocado Toast 11	Lentils with Artichoke, Tomato, and Feta 28	Roasted Portobello Mushrooms with Kale and Red Onion 60	Savory Mackerel & Goat'S Cheese "Paradox" Balls 86
5	Harissa Shakshuka with Bell Peppers and Tomatoes 11	Pesto Rice with Olives and Goat Cheese 29	Quinoa Lentil "Meatballs" with Quick Tomato Sauce 61	Charred Eggplant Dip with Feta and Mint
6	Savory Zucchini Muffins 14	Couscous with Apricots 29	Cheese Stuffed Zucchini 61	Roasted Rosemary Olives 90
7	Grilled Halloumi with Whole-Wheat Pita Bread 15	White Bean Cassoulet 32	Farro with Roasted Tomatoes and Mushrooms 63	Mediterranean Mini Spinach Quiche 86
8	Spanish Tuna Tortilla with Roasted Peppers 16	Lemon Orzo with Fresh Herbs 29	Moroccan Vegetable Tagine 61	Burrata Caprese Stack 89
9	Ricotta and Fruit Bruschetta 12	Spanish Rice 27	Spinach-Artichoke Stuffed Mushrooms 64	Salted Almonds 89
10	Crostini with Smoked Trout 13	Mediterranean Lentils and Rice 29	Mediterranean Pan Pizza 64	Sfougato 87
11	Lemon–Olive Oil Breakfast Cakes with Berry Syrup 13	Baked Tofu with Sun-Dried Tomatoes and Artichokes 60	Warm Fennel, Cherry Tomato, and Spinach Salad 73	Herbed Labneh Vegetable Parfaits 87
12	Egg and Pepper Pita 11	Crustless Spanakopita 63	No-Mayo Florence Tuna Salad 77	Lemony Olives and Feta Medley 87
13	Quinoa Porridge with Apricots 13	Vegetable Burgers 62	Tossed Green Mediterranean Salad 72	Marinated Olives 87
14	Blueberry-Banana Bowl with Quinoa 10	Broccoli-Cheese Fritters 62	Arugula and Fennel Salad with Fresh Basil 73	Sweet Potato Hummus 88
15	Oat and Fruit Parfait 13	Grilled Eggplant Stacks 62	Grain-Free Kale Tabbouleh 73	Greek Island Almond Cocoa Bites 65
16	Greek Egg and Tomato Scramble 14	Caprese Eggplant Stacks 64	Orange-Tarragon Chicken Salad Wrap 74	Fruit with Mint and Crème Fraîche 66

DAYS	BREAKFAST	LUNCH	DINNER	SNACK/DESSERT
17	Blender Cinnamon Pancakes with Cacao Cream Topping 15	Cauliflower Steaks with Olive Citrus Sauce 64	Arugula Salad with Grapes, Goat Cheese, and Za'atar Croutons 77	Ricotta with Balsamic Cherries and Black Pepper
18	Spinach and Mushroom Mini Quiche 16	Broccoli Crust Pizza	Pear-Fennel Salad with Pomegranate 74	Red Grapefruit Granita 66
19	Spinach, Sun-Dried Tomato, and Feta Egg Wraps 12	Cauliflower Steaks with Olive Citrus Sauce 64	Italian Summer Vegetable Barley Salad 72	Chocolate-Dipped Fruit Bites 66
20	Amaranth Breakfast Bowl with Chocolate and Almonds 15	Herbed Ricotta–Stuffed Mushrooms 63	Panzanella (Tuscan Tomato and Bread Salad) 74	Grilled Pineapple and Melon 69
21	Kagianas 12	Sicilian Salad 72	Black Chickpeas 30	Fruit Compote 70
22	Garlic Scrambled Eggs with Basil 12	Peachy Tomato Salad 77	Greek-Style Pea Casserole 27	Cherry-Stuffed Apples 69
23	Berry Breakfast Smoothie 15	Flank Steak Spinach Salad 76	Domatorizo (Greek Tomato Rice) 32	Frozen Raspberry Delight 70
24	Avocado Toast with Smoked Trout 17	Wild Greens Salad with Fresh Herbs 75	Lentils with Cilantro and Lime 31	Apricot and Mint No-Bake Parfait 67
25	Quickie Honey Nut Granola 14	Valencia-Inspired Salad 75	Lentil and Zucchini Boats 30	Blueberry Pomegranate Granita 65
26	Peachy Green Smoothie 17	Superfood Salmon Salad Bowl 75	Wild Mushroom Farrotto 28	Lemon Coconut Cake 67
27	Tortilla Española (Spanish Omelet) 16	Traditional Greek Salad 76	Moroccan Vegetables and Chickpeas 32	Chocolate Turtle Hummus 66
28	Garden Scramble 17	Tuna Niçoise 73	Risotto Primavera	S'mores 67

Smoky Sausage Patties

Prep time: 30 minutes | Cook time: 9 minutes | Serves 8

- 1 pound (454 g) ground pork
- 1 tablespoon coconut aminos
- 2 teaspoons liquid smoke
- 1 teaspoon dried sage
- 1 teaspoon sea salt
- ½ teaspoon fennel seeds
- ½ teaspoon dried thyme
- ½ teaspoon freshly ground black pepper
- ¼ teaspoon cayenne pepper

1. In a large bowl, combine the pork, coconut aminos, liquid smoke, sage, salt, fennel seeds, thyme, black pepper, and cayenne pepper. Work the meat with your hands until the seasonings are fully incorporated. 2. Shape the mixture into 8 equal-size patties. Using your thumb, make a dent in the center of each patty. Place the patties on a plate and cover with plastic wrap. Refrigerate the patties for at least 30 minutes. 3. Working in batches if necessary, place the patties in a single layer in the air fryer, being careful not to overcrowd them. 4. Set the air fryer to 400ºF (204ºC) and air fry for 5 minutes. Flip and cook for about 4 minutes more.

Per Serving:
calories: 70 | fat: 2g | protein: 12g | carbs: 0g | fiber: 0g | sodium: 329mg

Spinach Pie

Prep time: 10 minutes | Cook time: 25 minutes | Serves 8

- Nonstick cooking spray
- 2 tablespoons extra-virgin olive oil
- 1 onion, chopped
- 1 pound (454 g) frozen spinach, thawed
- ¼ teaspoon garlic salt
- ¼ teaspoon freshly ground black pepper
- ¼ teaspoon ground nutmeg
- 4 large eggs, divided
- 1 cup grated Parmesan cheese, divided
- 2 puff pastry doughs, (organic, if available), at room temperature
- 4 hard-boiled eggs, halved

1. Preheat the oven to 350°F(180°C). Spray a baking sheet with nonstick cooking spray and set aside. 2. Heat a large sauté pan or skillet over medium-high heat. Put in the oil and onion and cook for about 5 minutes, until translucent. 3. Squeeze the excess water from the spinach, then add to the pan and cook, uncovered, so that any excess water from the spinach can evaporate. Add the garlic salt, pepper, and nutmeg. Remove from heat and set aside to cool. 4. In a small bowl, crack 3 eggs and mix well. Add the eggs and ½ cup Parmesan cheese to the cooled spinach mix. 5. On the prepared baking sheet, roll out the pastry dough. Layer the spinach mix on top of dough, leaving 2 inches around each edge. 6. Once the spinach is spread onto the pastry dough, place hard-boiled egg halves evenly throughout the pie, then cover with the second pastry dough. Pinch the edges closed. 7. Crack the remaining egg in a small bowl and mix well. Brush the egg wash over the pastry dough. 8. Bake for 15 to 20 minutes, until golden brown and warmed through.

Per Serving:
calories: 417 | fat: 28g | protein: 17g | carbs: 25g | fiber: 3g | sodium: 490mg

Blueberry-Banana Bowl with Quinoa

Prep time: 5 minutes | Cook time: 20 minutes | Serves 4

- 1½ cups water
- ¾ cup uncooked quinoa, rinsed
- 2 tablespoons honey, divided
- 1 cup blueberries (preferably frozen)
- 2 bananas (preferably frozen), sliced
- ½ cup sliced almonds or crushed walnuts
- ½ cup dried cranberries
- 1 cup granola
- 1 cup milk or nondairy milk of your choice

1. Combine the water and quinoa in a medium saucepan. Bring to a boil over medium-high heat, cover, reduce the heat to low, and simmer for 15 to 20 minutes, until the water has been absorbed. Remove from the heat and fluff the quinoa with a fork. 2. Evenly divide the quinoa among four bowls, about ½ cup for each bowl. Evenly divide the honey among the bowls and mix it in well. Top evenly with the blueberries, bananas, almonds, cranberries, granola, and milk. Serve.

Per Serving:
calories: 469 | fat: 15g | protein: 12g | carbs: 77g | fiber: 9g | sodium: 31mg

Egg and Pepper Pita

Prep time: 10 minutes | Cook time: 10 minutes | Serves 4

- 2 pita breads
- 2 tablespoons olive oil
- 1 red or yellow bell pepper, diced
- 2 zucchini, quartered lengthwise and sliced
- 4 large eggs, beaten
- Sea salt
- Freshly ground black pepper
- Pinch dried oregano
- 2 avocados, sliced
- ½ to ¾ cup crumbled feta cheese
- 2 tablespoons chopped scallion, green part only, for garnish
- Hot sauce, for serving

1. In a large skillet, heat the pitas over medium heat until warmed through and lightly toasted, about 2 minutes. Remove the pitas from the skillet and set aside. 2. In the same skillet, heat the olive oil over medium heat. Add the bell pepper and zucchini and sauté for 4 to 5 minutes. Add the eggs and season with salt, black pepper, and the oregano. Cook, stirring, for 2 to 3 minutes, until the eggs are cooked through. Remove from the heat. 3. Slice the pitas in half crosswise and fill each half with the egg mixture. Divide the avocado and feta among the pita halves. Garnish with the scallion and serve with hot sauce.

Per Serving:
calories: 476 | fat: 31g | protein: 17g | carbs: 36g | fiber: 11g | sodium: 455mg

Harissa Shakshuka with Bell Peppers and Tomatoes

Prep time: 10 minutes | Cook time: 20 minutes | Serves 4

- 1½ tablespoons extra-virgin olive oil
- 2 tablespoons harissa
- 1 tablespoon tomato paste
- ½ onion, diced
- 1 bell pepper, seeded and diced
- 3 garlic cloves, minced
- 1 (28-ounce / 794-g) can no-salt-added diced tomatoes
- ½ teaspoon kosher salt
- 4 large eggs
- 2 to 3 tablespoons fresh basil, chopped or cut into ribbons

1. Preheat the oven to 375°F (190°C). 2. Heat the olive oil in a 12-inch cast-iron pan or ovenproof skillet over medium heat. Add the harissa, tomato paste, onion, and bell pepper; sauté for 3 to 4 minutes. Add the garlic and cook until fragrant, about 30 seconds. Add the diced tomatoes and salt and simmer for about 10 minutes. 3. Make 4 wells in the sauce and gently break 1 egg into each. Transfer to the oven and bake until the whites are cooked and the yolks are set, 10 to 12 minutes. 4. Allow to cool for 3 to 5 minutes, garnish with the basil, and carefully spoon onto plates.

Per Serving:
calories: 190 | fat: 10g | protein: 9g | carbs: 15g | fiber: 4g | sodium: 255mg

Berry Warming Smoothie

Prep time: 5 minutes | Cook time: 0 minutes | Serves 1

- ⅔ cup plain kefir or plain yogurt
- ½ cup frozen mixed berries
- ½ cup baby spinach
- ½ cup cucumber, chopped
- 2 tablespoons unsweetened shredded coconut
- ¼ teaspoon grated ginger
- ¼ teaspoon ground cinnamon
- ¼ teaspoon ground nutmeg
- ⅛ teaspoon ground cardamom
- ¼ teaspoon vanilla extract (optional)

1. In a blender or Vitamix, add all the ingredients. Blend to combine.

Per Serving:
calories: 165 | fat: 7g | protein: 7g | carbs: 20g | fiber: 4g | sodium: 100mg

Mashed Chickpea, Feta, and Avocado Toast

Prep time: 10 minutes |Cook time: 0 minutes| Serves: 4

- 1 (15-ounce / 425-g) can chickpeas, drained and rinsed
- 1 avocado, pitted
- ½ cup diced feta cheese (about 2 ounces / 57 g)
- 2 teaspoons freshly squeezed
- lemon juice or 1 tablespoon orange juice
- ½ teaspoon freshly ground black pepper
- 4 pieces multigrain toast
- 2 teaspoons honey

1. Put the chickpeas in a large bowl. Scoop the avocado flesh into the bowl. 2. With a potato masher or large fork, mash the ingredients together until the mix has a spreadable consistency. It doesn't need to be totally smooth. 3. Add the feta, lemon juice, and pepper, and mix well. 4. Evenly divide the mash onto the four pieces of toast and spread with a knife. Drizzle with honey and serve.

Per Serving:
calories: 301 | fat: 14g | protein: 12g | carbs: 35g | fiber: 11g | sodium: 450mg

Spinach, Sun-Dried Tomato, and Feta Egg Wraps

Prep time: 10 minutes | Cook time: 7 minutes | Serves 2

- 1 tablespoon olive oil
- ¼ cup minced onion
- 3 to 4 tablespoons minced sun-dried tomatoes in olive oil and herbs
- 3 large eggs, beaten
- 1½ cups packed baby spinach
- 1 ounce (28 g) crumbled feta cheese
- Salt
- 2 (8-inch) whole-wheat tortillas

1. In a large skillet, heat the olive oil over medium-high heat. Add the onion and tomatoes and sauté for about 3 minutes. 2. Turn the heat down to medium. Add the beaten eggs and stir to scramble them. 3. Add the spinach and stir to combine. Sprinkle the feta cheese over the eggs. Add salt to taste. 4. Warm the tortillas in the microwave for about 20 seconds each. 5. Fill each tortilla with half of the egg mixture. Fold in half or roll them up and serve.

Per Serving:

calories: 435 | fat: 28g | protein: 17g | carbs: 31g | fiber: 6g | sodium: 552mg

Kagianas

Prep time: 5 minutes | Cook time: 10 minutes | Serves 2

- 2 teaspoons extra virgin olive oil
- 2 tablespoons finely chopped onion (any variety)
- ¼ teaspoon fine sea salt, divided
- 1 medium tomato (any variety), chopped
- 2 eggs
- 1 ounce (28 g) crumbled feta
- ½ teaspoon dried oregano
- 1 teaspoon chopped fresh mint
- Pinch of freshly ground black pepper for serving

1. Heat the olive oil in a small pan placed over medium heat. When the oil begins to shimmer, add the onions along with ⅛ teaspoon sea salt. Sauté for about 3 minutes or until the onions are soft. 2. Add the tomatoes, stir, then reduce the heat to low and simmer for 8 minutes or until the mixture thickens. 3. While the tomatoes are cooking, beat the eggs in a small bowl. 4. When the tomatoes have thickened, pour the eggs into the pan and increase the heat to medium. Continue cooking, using a spatula to stir the eggs and tomatoes continuously, for 2–3 minutes or until the eggs are set. Remove the pan from the heat. 5. Add the feta, oregano, and mint, and stir to combine. 6. Transfer to a plate. Top with a pinch of black pepper and the remaining ⅛ teaspoon sea salt. Serve promptly.

Per Serving:

calories: 156 | fat: 12g | protein: 8g | carbs: 4g | fiber: 1g | sodium: 487mg

Garlic Scrambled Eggs with Basil

Prep time: 5 minutes | Cook time: 5 minutes | Serves 2

- 4 large eggs
- 2 tablespoons finely chopped fresh basil
- 2 tablespoons grated Gruyère cheese
- 1 tablespoon cream
- 1 tablespoon olive oil
- 2 cloves garlic, minced
- Sea salt and freshly ground pepper, to taste

1. In a large bowl, beat together the eggs, basil, cheese, and cream with a whisk until just combined. 2. Heat the oil in a large, heavy nonstick skillet over medium-low heat. Add the garlic and cook until golden, about 1 minute. 3. Pour the egg mixture into the skillet over the garlic. Work the eggs continuously and cook until fluffy and soft. 4. Season with sea salt and freshly ground pepper to taste. Divide between 2 plates and serve immediately.

Per Serving:

calories: 267 | fat: 21g | protein: 16g | carbs: 3g | fiber: 0g | sodium: 394mg

Ricotta and Fruit Bruschetta

Prep time: 5 minutes | Cook time: 0 minutes | Serves 2

- ¼ cup full-fat ricotta cheese
- 1½ teaspoons honey, divided
- 3 drops almond extract
- 2 slices whole-grain bread, toasted
- ½ medium banana, peeled
- and cut into ¼-inch slices
- ½ medium pear (any variety), thinly sliced
- 2 teaspoons chopped walnuts
- 2 pinches of ground cinnamon

1. In a small bowl, combine the ricotta, ¼ teaspoon honey, and the almond extract. Stir well. 2. Spread 1½ tablespoons of the ricotta mixture over each slice of toast. 3. Divide the pear slices and banana slices equally on top of each slice of toast. 4. Drizzle equal amounts of the remaining honey over each slice, and sprinkle 1 teaspoon of the walnuts over each slice. Top each serving with a pinch of cinnamon.

Per Serving:

calories: 207 | fat: 7g | protein: 8g | carbs: 30g | fiber: 4g | sodium: 162mg

Crostini with Smoked Trout

Prep time: 10 minutes | Cook time: 5 minutes | Serves 4

- ½ French baguette, cut into 1-inch-thick slices
- 1 tablespoon olive oil
- ¼ teaspoon onion powder
- 1 (4-ounce / 113-g) can

- smoked trout
- ¼ cup crème fraîche
- ¼ teaspoon chopped fresh dill, for garnish

1. Drizzle the bread on both sides with the olive oil and sprinkle with the onion powder. 2. Place the bread in a single layer in a large skillet and toast over medium heat until lightly browned on both sides, 3 to 4 minutes total. 3. Transfer the toasted bread to a serving platter and place 1 or 2 pieces of the trout on each slice. Top with the crème fraîche, garnish with the dill, and serve immediately.

Per Serving:

calories: 206 | fat: 10g | protein: 13g | carbs: 15g | fiber: 1g | sodium: 350mg

Lemon–Olive Oil Breakfast Cakes with Berry Syrup

Prep time: 5 minutes | Cook time: 10 minutes | Serves 4

For the Pancakes:
- 1 cup almond flour
- 1 teaspoon baking powder
- ¼ teaspoon salt
- 6 tablespoon extra-virgin olive oil, divided

- 2 large eggs
- Zest and juice of 1 lemon
- ½ teaspoon almond or vanilla extract

For the Berry Sauce:
- 1 cup frozen mixed berries
- 1 tablespoon water or lemon

- juice, plus more if needed
- ½ teaspoon vanilla extract

Make the Pancakes: 1. In a large bowl, combine the almond flour, baking powder, and salt and whisk to break up any clumps. 2. Add the 4 tablespoons olive oil, eggs, lemon zest and juice, and almond extract and whisk to combine well. 3. In a large skillet, heat 1 tablespoon of olive oil and spoon about 2 tablespoons of batter for each of 4 pancakes. Cook until bubbles begin to form, 4 to 5 minutes, and flip. Cook another 2 to 3 minutes on second side. Repeat with remaining 1 tablespoon olive oil and batter. Make the Berry Sauce 1. In a small saucepan, heat the frozen berries, water, and vanilla extract over medium-high for 3 to 4 minutes, until bubbly, adding more water if mixture is too thick. Using the back of a spoon or fork, mash the berries and whisk until smooth.

Per Serving:

calories: 381 | fat: 35g | protein: 8g | carbs: 12g | fiber: 4g | sodium: 183mg

Quinoa Porridge with Apricots

Prep time: 10 minutes | Cook time: 12 minutes | Serves 4

- 1½ cups quinoa, rinsed and drained
- 1 cup chopped dried apricots
- 2½ cups water

- 1 cup almond milk
- 1 tablespoon rose water
- ½ teaspoon cardamom
- ¼ teaspoon salt

1. Place all ingredients in the Instant Pot®. Stir to combine. Close lid, set steam release to Sealing, press the Rice button, and set time to 12 minutes. When the timer beeps, let pressure release naturally, about 20 minutes. 2. Press the Cancel button, open lid, and fluff quinoa with a fork. Serve warm.

Per Serving:

calories: 197 | fat: 2g | protein: 3g | carbs: 44g | fiber: 4g | sodium: 293mg

Oat and Fruit Parfait

Prep time: 5 minutes | Cook time: 12 minutes | Serves 2

- ½ cup whole-grain rolled or quickcooking oats (not instant)
- ½ cup walnut pieces
- 1 teaspoon honey

- 1 cup sliced fresh strawberries
- 1½ cups vanilla low-fat Greek yogurt
- Fresh mint leaves for garnish

1. Preheat the oven to 300°F(150°C). 2. Spread the oats and walnuts in a single layer on a baking sheet. 3. Toast the oats and nuts just until you begin to smell the nuts, 10 to 12 minutes. Remove the pan from the oven and set aside. 4. In a small microwave-safe bowl, heat the honey just until warm, about 30 seconds. Add the strawberries and stir to coat. 5. Place 1 tablespoon of the strawberries in the bottom of each of 2 dessert dishes or 8-ounce glasses. Add a portion of yogurt and then a portion of oats and repeat the layers until the containers are full, ending with the berries. Serve immediately or chill until ready to eat.

Per Serving:

calories: 541 | fat: 25g | protein: 21g | carbs: 66g | fiber: 8g | sodium: 124mg

Greek Egg and Tomato Scramble

Prep time: 10 minutes | Cook time: 25 minutes | Serves 4

- ¼ cup extra-virgin olive oil, divided
- 1½ cups chopped fresh tomatoes
- ¼ cup finely minced red onion
- 2 garlic cloves, minced
- ½ teaspoon dried oregano or 1 to 2 teaspoons chopped fresh oregano
- ½ teaspoon dried thyme or 1 to 2 teaspoons chopped fresh thyme
- 8 large eggs
- ½ teaspoon salt
- ¼ teaspoon freshly ground black pepper
- ¾ cup crumbled feta cheese
- ¼ cup chopped fresh mint leaves

1. In large skillet, heat the olive oil over medium heat. Add the chopped tomatoes and red onion and sauté until tomatoes are cooked through and soft, 10 to 12 minutes. 2. Add the garlic, oregano, and thyme and sauté another 2 to 4 minutes, until fragrant and liquid has reduced. 3. In a medium bowl, whisk together the eggs, salt, and pepper until well combined. 4. Add the eggs to the skillet, reduce the heat to low, and scramble until set and creamy, using a spatula to move them constantly, 3 to 4 minutes. Remove the skillet from the heat, stir in the feta and mint, and serve warm.

Per Serving:
calories: 355 | fat: 29g | protein: 17g | carbs: 6g | fiber: 1g | sodium: 695mg

Savory Zucchini Muffins

Prep time: 10 minutes | Cook time: 35 minutes | Serves 13

- 1 tablespoon extra virgin olive oil plus extra for brushing
- 2 medium zucchini, grated
- ⅛ teaspoon fine sea salt
- 1 large egg, lightly beaten
- 1½ ounces (43 g) crumbled feta
- ¼ medium onion (any variety), finely chopped
- 1 tablespoon chopped fresh parsley
- 1 tablespoon chopped fresh dill
- 1 tablespoon chopped fresh mint
- ¼ teaspoon freshly ground black pepper
- 3 tablespoons unseasoned breadcrumbs
- 1 tablespoon grated Parmesan cheese

1. Preheat the oven to 400°F (205°C), and line a medium muffin pan with 6 muffin liners. Lightly brush the bottoms of the liners with olive oil. 2. Place the grated zucchini in a colander and sprinkle with the sea salt. Set aside for 10 minutes to allow the salt to penetrate. 3. Remove the zucchini from the colander, and place it on a tea towel. Pull the edges of the towel in and then twist and squeeze the towel to remove as much of the water from the zucchini as possible. (This will prevent the muffins from becoming soggy.) 4. In a large bowl, combine the egg, feta, onions, parsley, dill, mint, pepper, and the remaining tablespoon of olive oil. Mix well, and add the zucchini to the bowl. Mix again, and add the breadcrumbs. Use a fork to mash the ingredients until well combined. 5. Divide the mixture among the prepared muffins liners and then sprinkle ½ teaspoon grated Parmesan over each muffin. Transfer to the oven, and bake for 35 minutes or until the muffins turn golden brown. 6. When the baking time is complete, remove the muffins from the oven and set aside to cool for 5 minutes before removing from the pan. Store in an airtight container in the refrigerator for 3 days, or tightly wrap individual muffins in plastic wrap and freeze for up to 3 months.

Per Serving:
calories: 39 | fat: 2g | protein: 2g | carbs: 3g | fiber: 1g | sodium: 80mg

Quickie Honey Nut Granola

Prep time: 10 minutes |Cook time: 20 minutes| Serves: 6

- 2½ cups regular rolled oats
- ⅓ cup coarsely chopped almonds
- ⅛ teaspoon kosher or sea salt
- ½ teaspoon ground cinnamon
- ½ cup chopped dried apricots
- 2 tablespoons ground flaxseed
- ¼ cup honey
- ¼ cup extra-virgin olive oil
- 2 teaspoons vanilla extract

1. Preheat the oven to 325°F(165°C). Line a large, rimmed baking sheet with parchment paper. 2. In a large skillet, combine the oats, almonds, salt, and cinnamon. Turn the heat to medium-high and cook, stirring often, to toast, about 6 minutes. 3. While the oat mixture is toasting, in a microwave-safe bowl, combine the apricots, flaxseed, honey, and oil. Microwave on high for about 1 minute, or until very hot and just beginning to bubble. (Or heat these ingredients in a small saucepan over medium heat for about 3 minutes.) 4. Stir the vanilla into the honey mixture, then pour it over the oat mixture in the skillet. Stir well. 5. Spread out the granola on the prepared baking sheet. Bake for 15 minutes, until lightly browned. Remove from the oven and cool completely. 6. Break the granola into small pieces, and store in an airtight container in the refrigerator for up to 2 weeks (if it lasts that long!).

Per Serving:
calories: 449 | fat: 17g | protein: 13g | carbs: 64g | fiber: 9g | sodium: 56mg

Blender Cinnamon Pancakes with Cacao Cream Topping

Prep time: 10 minutes | Cook time: 10 minutes | Serves 4

Cinnamon Pancakes:
- 2 cups pecans
- 4 large eggs
- 1 tablespoon cinnamon
- ½ teaspoon baking soda

Cacao Cream Topping:
- 1 cup coconut cream
- 1½ tablespoons raw cacao powder
- Optional: low-carb sweetener, to taste
- 1 teaspoon fresh lemon juice or apple cider vinegar
- 1 tablespoon virgin coconut oil or ghee

To Serve:
- 9 medium strawberries, sliced
- 1 tablespoon unsweetened shredded coconut

1. To make the pancakes: Place the pecans in a blender and process until powdered. Add all of the remaining ingredients apart from the ghee. Blend again until smooth. 2. Place a nonstick pan greased with 1 teaspoon of the coconut oil over low heat. Using a ¼-cup (60 ml) measure per pancake, cook in batches of 2 to 3 small pancakes over low heat until bubbles begin to form on the pancakes. Use a spatula to flip over, then cook for 30 to 40 seconds and place on a plate. Grease the pan with more coconut oil between batches. Transfer the pancakes to a plate. 3. To make the cacao cream topping: Place the coconut cream in a bowl. Add the cacao powder and sweetener, if using. Whisk until well combined and creamy. 4. Serve the pancakes with the cacao cream, sliced strawberries and a sprinkle of shredded coconut. You can enhance the flavor of the shredded coconut by toasting it in a dry pan for about 1 minute.

Per Serving:

calories: 665 | fat: 65g | protein: 14g | carbs: 17g | fiber: 9g | sodium: 232mg

Amaranth Breakfast Bowl with Chocolate and Almonds

Prep time: 10 minutes | Cook time: 6 minutes | Serves 6

- 2 cups amaranth, rinsed and drained
- 2 cups almond milk
- 2 cups water
- ¼ cup maple syrup
- 3 tablespoons cocoa powder
- 1 teaspoon vanilla extract
- ¼ teaspoon salt
- ½ cup toasted sliced almonds
- ⅓ cup miniature semisweet chocolate chips

1. Place amaranth, almond milk, water, maple syrup, cocoa powder, vanilla, and salt in the Instant Pot®. Stir to combine. Close lid, set steam release to Sealing, press the Rice button, and set time to 6 minutes. When the timer beeps, quick-release the pressure until the float valve drops, press the Cancel button, open lid, and stir well. 2. Serve hot, topped with almonds and chocolate chips.

Per Serving:

calories: 263 | fat: 12g | protein: 5g | carbs: 35g | fiber: 5g | sodium: 212mg

Berry Breakfast Smoothie

Prep time: 5 minutes | Cook time: 0 minutes | Serves 1

- ½ cup vanilla low-fat Greek yogurt
- ¼ cup low-fat milk
- ½ cup fresh or frozen
- blueberries or strawberries (or a combination)
- 6 to 8 ice cubes

1. Place the Greek yogurt, milk, and berries in a blender and blend until the berries are liquefied. Add the ice cubes and blend on high until thick and smooth. Serve immediately.

Per Serving:

calories: 158 | fat: 3g | protein: 9g | carbs: 25g | fiber: 1g | sodium: 110mg

Grilled Halloumi with Whole-Wheat Pita Bread

Prep time: 5 minutes | Cook time: 10 minutes | Serves 4

- 2 teaspoons olive oil
- 8 (½-inch-thick) slices of halloumi cheese
- 4 whole-wheat pita rounds
- 1 Persian cucumber, thinly sliced
- 1 large tomato, sliced
- ½ cup pitted Kalamata olives

1. Brush a bit of olive oil on a grill pan and heat it over medium-high heat. 2. Brush the cheese slices all over with olive oil. Add the cheese slices in a single layer and cook until grill marks appear on the bottom, about 3 minutes. Flip the slices over and grill until grill marks appear on the second side, about 2 to 3 minutes more. 3. While the cheese is cooking, heat the pita bread, either in a skillet or in a toaster. 4. Serve the cheese inside of the pita pockets with the sliced cucumber, tomato, and olives.

Per Serving:

calories: 358 | fat: 24g | protein: 17g | carbs: 21g | fiber: 4g | sodium: 612mg

Spanish Tuna Tortilla with Roasted Peppers

Prep time: 15 minutes | Cook time: 15 minutes | Serves 4

- 6 large eggs
- ¼ cup olive oil
- 2 small russet potatoes, diced
- 1 small onion, chopped
- 1 roasted red bell pepper, sliced
- 1 (7-ounce / 198-g) can tuna packed in water, drained well and flaked
- 2 plum tomatoes, seeded and diced
- 1 teaspoon dried tarragon

1. Preheat the broiler on high. 2. Crack the eggs in a large bowl and whisk them together until just combined. Heat the olive oil in a large, oven-safe, nonstick or cast-iron skillet over medium-low heat. 3. Add the potatoes and cook until slightly soft, about 7 minutes. Add the onion and the peppers and cook until soft, 3–5 minutes. 4. Add the tuna, tomatoes, and tarragon to the skillet and stir to combine, then add the eggs. 5. Cook for 7–10 minutes until the eggs are bubbling from the bottom and the bottom is slightly brown. 6. Place the skillet into the oven on 1 of the first 2 racks, and cook until the middle is set and the top is slightly brown. 7. Slice into wedges and serve warm or at room temperature.

Per Serving:

calories: 247 | fat: 14g | protein: 12g | carbs: 19g | fiber: 2g | sodium: 130mg

Tortilla Española (Spanish Omelet)

Prep time: 10 minutes | Cook time: 40 minutes | Serves 4

- 1½ pounds (680 g) Yukon gold potatoes, scrubbed and thinly sliced
- 3 tablespoons olive oil, divided
- 1 teaspoon kosher salt, divided
- 1 sweet white onion, thinly sliced
- 3 cloves garlic, minced
- 8 eggs
- ½ teaspoon ground black pepper

1. Preheat the oven to 350°F(180°C). Line 2 baking sheets with parchment paper. 2. In a large bowl, toss the potatoes with 1 tablespoon of the oil and ½ teaspoon of the salt until well coated. Spread over the 2 baking sheets in a single layer. Roast the potatoes, rotating the baking sheets halfway through cooking, until tender but not browned, about 15 minutes. Using a spatula, remove the potatoes from the baking sheets and let cool until warm. 3. Meanwhile, in a medium skillet over medium-low heat, cook the onion in 1 tablespoon of the oil, stirring, until soft and golden, about 10 minutes. Add the garlic and cook until fragrant, about 2 minutes. Transfer the onion and garlic to a plate and let cool until warm. 4. In a large bowl, beat the eggs, pepper, and the remaining ½ teaspoon salt vigorously until the yolks and whites are completely combined and slightly frothy. Stir in the potatoes and onion and garlic and combine well, being careful not to break too many potatoes. 5. In the same skillet over medium-high heat, warm the remaining 1 tablespoon oil until shimmering, swirling to cover the whole surface. Pour in the egg mixture and spread the contents evenly. Cook for 1 minute and reduce the heat to medium-low. Cook until the edges of the egg are set and the center is slightly wet, about 8 minutes. Using a spatula, nudge the omelet to make sure it moves freely in the skillet. 6. Place a rimless plate, the size of the skillet, over the omelet. Place one hand over the plate and, in a swift motion, flip the omelet onto the plate. Slide the omelet back into the skillet, cooked side up. Cook until completely set, a toothpick inserted into the middle comes out clean, about 6 minutes. 7. Transfer to a serving plate and let cool for 5 minutes. Serve warm or room temperature.

Per Serving:

calories: 376 | fat: 19g | protein: 15g | carbs: 37g | fiber: 5g | sodium: 724mg

Spinach and Mushroom Mini Quiche

Prep time: 10 minutes | Cook time: 15 minutes | Serves 4

- 1 teaspoon olive oil, plus more for spraying
- 1 cup coarsely chopped mushrooms
- 1 cup fresh baby spinach, shredded
- 4 eggs, beaten
- ½ cup shredded Cheddar cheese
- ½ cup shredded Mozzarella cheese
- ¼ teaspoon salt
- ¼ teaspoon black pepper

1. Spray 4 silicone baking cups with olive oil and set aside. 2. In a medium sauté pan over medium heat, warm 1 teaspoon of olive oil. Add the mushrooms and sauté until soft, 3 to 4 minutes. 3. Add the spinach and cook until wilted, 1 to 2 minutes. Set aside. 4. In a medium bowl, whisk together the eggs, Cheddar cheese, Mozzarella cheese, salt, and pepper. 5. Gently fold the mushrooms and spinach into the egg mixture. 6. Pour ¼ of the mixture into each silicone baking cup. 7. Place the baking cups into the air fryer basket and air fry at 350°F (177°C) for 5 minutes. Stir the mixture in each ramekin slightly and air fry until the egg has set, an additional 3 to 5 minutes.

Per Serving:

calories: 156 | fat: 10g | protein: 14g | carbs: 2g | fiber: 1g | sodium: 411mg

Smoked Salmon Egg Scramble with Dill and Chives

Prep time: 5 minutes | Cook time: 5 minutes | Serves 2

- 4 large eggs
- 1 tablespoon milk
- 1 tablespoon fresh chives, minced
- 1 tablespoon fresh dill, minced
- ¼ teaspoon kosher salt
- ⅛ teaspoon freshly ground black pepper
- 2 teaspoons extra-virgin olive oil
- 2 ounces (57 g) smoked salmon, thinly sliced

1. In a large bowl, whisk together the eggs, milk, chives, dill, salt, and pepper. 2. Heat the olive oil in a medium skillet or sauté pan over medium heat. Add the egg mixture and cook for about 3 minutes, stirring occasionally. 3. Add the salmon and cook until the eggs are set but moist, about 1 minute.

Per Serving:
calories: 325 | fat: 26g | protein: 23g | carbs: 1g | fiber: 0g | sodium: 455mg

Garden Scramble

Prep time: 10 minutes | Cook time: 10 minutes | Serves 4

- 1 teaspoon extra-virgin olive oil
- ½ cup diced yellow squash
- ½ cup diced green bell pepper
- ¼ cup diced sweet white onion
- 6 cherry tomatoes, halved
- 1 tablespoon chopped fresh basil
- 1 tablespoon chopped fresh parsley
- ½ teaspoon salt
- ¼ teaspoon freshly ground black pepper
- 8 large eggs, beaten

1. In a large nonstick skillet, heat the olive oil over medium heat. Add the squash, pepper, and onion and sauté until the onion is translucent, 3 to 4 minutes. 2. Add the tomatoes, basil, and parsley and season with salt and pepper. Sauté for 1 minute, then pour the beaten eggs over the vegetables. Cover the pan and reduce the heat to low. 3. Cook until the eggs are cooked through, 5 to 6 minutes,

making sure that the center is no longer runny. 4. To serve, slide the frittata onto a platter and cut into wedges.

Per Serving:
calories: 165 | fat: 11g | protein: 13g | carbs: 3g | fiber: 1g | sodium: 435mg

Peachy Green Smoothie

Prep time: 10 minutes | Cook time: 0 minutes | Serves 2

- 1 cup almond milk
- 3 cups kale or spinach
- 1 banana, peeled
- 1 orange, peeled
- 1 small green apple
- 1 cup frozen peaches
- ¼ cup vanilla Greek yogurt

1. Put the ingredients in a blender in the order listed and blend on high until smooth. 2. Serve and enjoy.

Per Serving:
calories: 257 | fat: 5g | protein: 9g | carbs: 50g | fiber: 7g | sodium: 87mg

Avocado Toast with Smoked Trout

Prep time: 10 minutes | Cook time: 0 minutes | Serves 2

- 1 avocado, peeled and pitted
- 2 teaspoons lemon juice, plus more for serving
- ¾ teaspoon ground cumin
- ¼ teaspoon kosher salt
- ¼ teaspoon red pepper flakes,
- plus more for sprinkling
- ¼ teaspoon lemon zest
- 2 pieces whole-wheat bread, toasted
- 1 (3.75-ounce / 106-g) can smoked trout

1. In a medium bowl, mash together the avocado, lemon juice, cumin, salt, red pepper flakes, and lemon zest. 2. Spread half the avocado mixture on each piece of toast. Top each piece of toast with half the smoked trout. Garnish with a pinch of red pepper flakes (if desired), and/or a sprinkle of lemon juice (if desired).

Per Serving:
calories: 300 | fat: 20g | protein: 11g | carbs: 21g | fiber: 6g | sodium: 390mg

Chapter 4 Poultry

Chicken Skewers

Prep time: 10 minutes | Cook time: 7 minutes | Serves 4

- ¼ cup olive oil
- Zest of 1 lemon
- Juice of 2 lemons
- 2 tablespoons dried oregano
- 1 tablespoon dried thyme
- 2 garlic cloves, minced
- Sea salt
- Freshly ground black pepper
- 3 pounds (1.4 kg) boneless, skinless chicken breasts, cut into 2-inch cubes

1. In a large bowl, stir together the olive oil, lemon zest, lemon juice, oregano, thyme, and garlic. Season with salt and pepper and mix well. Add the chicken and stir to coat thoroughly. Cover the bowl and refrigerate for at least 20 to 30 minutes. 2. Remove the chicken from the refrigerator and thread the chicken pieces onto skewers, using 4 or 5 pieces per skewer. 3. Heat a cast-iron skillet over medium-high heat. Working in batches, place the skewers in the skillet, about 3 per batch, and cook, turning frequently, for 5 to 7 minutes, until the chicken is cooked through and has an internal temperature of 165°F (74°C). Repeat with the remaining skewers. Serve.

Per Serving:
calories: 504 | fat: 19g | protein: 76g | carbs: 4g | fiber: 1g | sodium: 214mg

Pecan Turkey Cutlets

Prep time: 10 minutes | Cook time: 10 to 12 minutes per batch | Serves 4

- ¾ cup panko bread crumbs
- ¼ teaspoon salt
- ¼ teaspoon pepper
- ¼ teaspoon dry mustard
- ¼ teaspoon poultry seasoning
- ½ cup pecans
- ¼ cup cornstarch
- 1 egg, beaten
- 1 pound (454 g) turkey cutlets, ½-inch thick
- Salt and pepper, to taste
- Oil for misting or cooking spray

1. Place the panko crumbs, ¼ teaspoon salt, ¼ teaspoon pepper, mustard, and poultry seasoning in food processor. Process until crumbs are finely crushed. Add pecans and process in short pulses just until nuts are finely chopped. Go easy so you don't overdo it! 2. Preheat the air fryer to 360°F (182°C). 3. Place cornstarch in one shallow dish and beaten egg in another. Transfer coating mixture from food processor into a third shallow dish. 4. Sprinkle turkey cutlets with salt and pepper to taste. 5. Dip cutlets in cornstarch and shake off excess. Then dip in beaten egg and roll in crumbs, pressing to coat well. Spray both sides with oil or cooking spray. 6. Place 2 cutlets in air fryer basket in a single layer and cook for 10 to 12 minutes or until juices run clear. 7. Repeat step 6 to cook remaining cutlets.

Per Serving:
calories: 340 | fat: 13g | protein: 31g | carbs: 24g | fiber: 4g | sodium: 447mg

Punjabi Chicken Curry

Prep time: 20 minutes | Cook time: 4 to 6 hours | Serves 6

- 2 tablespoons vegetable oil
- 3 onions, finely diced
- 6 garlic cloves, finely chopped
- 1 heaped tablespoon freshly grated ginger
- 1 (14-ounce / 397-g) can plum tomatoes
- 1 teaspoon salt
- 1 teaspoon turmeric
- 1 teaspoon chili powder
- Handful coriander stems, finely chopped
- 3 fresh green chiles, finely chopped
- 12 pieces chicken, mixed thighs and drumsticks, or a whole chicken, skinned, trimmed, and chopped
- 2 teaspoons garam masala
- Handful fresh coriander leaves, chopped

1. Heat the oil in a frying pan (or in the slow cooker if you have a sear setting). Add the diced onions and cook for 5 minutes. Add the garlic and continue to cook for 10 minutes until the onions are brown. 2. Heat the slow cooker to high and add the onion-and-garlic mixture. Stir in the ginger, tomatoes, salt, turmeric, chili powder, coriander stems, and chiles. 3. Add the chicken pieces. Cover and cook on low for 6 hours, or on high for 4 hours. 4. Once cooked, check the seasoning, and then stir in the garam masala and coriander leaves.

Per Serving:
calories: 298 | fat: 9g | protein: 35g | carbs: 19g | fiber: 3g | sodium: 539mg

Tuscan Turkey

Prep time: 15 minutes | Cook time: 6 to 8 hours | Serves 4

- 1 pound (454 g) new potatoes, halved
- 1 red bell pepper, seeded and sliced
- 1 small onion, sliced
- 4 boneless, skinless turkey breast fillets (about 2 pounds / 907 g)
- 1 cup low-sodium chicken broth
- ½ cup grated Parmesan cheese
- 3 garlic cloves, minced
- 1 teaspoon dried oregano
- 1 teaspoon dried rosemary
- ½ teaspoon sea salt
- ½ teaspoon freshly ground black pepper
- ½ teaspoon dried thyme
- ¼ cup chopped fresh basil

1. In a slow cooker, combine the potatoes, bell pepper, and onion. Stir to mix well. 2. Place the turkey on top of the vegetables. 3. In a small bowl, whisk together the chicken broth, Parmesan cheese, garlic, oregano, rosemary, salt, black pepper, and thyme until blended. Pour the sauce over the turkey. 4. Cover the cooker and cook for 6 to 8 hours on Low heat. 5. Garnish with fresh basil for serving.

Per Serving:
calories: 402 | fat: 5g | protein: 65g | carbs: 24g | fiber: 3g | sodium: 673mg

Catalonian Chicken with Spiced Lemon Rice

Prep time: 10 minutes | Cook time: 4 hours 10 minutes | Serves 4

- 3 tablespoons all-purpose flour
- 2 tablespoons paprika
- 1 tablespoon garlic powder
- Sea salt
- Black pepper
- 6 chicken thighs
- ¼ cup olive oil
- 1 (15-ounce / 425-g) can diced tomatoes, with the juice
- 2 green bell peppers, diced into 2-inch pieces
- 1 large yellow onion, sliced into thick pieces
- 2 tablespoons tomato paste
- 4 cups chicken stock
- 1 cup uncooked brown rice
- ½ teaspoon red pepper flakes
- Zest and juice from 1 lemon
- ½ cup pitted green olives

1. In a large resealable bag, mix together the flour, paprika, and garlic powder and season with salt and pepper. Add the chicken, reseal the bag, and toss to coat. 2. In a large skillet over medium heat, heat the olive oil. Add the chicken and brown on both sides, 3 to 4 minutes per side. 3. While the chicken is cooking, add the tomatoes, bell peppers, and onion to the slow cooker. 4. Place the browned chicken thighs in the slow cooker. 5. In same skillet used to brown the chicken, add the tomato paste and cook for 1 minute, stirring constantly. 6. Add 2 cups of the chicken stock to the skillet and bring to a simmer, stirring with a wooden spoon to scrape up the flavorful browned bits off the bottom of the pan. Pour over the top of the chicken in the slow cooker. 7. Cook on low for 4 hours, or until the chicken is extremely tender. 8. In a heavy medium saucepan over medium-high heat, combine the remaining 2 cups stock, the rice, red pepper flakes, lemon zest, and juice of one-half of the lemon, and season with salt. Bring to a boil, reduce the heat to low, and simmer, covered, until the rice is tender and has absorbed all the liquid, about 25 minutes. 9. To serve, spoon the rice onto plates and ladle the Catalonian chicken and vegetables over the top. Garnish with the olives and squeeze the juice from the remaining one-half lemon over the dish.

Per Serving:
calories: 791 | fat: 31g | protein: 69g | carbs: 60g | fiber: 8g | sodium: 497mg

Fried Chicken Breasts

Prep time: 30 minutes | Cook time: 12 to 14 minutes | Serves 4

- 1 pound (454 g) boneless, skinless chicken breasts
- ¾ cup dill pickle juice
- ¾ cup finely ground blanched almond flour
- ¾ cup finely grated Parmesan
- cheese
- ½ teaspoon sea salt
- ½ teaspoon freshly ground black pepper
- 2 large eggs
- Avocado oil spray

1. Place the chicken breasts in a zip-top bag or between two pieces of plastic wrap. Using a meat mallet or heavy skillet, pound the chicken to a uniform ½-inch thickness. 2. Place the chicken in a large bowl with the pickle juice. Cover and allow to brine in the refrigerator for up to 2 hours. 3. In a shallow dish, combine the almond flour, Parmesan cheese, salt, and pepper. In a separate, shallow bowl, beat the eggs. 4. Drain the chicken and pat it dry with paper towels. Dip in the eggs and then in the flour mixture, making sure to press the coating into the chicken. Spray both sides of the coated breasts with oil. 5. Spray the air fryer basket with oil and put the chicken inside. Set the temperature to 400ºF (204ºC) and air fry for 6 to 7 minutes. 6. Carefully flip the breasts with a spatula. Spray the breasts again with oil and continue cooking for 6 to 7 minutes more, until golden and crispy.

Per Serving:
calories: 319 | fat: 17g | protein: 37g | carbs: 5g | fiber: 3g | sodium: 399mg

Classic Whole Chicken

Prep time: 5 minutes | Cook time: 50 minutes | Serves 4

- Oil, for spraying
- 1 (4-pound / 1.8-kg) whole chicken, giblets removed
- 1 tablespoon olive oil
- 1 teaspoon paprika
- ½ teaspoon granulated garlic
- ½ teaspoon salt
- ½ teaspoon freshly ground black pepper
- ¼ teaspoon finely chopped fresh parsley, for garnish

1. Line the air fryer basket with parchment and spray lightly with oil. 2. Pat the chicken dry with paper towels. Rub it with the olive oil until evenly coated. 3. In a small bowl, mix together the paprika, garlic, salt, and black pepper and sprinkle it evenly over the chicken. 4. Place the chicken in the prepared basket, breast-side down. 5. Air fry at 360ºF (182ºC) for 30 minutes, flip, and cook for another 20 minutes, or until the internal temperature reaches 165ºF (74ºC) and the juices run clear. 6. Sprinkle with the parsley before serving.

Per Serving:
calories: 549 | fat: 11g | protein: 105g | carbs: 0g | fiber: 0g | sodium: 523mg

Tex-Mex Chicken Roll-Ups

Prep time: 10 minutes | Cook time: 14 to 17 minutes | Serves 8

- 2 pounds (907 g) boneless, skinless chicken breasts or thighs
- 1 teaspoon chili powder
- ½ teaspoon smoked paprika
- ½ teaspoon ground cumin
- Sea salt and freshly ground
- black pepper, to taste
- 6 ounces (170 g) Monterey Jack cheese, shredded
- 4 ounces (113 g) canned diced green chiles
- Avocado oil spray

1. Place the chicken in a large zip-top bag or between two pieces of plastic wrap. Using a meat mallet or heavy skillet, pound the chicken until it is about ¼ inch thick. 2. In a small bowl, combine the chili powder, smoked paprika, cumin, and salt and pepper to taste. Sprinkle both sides of the chicken with the seasonings. 3. Sprinkle the chicken with the Monterey Jack cheese, then the diced green chiles. 4. Roll up each piece of chicken from the long side, tucking in the ends as you go. Secure the roll-up with a toothpick. 5. Set the air fryer to 350ºF (177ºC). Spray the outside of the chicken with avocado oil. Place the chicken in a single layer in the basket, working in batches if necessary, and roast for 7 minutes. Flip and cook for another 7 to 10 minutes, until an instant-read thermometer reads 160ºF (71ºC). 6. Remove the chicken from the air fryer and allow it to rest for about 5 minutes before serving.

Per Serving:
calories: 220 | fat: 10g | protein: 31g | carbs: 1g | fiber: 0g | sodium: 355mg

Chicken Korma

Prep time: 20 minutes | Cook time: 3 to 4 hours | Serves 6

Marinade:
- 1 tablespoon coriander seeds, ground
- 1 teaspoon salt
- 6 whole black peppercorns
- 1-inch piece fresh ginger, roughly chopped
- 3 garlic cloves, roughly

Korma:
- 1 tablespoon ghee or vegetable oil
- 3 cloves
- 3 green cardamom pods
- 1-inch piece cassia bark
- 1 to 3 dried red chiles
- 2 onions, minced
- ⅓ cup creamed coconut
- 2 heaped tablespoons ground almonds

- chopped
- 12 boneless chicken thighs, skinned and chopped into chunks
- 1 cup Greek yogurt
- 1 heaped teaspoon gram flour
- 1 teaspoon turmeric

- 1 teaspoon ground white poppy seeds
- Pinch of saffron
- 2 tablespoons milk
- 1 teaspoon garam masala
- Handful fresh coriander leaves, finely chopped
- 1 tablespoon chopped toasted almonds
- Squeeze of lemon juice

Make the Marinade: 1. Place the coriander seeds, salt, and peppercorns into a mortar and pestle and crush, or grind them in a spice grinder. Then add the roughly chopped ginger and garlic, and pound (or grind) to create an aromatic paste. 2. Place the chicken in a large bowl and add the yogurt, gram flour, turmeric, and spice paste. Stir thoroughly, cover, and leave to marinate for an hour, or longer if possible, in the refrigerator. Make the Korma: 3. Heat the slow cooker to high and add the oil. Add the cloves, cardamom pods, cassia bark, and the dried red chiles, and toast until fragrant, about 1 minute. 4. Add the minced onions, and then add the marinated chicken. Cover and cook for 2 hours on low, or for 1 hour on high. 5. Pour in the creamed coconut, ground almonds, and poppy seeds, then stir. Cover and cook on low for 2 more hours. 6. Crumble the saffron into a small bowl, add the milk, and leave to steep for 20 minutes. 7. Once cooked through and the sauce has thickened, pour in the saffron milk for added decadence, if using. Then add the garam masala. Garnish with the fresh coriander leaves and chopped almonds. You can also add a squeeze of lemon juice for added freshness, then serve.

Per Serving:
calories: 568 | fat: 23g | protein: 79g | carbs: 9g | fiber: 2g | sodium: 779mg

Broccoli Cheese Chicken

Prep time: 10 minutes | Cook time: 19 to 24 minutes | Serves 6

- 1 tablespoon avocado oil
- ¼ cup chopped onion
- ½ cup finely chopped broccoli
- 4 ounces (113 g) cream cheese, at room temperature
- 2 ounces (57 g) Cheddar cheese, shredded
- 1 teaspoon garlic powder
- ½ teaspoon sea salt, plus

- additional for seasoning, divided
- ¼ freshly ground black pepper, plus additional for seasoning, divided
- 2 pounds (907 g) boneless, skinless chicken breasts
- 1 teaspoon smoked paprika

1. Heat a medium skillet over medium-high heat and pour in the avocado oil. Add the onion and broccoli and cook, stirring occasionally, for 5 to 8 minutes, until the onion is tender. 2. Transfer to a large bowl and stir in the cream cheese, Cheddar cheese, and garlic powder, and season to taste with salt and pepper. 3. Hold a sharp knife parallel to the chicken breast and cut a long pocket into one side. Stuff the chicken pockets with the broccoli mixture, using toothpicks to secure the pockets around the filling. 4. In a small dish, combine the paprika, ½ teaspoon salt, and ¼ teaspoon pepper. Sprinkle this over the outside of the chicken. 5. Set the air fryer to 400°F (204°C). Place the chicken in a single layer in the air fryer basket, cooking in batches if necessary, and cook for 14 to 16 minutes, until an instant-read thermometer reads 160°F (71°C). Place the chicken on a plate and tent a piece of aluminum foil over the chicken. Allow to rest for 5 to 10 minutes before serving.

Per Serving:
calorie: 287 | fat: 16g | protein: 32g | carbs: 1g | fiber: 0g | sodium: 291mg

Chicken Shawarma

Prep time: 30 minutes | Cook time: 15 minutes | Serves 4

Shawarma Spice:
- 2 teaspoons dried oregano
- 1 teaspoon ground cinnamon
- 1 teaspoon ground cumin
- 1 teaspoon ground coriander

Chicken:
- 1 pound (454 g) boneless, skinless chicken thighs, cut

For Serving:
- Tzatziki

- 1 teaspoon kosher salt
- ½ teaspoon ground allspice
- ½ teaspoon cayenne pepper

- into large bite-size chunks
- 2 tablespoons vegetable oil

- Pita bread

1. For the shawarma spice: In a small bowl, combine the oregano, cayenne, cumin, coriander, salt, cinnamon, and allspice. 2. For the chicken: In a large bowl, toss together the chicken, vegetable oil, and shawarma spice to coat. Marinate at room temperature for 30 minutes or cover and refrigerate for up to 24 hours. 3. Place the chicken in the air fryer basket. Set the air fryer to 350°F (177°C) for 15 minutes, or until the chicken reaches an internal temperature of 165°F (74°C). 4. Transfer the chicken to a serving platter. Serve with tzatziki and pita bread.

Per Serving:
calories: 202 | fat: 12g | protein: 23g | carbs: 1g | fiber: 1g | sodium: 690mg

Chicken and Olives with Couscous

Prep time: 15 minutes | Cook time: 1 hour | Serves 6

- 2 tablespoons olive oil, divided
- 8 bone-in, skin-on chicken thighs
- ½ teaspoon kosher salt
- ¼ teaspoon ground black pepper
- 2 cloves garlic, chopped
- 1 small red onion, chopped
- 1 red bell pepper, seeded and chopped
- 1 green bell pepper, seeded and chopped

- 1 tablespoon fresh thyme leaves
- 2 teaspoons fresh oregano leaves
- 1 (28-ounce / 794-g) can no-salt-added diced tomatoes
- 1 cup low-sodium chicken broth
- 1 cup pitted green olives, coarsely chopped
- 2 cups whole wheat couscous
- Chopped flat-leaf parsley, for garnish

1. Preheat the oven to 350°F(180°C). 2. In a large ovenproof or cast-iron skillet over medium heat, warm 1 tablespoon of the oil. Pat the chicken thighs dry with a paper towel, season with the salt and black pepper, and cook, turning once, until golden and crisp, 8 to 10 minutes per side. Remove the chicken from the skillet and set aside. 3. Add the remaining 1 tablespoon oil to the skillet. Cook the garlic, onion, bell peppers, thyme, and oregano until softened, about 5 minutes. Add the tomatoes and broth and bring to a boil. Return the chicken to the skillet, add the olives, cover, and place the skillet in the oven. Roast until the chicken is tender and a thermometer inserted in the thickest part registers 165°F(74°C), 40 to 50 minutes. 4. While the chicken is cooking, prepare the couscous according to package directions. 5. To serve, pile the couscous on a serving platter and nestle the chicken on top. Pour the vegetables and any pan juices over the chicken and couscous. Sprinkle with the parsley and serve.

Per Serving:
calories: 481 | fat: 15g | protein: 29g | carbs: 61g | fiber: 11g | sodium: 893mg

Chicken with Lemon and Artichokes

Prep time: 10 minutes | Cook time: 6 to 8 hours | Serves 4

- 2 pounds (907 g) bone-in, skin-on chicken thighs
- 1 large onion, sliced
- 1 (15-ounce / 425-g) can artichoke hearts, drained, rinsed, and chopped
- ¼ cup freshly squeezed lemon juice
- 1 tablespoon extra-virgin olive oil
- 3 garlic cloves, minced
- 2 teaspoons dried thyme
- 1 teaspoon sea salt
- ½ teaspoon freshly ground black pepper
- 1 lemon, thinly sliced

1. In a slow cooker, combine the chicken and onion. Top with the artichoke hearts. 2. In a small bowl, whisk together the lemon juice, olive oil, garlic, thyme, salt, and pepper. Pour the sauce into the slow cooker. Top the chicken with lemon slices. 3. Cover the cooker and cook for 6 to 8 hours on Low heat.

Per Serving:
calories: 608 | fat: 41g | protein: 42g | carbs: 19g | fiber: 7g | sodium: 584mg

Chicken Pesto Parmigiana

Prep time: 10 minutes | Cook time: 23 minutes | Serves 4

- 2 large eggs
- 1 tablespoon water
- Fine sea salt and ground black pepper, to taste
- 1 cup powdered Parmesan cheese (about 3 ounces / 85 g)
- 2 teaspoons Italian seasoning
- 4 (5-ounce / 142-g) boneless, skinless chicken breasts or
- thighs, pounded to ¼ inch thick
- 1 cup pesto
- 1 cup shredded Mozzarella cheese (about 4 ounces / 113 g)
- Finely chopped fresh basil, for garnish (optional)
- Grape tomatoes, halved, for serving (optional)

1. Spray the air fryer basket with avocado oil. Preheat the air fryer to 400°F (204°C). 2. Crack the eggs into a shallow baking dish, add the water and a pinch each of salt and pepper, and whisk to combine. In another shallow baking dish, stir together the Parmesan and Italian seasoning until well combined. 3. Season the chicken breasts well on both sides with salt and pepper. Dip one chicken breast in the eggs and let any excess drip off, then dredge both sides of the breast in the Parmesan mixture. Spray the breast with avocado oil and place it in the air fryer basket. Repeat with the remaining 3 chicken breasts. 4. Air fry the chicken in the air fryer for 20 minutes, or until the internal temperature reaches 165°F (74°C) and the breading is golden brown, flipping halfway through. 5. Dollop each chicken breast with ¼ cup of the pesto and top with the Mozzarella. Return the breasts to the air fryer and cook for 3 minutes, or until the cheese is melted. Garnish with basil and serve with halved grape tomatoes on the side, if desired. 6. Store leftovers in an airtight container in the refrigerator for up to 4 days. Reheat in a preheated 400°F (204°C) air fryer for 5 minutes, or until warmed through.

Per Serving:
calories: 631 | fat: 45g | protein: 52g | carbs: 4g | fiber: 0g | sodium: 607mg

Seared Duck Breast with Orange Ouzo Sauce

Prep time: 10 minutes | Cook time: 15 minutes | Serves 4

- 2 duck breast halves
- 1 teaspoon salt, plus a pinch
- 1 tablespoon olive oil
- 1 shallot, minced
- 1 Thai chile, or other small, hot chile, halved lengthwise
- ½ cup chopped fennel bulb,
- plus a handful of the minced fronds for garnish
- ¼ cup ouzo
- 1 cup chicken broth
- Juice of one orange, about ½ cup
- Freshly ground black pepper

1. Using a very sharp knife, score a cross-hatch pattern into the skin of each duck breast, cutting through the skin and the fat layer, but not into the meat. Sprinkle the salt evenly over them and let stand at room temperature for about 15 minutes. 2. Heat the olive oil in a large skillet over medium-high heat. Add the duck breasts, skin-side down, and cook over medium heat until the skin is nicely browned and a good amount of fat has been rendered, about 8 to 10 minutes. Turn the breasts over and cook until the meat is medium-rare, about 3 more minutes. Remove the breasts from the pan, tent with foil, and let rest for about 10 minutes. 3. While the duck is resting, make the sauce. In the same skillet over medium heat, cook the shallot, chile, and fennel bulb, until the vegetables begin to soften, about 3 minutes. Remove the pan from the heat and add the ouzo (be careful not to let it catch fire). Cook, scraping up any browned bits from the pan, until the liquid is reduced by half. 4. Add the broth and orange juice, along with a pinch of salt, and bring to a boil. Let the sauce boil until it is thick and syrupy, about 5 minutes more. Remove from the heat. 5. Slice the duck breast against the grain into ⅛-inch-thick slices. Arrange the slices onto 4 serving plates and drizzle the sauce over the top. Garnish with the chopped fennel fronds and serve immediately.

Per Serving:
calories: 229 | fat: 9g | protein: 27g | carbs: 7g | fiber: 1g | sodium: 781mg

Greek-Style Roast Turkey Breast

Prep time: 10 minutes | Cook time: 7½ hours | Serves 8

- 1 (4-pound / 1.8-kg) turkey breast, trimmed of fat
- ½ cup chicken stock
- 2 tablespoons fresh lemon juice
- 2 cups chopped onions
- ½ cup pitted kalamata olives
- ½ cup oil-packed sun-dried tomatoes, drained and thinly sliced
- 1 clove garlic, minced
- 1 teaspoon dried oregano
- ½ teaspoon ground cinnamon
- ½ teaspoon ground dill
- ¼ teaspoon ground nutmeg
- ¼ teaspoon cayenne pepper
- 1 teaspoon sea salt
- ¼ teaspoon black pepper
- 3 tablespoons all-purpose flour

1. Place the turkey breast, ¼ cup of the chicken stock, lemon juice, onions, Kalamata olives, garlic, and sun-dried tomatoes into the slow cooker. Sprinkle with the oregano, cinnamon, dill, nutmeg, cayenne pepper, salt, and black pepper. Cover and cook on low for 7 hours. 2. Combine the remaining ¼ cup chicken stock and the flour in a small bowl. Whisk until smooth. Stir into the slow cooker. Cover and cook on low for an additional 30 minutes. 3. Serve hot over rice, pasta, potatoes, or another starch of your choice.

Per Serving:

calories: 386 | fat: 7g | protein: 70g | carbs: 8g | fiber: 2g | sodium: 601mg

Taco Chicken

Prep time: 10 minutes | Cook time: 23 minutes | Serves 4

- 2 large eggs
- 1 tablespoon water
- Fine sea salt and ground black pepper, to taste
- 1 cup pork dust
- 1 teaspoon ground cumin
- 1 teaspoon smoked paprika
- 4 (5 ounces / 142 g) boneless, skinless chicken breasts or
- thighs, pounded to ¼ inch thick
- 1 cup salsa
- 1 cup shredded Monterey Jack cheese (about 4 ounces / 113 g) (omit for dairy-free)
- Sprig of fresh cilantro, for garnish (optional)

1. Spray the air fryer basket with avocado oil. Preheat the air fryer to 400°F (204°C). 2. Crack the eggs into a shallow baking dish, add the water and a pinch each of salt and pepper, and whisk to combine. In another shallow baking dish, stir together the pork dust, cumin, and paprika until well combined. 3. Season the chicken breasts well on both sides with salt and pepper. Dip 1 chicken breast in the eggs and let any excess drip off, then dredge both sides of the chicken breast in the pork dust mixture. Spray the breast with avocado oil and place it in the air fryer basket. Repeat with the remaining 3 chicken breasts. 4. Air fry the chicken in the air fryer for 20 minutes, or until the internal temperature reaches 165°F (74°C) and the breading is golden brown, flipping halfway through. 5. Dollop each chicken breast with ¼ cup of the salsa and top with ¼ cup of the cheese. Return the breasts to the air fryer and cook for 3 minutes, or until the cheese is melted. Garnish with cilantro before serving, if desired. 6. Store leftovers in an airtight container in the refrigerator for up to 4 days. Reheat in a preheated 400°F (204°C) air fryer for 5 minutes, or until warmed through.

Per Serving:

calories: 360 | fat: 15g | protein: 20g | carbs: 4g | fiber: 1g | sodium: 490mg

Moroccan-Spiced Chicken Thighs with Saffron Basmati Rice

Prep time: 15 minutes | Cook time: 15 minutes | Serves 2

For the chicken
- ½ teaspoon paprika
- ½ teaspoon cumin
- ½ teaspoon cinnamon
- ¼ teaspoon salt
- ¼ teaspoon garlic powder
- ¼ teaspoon ginger powder
- ¼ teaspoon coriander

For the rice
- 1 tablespoon olive oil
- ½ small onion, minced
- ½ cup basmati rice
- 2 pinches saffron

- ⅛ teaspoon cayenne pepper (a pinch—or more if you like it spicy)
- 10 ounces (283 g) boneless, skinless chicken thighs (about 4 pieces)

- ¼ teaspoon salt
- 1 cup low-sodium chicken stock

Make the chicken 1. Preheat the oven to 350°F (180°C) and set the rack to the middle position. 2. In a small bowl, combine the paprika, cumin, cinnamon, salt, garlic powder, ginger powder, coriander, and cayenne pepper. Add chicken thighs and toss, rubbing the spice mix into the chicken. 3. Place the chicken in a baking dish and roast it for 35 to 40 minutes, or until the chicken reaches an internal temperature of 165°F(74°C). Let the chicken rest for 5 minutes before serving. Make the rice 1. While the chicken is roasting, heat the oil in a sauté pan over medium-high heat. Add the onion and sauté for 5 minutes. 2. Add the rice, saffron, salt, and chicken stock. Cover the pot with a tight-fitting lid and reduce the heat to low. Let the rice simmer for 15 minutes, or until it is light and fluffy and the liquid has been absorbed.

Per Serving:

calories: 401 | fat: 10g | protein: 37g | carbs: 41g | fiber: 2g | sodium: 715mg

Crispy Dill Chicken Strips

Prep time: 30 minutes | Cook time: 10 minutes | Serves 4

- 2 whole boneless, skinless chicken breasts (about 1 pound / 454 g each), halved lengthwise
- 1 cup Italian dressing
- 3 cups finely crushed potato chips
- 1 tablespoon dried dill weed
- 1 tablespoon garlic powder
- 1 large egg, beaten
- 1 to 2 tablespoons oil

1. In a large resealable bag, combine the chicken and Italian dressing. Seal the bag and refrigerate to marinate at least 1 hour. 2. In a shallow dish, stir together the potato chips, dill, and garlic powder. Place the beaten egg in a second shallow dish. 3. Remove the chicken from the marinade. Roll the chicken pieces in the egg and the potato chip mixture, coating thoroughly. 4. Preheat the air fryer to 325°F (163°C). Line the air fryer basket with parchment paper. 5. Place the coated chicken on the parchment and spritz with oil. 6. Cook for 5 minutes. Flip the chicken, spritz it with oil, and cook for 5 minutes more until the outsides are crispy and the insides are no longer pink.

Per Serving:
calories: 349 | fat: 16g | protein: 30g | carbs: 20g | fiber: 2g | sodium: 92mg

Old Delhi Butter Chicken

Prep time: 15 minutes | Cook time: 3 to 7 hours | Serves 6

Tomato Sauce:
- 3 medium red onions, roughly chopped
- 2 to 3 fresh green chiles
- 1 tablespoon freshly grated ginger
- 6 garlic cloves, roughly chopped
- 2¾-inch piece cassia bark
- 5 green cardamom pods
- 4 cloves
- 10 black peppercorns
Chicken:
- 2 tablespoons ghee or butter
- 1 tablespoon cumin seeds
- 12 chicken thighs, skinned, trimmed, and cut into cubes
- 1 to 2 tablespoons honey
- 1 tablespoon dried fenugreek
- 1 teaspoon salt
- 10 ripe red tomatoes, roughly chopped, or 1 (14-ounce / 397-g) can plum tomatoes
- 1 tablespoon tomato paste
- ½ teaspoon turmeric
- 1 tablespoon Kashmiri chili powder
- 2 teaspoons coriander seeds, ground
- 2 cups hot water

leaves
- ⅓ cup heavy cream (optional)
- 1 tablespoon butter (optional)
- Coriander leaves to garnish (optional)

Make the Tomato Sauce: 1. Heat the slow cooker to high and add the onion, chiles, ginger, garlic, cassia bark, green cardamom pods, cloves, black peppercorns, salt, tomatoes, tomato paste, turmeric, chili powder, ground coriander seeds, and water. 2. Cover and cook on high for 1 to 2 hours, or on low for 3 hours. By the end, the tomatoes should have broken down. 3. Remove the cassia bark (this is important, because if you grind the cassia in the sauce it will turn out much darker) and blend the sauce with an immersion or regular blender until it's smooth. You can strain this to get a fine, glossy sauce, if you'd like, or leave it as it is. Return the sauce to the slow cooker. Make the Chicken: 4. In a frying pan, heat the ghee. Add cumin seeds and cook until fragrant, about 1 minute. Pour into the sauce in the slow cooker. 5. Add the diced chicken, cover the slow cooker, and cook on high for 2 hours, or on low for 4 hours. 6. When the chicken is cooked, stir in the honey, dried fenugreek leaves, and cream (if using). If you want to thicken the sauce you can turn the cooker to high and reduce for a while with the cover off. Add some butter, a little extra drizzle of cream, and garnish with coriander leaves (if using) just before serving.

Per Serving:
calories: 600 | fat: 21g | protein: 80g | carbs: 22g | fiber: 5g | sodium: 814mg

Garlic Chicken (Shish Tawook)

Prep time: 15 minutes | Cook time: 15 minutes | Serves 4 to 6

- 2 tablespoons garlic, minced
- 2 tablespoons tomato paste
- 1 teaspoon smoked paprika
- ½ cup lemon juice
- ½ cup extra-virgin olive oil
- 1½ teaspoons salt
- ½ teaspoon freshly ground
- black pepper
- 2 pounds (907 g) boneless and skinless chicken (breasts or thighs)
- Rice, tzatziki, or hummus, for serving (optional)

1. In a large bowl, add the garlic, tomato paste, paprika, lemon juice, olive oil, salt, and pepper and whisk to combine. 2. Cut the chicken into ½-inch cubes and put them into the bowl; toss to coat with the marinade. Set aside for at least 10 minutes. 3. To grill, preheat the grill on high. Thread the chicken onto skewers and cook for 3 minutes per side, for a total of 9 minutes. 4. To cook in a pan, preheat the pan on high heat, add the chicken, and cook for 9 minutes, turning over the chicken using tongs. 5. Serve the chicken with rice, tzatziki, or hummus, if desired.

Per Serving:
calories: 350 | fat: 22g | protein: 34g | carbs: 3g | fiber: 0g | sodium: 586mg

Kale and Orzo Chicken

Prep time: 10 minutes | Cook time: 16 minutes | Serves 4

- 3 tablespoons light olive oil
- 1 pound (454 g) boneless, skinless chicken breasts
- ½ teaspoon salt
- ½ teaspoon ground black pepper
- ½ medium yellow onion, peeled and chopped
- 4 cups chopped kale
- ¼ teaspoon crushed red pepper flakes
- 2 cups low-sodium chicken broth
- 1½ cups orzo
- ½ cup crumbled feta cheese

1. Press the Sauté button on the Instant Pot® and heat oil. Season chicken with salt and pepper and add to the pot. Brown well on both sides, about 4 minutes per side. Transfer chicken to a plate and set aside. 2. Add onion and cook until just tender, about 2 minutes. Add kale and crushed red pepper flakes, and cook until kale is just wilted, about 2 minutes. Press the Cancel button. 3. Add broth and orzo to the Instant Pot® and stir well. Top with chicken breasts. Close lid, set steam release to Sealing, press the Manual button, and set time to 4 minutes. When the timer beeps, quick-release the pressure until the float valve drops. Press the Cancel button and open lid. Transfer chicken to a cutting board and cut into ½" slices. Arrange slices on a platter along with orzo and kale. Top with feta and serve hot.

Per Serving:
calories: 690 | fat: 19g | protein: 56g | carbs: 72g | fiber: 7g | sodium: 835mg

Skillet Creamy Tarragon Chicken and Mushrooms

Prep time: 10 minutes | Cook time: 20 minutes | Serves 2

- 2 tablespoons olive oil, divided
- ½ medium onion, minced
- 4 ounces (113 g) baby bella (cremini) mushrooms, sliced
- 2 small garlic cloves, minced
- 8 ounces (227 g) chicken cutlets
- 2 teaspoons tomato paste
- 2 teaspoons dried tarragon
- 2 cups low-sodium chicken stock
- 6 ounces (170 g) pappardelle pasta
- ¼ cup plain full-fat Greek yogurt
- Salt
- Freshly ground black pepper

1. Heat 1 tablespoon of the olive oil in a sauté pan over medium-high heat. Add the onion and mushrooms and sauté for 5 minutes. Add the garlic and cook for 1 minute more. 2. Move the vegetables to the edges of the pan and add the remaining 1 tablespoon of olive oil to the center of the pan. Place the cutlets in the center and let them cook for about 3 minutes, or until they lift up easily and are golden brown on the bottom. 3. Flip the chicken and cook for another 3 minutes. 4. Mix in the tomato paste and tarragon. Add the chicken stock and stir well to combine everything. Bring the stock to a boil. 5. Add the pappardelle. Break up the pasta if needed to fit into the pan. Stir the noodles so they don't stick to the bottom of the pan. 6. Cover the sauté pan and reduce the heat to medium-low. Let the chicken and noodles simmer for 15 minutes, stirring occasionally, until the pasta is cooked and the liquid is mostly absorbed. If the liquid absorbs too quickly and the pasta isn't cooked, add more water or chicken stock, about ¼ cup at a time as needed. 7. Remove the pan from the heat. 8. Stir 2 tablespoons of the hot liquid from the pan into the yogurt. Pour the tempered yogurt into the pan and stir well to mix it into the sauce. Season with salt and pepper. 9. The sauce will tighten up as it cools, so if it seems too thick, add a few tablespoons of water.

Per Serving:
calories: 556 | fat: 18g | protein: 42g | carbs: 56g | fiber: 2g | sodium: 190mg

Chicken and Chickpea Skillet with Berbere Spice

Prep time: 15 minutes | Cook time: 45 minutes | Serves 6

- 2 tablespoons olive oil
- 1 (3-to 4-pound / 1.4-to 1.8-kg) whole chicken, cut into 8 pieces
- 3 teaspoons Berbere or baharat spice blend
- 1 large onion, preferably Spanish, thinly sliced into half-moons
- 2 garlic cloves, minced
- 2 cups 1-inch cubes peeled butternut squash, or 1 (12-ounce / 340-g) bag pre-cut squash
- 1 (15-ounce / 425-g) can no-salt-added chickpeas, undrained
- ½ cup golden raisins
- Hot cooked rice, for serving

1. In a 12-inch skillet, heat 1 tablespoon olive oil over medium-high heat. Sprinkle the chicken with 2 teaspoons of the Berbere spice. Add half the chicken to the skillet and cook until browned, 4 to 6 minutes per side. Transfer the chicken to a plate and repeat to brown the remaining chicken. Set aside. 2. In the same skillet, heat the remaining 1 tablespoon olive oil. Add the onion and cook, stirring, until softened, about 5 minutes. Add the remaining 1 teaspoon Berbere spice, the garlic, squash, chickpeas, and raisins and stir to combine. Return the chicken to skillet, pushing the pieces between the vegetables, and bring to a boil. Reduce the heat to maintain a simmer, cover tightly, and cook for 20 to 25 minutes, until the chicken is cooked through and an instant-read thermometer inserted into the thickest part registers 165°F (74°C), and the squash is tender. 3. Serve over hot cooked rice.

Per Serving:

1 cup: calories: 507 | fat: 26g | protein: 42g | carbs: 33g | fiber: 9g | sodium: 218mg

Tahini Chicken Rice Bowls

Prep time: 10 minutes |Cook time: 15 minutes| Serves: 4

- 1 cup uncooked instant brown rice
- ¼ cup tahini or peanut butter (tahini for nut-free)
- ¼ cup 2% plain Greek yogurt
- 2 tablespoons chopped scallions, green and white parts (2 scallions)
- 1 tablespoon freshly squeezed lemon juice (from ½ medium lemon)
- 1 tablespoon water
- 1 teaspoon ground cumin
- ¾ teaspoon ground cinnamon
- ¼ teaspoon kosher or sea salt
- 2 cups chopped cooked chicken breast (about 1 pound / 454 g)
- ½ cup chopped dried apricots
- 2 cups peeled and chopped seedless cucumber (1 large cucumber)
- 4 teaspoons sesame seeds
- Fresh mint leaves, for serving (optional)

1. Cook the brown rice according to the package instructions. 2. While the rice is cooking, in a medium bowl, mix together the tahini, yogurt, scallions, lemon juice, water, cumin, cinnamon, and salt. Transfer half the tahini mixture to another medium bowl. Mix the chicken into the first bowl. 3. When the rice is done, mix it into the second bowl of tahini (the one without the chicken). 4. To assemble, divide the chicken among four bowls. Spoon the rice mixture next to the chicken in each bowl. Next to the chicken, place the dried apricots, and in the remaining empty section, add the cucumbers. Sprinkle with sesame seeds, and top with mint, if desired, and serve.

Per Serving:

calories: 448 | fat: 13g | protein: 30g | carbs: 53g | fiber: 5g | sodium: 243mg

Chapter 5 Beans and Grains

Spanish Rice

Prep time: 10 minutes | Cook time: 20 minutes | Serves 4

- 2 tablespoons extra-virgin olive oil
- 1 medium onion, finely chopped
- 1 large tomato, finely diced
- 2 tablespoons tomato paste
- 1 teaspoon smoked paprika
- 1 teaspoon salt
- 1½ cups basmati rice
- 3 cups water

1. In a medium pot over medium heat, cook the olive oil, onion, and tomato for 3 minutes. 2. Stir in the tomato paste, paprika, salt, and rice. Cook for 1 minute. 3. Add the water, cover the pot, and turn the heat to low. Cook for 12 minutes. 4. Gently toss the rice, cover, and cook for another 3 minutes.

Per Serving:

calories: 328 | fat: 7g | protein: 6g | carbs: 60g | fiber: 2g | sodium: 651mg

Tomato Rice

Prep time: 10 minutes | Cook time: 25 minutes | Serves 3

- 2 tablespoons extra virgin olive oil
- 1 medium onion (any variety), chopped
- 1 garlic clove, finely chopped
- 1 cup uncooked medium-grain rice
- 1 tablespoon tomato paste
- 1 pound (454 g) canned
- crushed tomatoes, or 1 pound (454 g) fresh tomatoes (puréed in a food processor)
- ¾ teaspoon fine sea salt
- 1 teaspoon granulated sugar
- 2 cups hot water
- 2 tablespoons chopped fresh mint or basil

1. Heat the olive oil in a wide, deep pan over medium heat. When the oil begins to shimmer, add the onion and sauté for 3–4 minutes or until soft, then add the garlic and sauté for an additional 30 seconds. 2. Add the rice and stir until the rice is coated with the oil, then add the tomato paste and stir rapidly. Add the tomatoes, sea salt, and sugar, and then stir again. 3. Add the hot water, stir, then reduce the heat to low and simmer, covered, for 20 minutes or until the rice is soft. (If the rice appears to need more cooking time, add a small amount of hot water to the pan and continue cooking.) Remove the pan from the heat. 4. Add the chopped mint or basil, and let the rice sit for 10 minutes before serving. Store covered in the refrigerator for up to 4 days.

Per Serving:

calories: 359 | fat: 11g | protein: 7g | carbs: 60g | fiber: 6g | sodium: 607mg

Greek-Style Pea Casserole

Prep time: 5 minutes | Cook time: 45 minutes | Serves 3

- ⅓ cup extra virgin olive oil
- 1 medium onion (any variety), diced
- 1 medium carrot, peeled and sliced
- 1 medium white potato, peeled and cut into bite-sized pieces
- 1 pound (454 g) peas (fresh or frozen)
- 3 tablespoons chopped fresh dill
- 2 medium tomatoes, grated, or 12 ounces (340 g) canned crushed tomatoes
- ½ teaspoon fine sea salt
- ¼ teaspoon freshly ground black pepper
- ½ cup hot water
- Salt to taste

1. Add the olive oil to a medium pot over medium heat. When the oil starts to shimmer, add the onions and sauté for 2 minutes. Add the carrots and potatoes, and sauté for 3 more minutes. 2. Add the peas and dill. Stir until the peas are coated in the olive oil. 3. Add the tomatoes, sea salt, black pepper, and hot water. Mix well.Bring to the mixture to a boil, then cover, reduce the heat to low, and simmer for 40 minutes or until the peas and carrots are soft and the casserole has thickened. (Check the water levels intermittently, adding more hot water if the mixture appears to be getting too dry.) 4. Remove the casserole from the heat, uncover, and set aside for 20 minutes. Add salt to taste before serving. Store covered in the refrigerator for up to 3 days.

Per Serving:

calories: 439 | fat: 26g | protein: 12g | carbs: 45g | fiber: 13g | sodium: 429mg

Garlicky Split Chickpea Curry

Prep time: 10 minutes | Cook time: 4 to 6 hours | Serves 6

- 1½ cups split gram
- 1 onion, finely chopped
- 2 tomatoes, chopped
- 1 tablespoon freshly grated ginger
- 1 teaspoon cumin seeds, ground or crushed with a mortar and pestle
- 2 teaspoons turmeric
- 2 garlic cloves, crushed
- 1 hot green Thai or other fresh chile, thinly sliced
- 3 cups hot water
- 1 teaspoon salt
- 2 tablespoons rapeseed oil
- 1 teaspoon cumin seeds, crushed
- 1 garlic clove, sliced
- 1 fresh green chile, sliced

1. Heat the slow cooker to high. Add the split gram, onion, tomatoes, ginger, crushed cumin seeds, turmeric, crushed garlic, hot chile, water, and salt, and then stir. 2. Cover and cook on high for 4 hours, or on low for 6 hours, until the split gram is tender. 3. Just before serving, heat the oil in a saucepan. When the oil is hot, add the cumin seeds with the sliced garlic. Cook until the garlic is golden brown, and then pour it over the dhal. 4. To serve, top with the sliced green chile.

Per Serving:
calories: 119 | fat: 5g | protein: 4g | carbs: 15g | fiber: 3g | sodium: 503mg

Wild Mushroom Farrotto

Prep time: 15 minutes | Cook time: 20 minutes | Serves 4 to 6

- 1½ cups whole farro
- 3 tablespoons extra-virgin olive oil, divided, plus extra for drizzling
- 12 ounces (340 g) cremini or white mushrooms, trimmed and sliced thin
- ½ onion, chopped fine
- ½ teaspoon table salt
- ¼ teaspoon pepper
- 1 garlic clove, minced
- ¼ ounce dried porcini
- mushrooms, rinsed and chopped fine
- 2 teaspoons minced fresh thyme or ½ teaspoon dried
- ¼ cup dry white wine
- 2½ cups chicken or vegetable broth, plus extra as needed
- 2 ounces (57 g) Parmesan cheese, grated (1 cup), plus extra for serving
- 2 teaspoons lemon juice
- ½ cup chopped fresh parsley

1. Pulse farro in blender until about half of grains are broken into smaller pieces, about 6 pulses. 2. Using highest sauté function, heat 2 tablespoons oil in Instant Pot until shimmering. Add cremini mushrooms, onion, salt, and pepper, partially cover, and cook until mushrooms are softened and have released their liquid, about 5 minutes. Stir in farro, garlic, porcini mushrooms, and thyme and cook until fragrant, about 1 minute. Stir in wine and cook until nearly evaporated, about 30 seconds. Stir in broth. 3. Lock lid in place and close pressure release valve. Select high pressure cook function and cook for 12 minutes. Turn off Instant Pot and quick-release pressure. Carefully remove lid, allowing steam to escape away from you. 4. If necessary adjust consistency with extra hot broth, or continue to cook farrotto, using highest sauté function, stirring frequently, until proper consistency is achieved. (Farrotto should be slightly thickened, and spoon dragged along bottom of multicooker should leave trail that quickly fills in.) Add Parmesan and remaining 1 tablespoon oil and stir vigorously until farrotto becomes creamy. Stir in lemon juice and season with salt and pepper to taste. Sprinkle individual portions with parsley and extra Parmesan, and drizzle with extra oil before serving.

Per Serving:
calories: 280 | fat: 10g | protein: 13g | carbs: 35g | fiber: 4g | sodium: 630mg

Lentils with Artichoke, Tomato, and Feta

Prep time: 10 minutes | Cook time: 12 minutes | Serves 6

- 2 cups dried red lentils, rinsed and drained
- ½ teaspoon salt
- 4 cups water
- 1 (12-ounce / 340-g) jar marinated artichokes, drained and chopped
- 2 medium vine-ripe tomatoes, chopped
- ½ medium red onion, peeled and diced
- ½ large English cucumber, diced
- ½ cup crumbled feta cheese
- ¼ cup chopped fresh flat-leaf parsley
- 3 tablespoons extra-virgin olive oil
- 2 tablespoons balsamic vinegar
- ½ teaspoon ground black pepper

1. Add lentils, salt, and water to the Instant Pot®. Close lid, set steam release to Sealing, press the Manual button, and set time to 12 minutes. When the timer beeps, quick-release the pressure until the float valve drops. Open lid and drain off any excess liquid. Let lentils cool to room temperature, about 30 minutes. 2. Add artichokes, tomatoes, onion, cucumber, feta, parsley, oil, vinegar, and pepper, and toss to mix. Transfer to a serving bowl. Serve at room temperature or refrigerate for at least 2 hours.

Per Serving:
calories: 332 | fat: 13g | protein: 17g | carbs: 40g | fiber: 6g | sodium: 552mg

Couscous with Apricots

Prep time: 10 minutes | Cook time: 15 minutes | Serves 4

- 2 tablespoons olive oil
- 1 small onion, diced
- 1 cup whole-wheat couscous
- 2 cups water or broth
- ½ cup dried apricots, soaked
- in water overnight
- ½ cup slivered almonds or pistachios
- ½ teaspoon dried mint
- ½ teaspoon dried thyme

1. Heat the olive oil in a large skillet over medium-high heat. Add the onion and cook until translucent and soft. 2. Stir in the couscous and cook for 2–3 minutes. 3. Add the water or broth, cover, and cook for 8–10 minutes until the water is mostly absorbed. 4. Remove from the heat and let stand for a few minutes. 5. Fluff with a fork and fold in the apricots, nuts, mint, and thyme.

Per Serving:
calories: 294 | fat: 15g | protein: 8g | carbs: 38g | fiber: 6g | sodium: 6mg

Mediterranean Lentils and Rice

Prep time: 5 minutes |Cook time: 25 minutes| Serves: 4

- 2¼ cups low-sodium or no-salt-added vegetable broth
- ½ cup uncooked brown or green lentils
- ½ cup uncooked instant brown rice
- ½ cup diced carrots (about 1 carrot)
- ½ cup diced celery (about 1 stalk)
- 1 (2¼-ounce / 64-g) can sliced olives, drained (about ½ cup)
- ¼ cup diced red onion (about
- ⅛ onion)
- ¼ cup chopped fresh curly-leaf parsley
- 1½ tablespoons extra-virgin olive oil
- 1 tablespoon freshly squeezed lemon juice (from about ½ small lemon)
- 1 garlic clove, minced (about ½ teaspoon)
- ¼ teaspoon kosher or sea salt
- ¼ teaspoon freshly ground black pepper

1. In a medium saucepan over high heat, bring the broth and lentils to a boil, cover, and lower the heat to medium-low. Cook for 8 minutes. 2. Raise the heat to medium, and stir in the rice. Cover the pot and cook the mixture for 15 minutes, or until the liquid is absorbed. Remove the pot from the heat and let it sit, covered, for 1 minute, then stir. 3. While the lentils and rice are cooking, mix together the carrots, celery, olives, onion, and parsley in a large serving bowl. 4. In a small bowl, whisk together the oil, lemon juice, garlic, salt, and pepper. Set aside. 5. When the lentils and rice are cooked, add them to the serving bowl. Pour the dressing on

top, and mix everything together. Serve warm or cold, or store in a sealed container in the refrigerator for up to 7 days.

Per Serving:
calories: 183 | fat: 6g | protein: 5g | carbs: 30g | fiber: 3g | sodium: 552mg

Pesto Rice with Olives and Goat Cheese

Prep time: 5 minutes | Cook time: 22 minutes | Serves 8

- 2 cups brown basmati rice
- 2¼ cups vegetable broth
- ½ cup pesto
- ½ cup chopped mixed olives
- ¼ cup chopped fresh basil
- ¼ cup crumbled goat cheese

1. Place rice, broth, and pesto in the Instant Pot® and stir well. Close lid, set steam release to Sealing, press the Manual button, and set time to 22 minutes. 2. When the timer beeps, let pressure release naturally for 10 minutes, then quick-release the remaining pressure. Open lid, add olives and basil, and fluff rice with a fork. Serve warm, topped with goat cheese.

Per Serving:
calories: 219 | fat: 6g | protein: 6g | carbs: 36g | fiber: 1g | sodium: 148mg

Lemon Orzo with Fresh Herbs

Prep time: 10 minutes | Cook time: 10 minutes | Serves 4

- 2 cups orzo
- ½ cup fresh parsley, finely chopped
- ½ cup fresh basil, finely chopped
- 2 tablespoons lemon zest
- ½ cup extra-virgin olive oil
- ⅓ cup lemon juice
- 1 teaspoon salt
- ½ teaspoon freshly ground black pepper

1. Bring a large pot of water to a boil. Add the orzo and cook for 7 minutes. Drain and rinse with cold water. Let the orzo sit in a strainer to completely drain and cool. 2. Once the orzo has cooled, put it in a large bowl and add the parsley, basil, and lemon zest. 3. In a small bowl, whisk together the olive oil, lemon juice, salt, and pepper. Add the dressing to the pasta and toss everything together. Serve at room temperature or chilled.

Per Serving:
calories: 568 | fat: 29g | protein: 11g | carbs: 65g | fiber: 4g | sodium: 586mg

Black Chickpeas

Prep time: 11 minutes | Cook time: 9 to 11 hours | Serves 6

- 1 tablespoon rapeseed oil
- 2 teaspoons cumin seeds
- 2 cups dried whole black chickpeas, washed
- 4 cups hot water
- 1 onion, roughly chopped
- 2-inch piece fresh ginger, peeled and roughly chopped
- 4 garlic cloves
- 3 fresh green chiles
- 1 tomato, roughly chopped
- 1 teaspoon turmeric
- 1 teaspoon Kashmiri chili powder
- 1 teaspoon sea salt
- Handful fresh coriander leaves, chopped
- Juice of 1 lemon

1. Heat the oil in a frying pan (or in the slow cooker if you have a sear setting). Add the cumin seeds until they sizzle, then pour them into the cooker. 2. Heat the slow cooker to high, and then add the chickpeas and water. 3. In a blender, purée the onion, ginger, garlic, chiles, and tomato to make a paste. Add it to the cooker, along with the turmeric, chili powder, and salt. 4. Cover and cook for 9 hours on high, or for 11 hours on low. 5. When the chickpeas are cooked, check the seasoning. Add the coriander leaves and lemon juice, and serve.

Per Serving:

calories: 129 | fat: 4g | protein: 5g | carbs: 19g | fiber: 5g | sodium: 525mg

Lentil and Zucchini Boats

Prep time: 15 minutes | Cook time: 50 minutes | Serves 4

- 1 cup dried green lentils, rinsed and drained
- ¼ teaspoon salt
- 2 cups water
- 1 tablespoon olive oil
- ½ medium red onion, peeled and diced
- 1 clove garlic, peeled and minced
- 1 cup marinara sauce
- ¼ teaspoon crushed red pepper flakes
- 4 medium zucchini, trimmed and cut lengthwise
- ½ cup shredded part-skim mozzarella cheese
- ¼ cup chopped fresh flat-leaf parsley

1. Add lentils, salt, and water to the Instant Pot®. Close lid, set steam release to Sealing, press the Manual button, and set time to 12 minutes. When the timer beeps, quick-release the pressure until the float valve drops. Press the Cancel button. Open lid and drain off any excess liquid. Transfer lentils to a medium bowl. Set aside. 2. Press the Sauté button and heat oil. Add onion and cook until tender, about 3 minutes. Add garlic and cook until fragrant,

about 30 seconds. Add marinara sauce and crushed red pepper flakes and stir to combine. Press the Cancel button. Stir in lentils. 3. Preheat oven to 350°F (180°C) and spray a 9" × 13" baking dish with nonstick cooking spray. 4. Using a teaspoon, hollow out each zucchini half. Lay zucchini in prepared baking dish. Divide lentil mixture among prepared zucchini. Top with cheese. Bake for 30–35 minutes, or until zucchini are tender and cheese is melted and browned. Top with parsley and serve hot.

Per Serving:

calories: 326 | fat: 10g | protein: 22g | carbs: 39g | fiber: 16g | sodium: 568mg

Barley Salad with Lemon-Tahini Dressing

Prep time: 15 minutes | Cook time: 10 minutes | Serves 4 to 6

- 1½ cups pearl barley
- 5 tablespoons extra-virgin olive oil, divided
- 1½ teaspoons table salt, for cooking barley
- ¼ cup tahini
- 1 teaspoon grated lemon zest plus ¼ cup juice (2 lemons)
- 1 tablespoon sumac, divided
- 1 garlic clove, minced
- ¾ teaspoon table salt
- 1 English cucumber, cut into ½-inch pieces
- 1 carrot, peeled and shredded
- 1 red bell pepper, stemmed, seeded, and chopped
- 4 scallions, sliced thin
- 2 tablespoons finely chopped jarred hot cherry peppers
- ¼ cup coarsely chopped fresh mint

1. Combine 6 cups water, barley, 1 tablespoon oil, and 1½ teaspoons salt in Instant Pot. Lock lid in place and close pressure release valve. Select high pressure cook function and cook for 8 minutes. Turn off Instant Pot and let pressure release naturally for 15 minutes. Quick-release any remaining pressure, then carefully remove lid, allowing steam to escape away from you. Drain barley, spread onto rimmed baking sheet, and let cool completely, about 15 minutes. 2. Meanwhile, whisk remaining ¼ cup oil, tahini, 2 tablespoons water, lemon zest and juice, 1 teaspoon sumac, garlic, and ¾ teaspoon salt in large bowl until combined; let sit for 15 minutes. 3. Measure out and reserve ½ cup dressing for serving. Add barley, cucumber, carrot, bell pepper, scallions, and cherry peppers to bowl with dressing and gently toss to combine. Season with salt and pepper to taste. Transfer salad to serving dish and sprinkle with mint and remaining 2 teaspoons sumac. Serve, passing reserved dressing separately.

Per Serving:

calories: 370 | fat: 18g | protein: 8g | carbs: 47g | fiber: 10g | sodium: 510mg

Creamy Lima Bean Soup

Prep time: 10 minutes | Cook time: 17 minutes | Serves 6

- 1 tablespoon olive oil
- 1 small onion, peeled and diced
- 1 clove garlic, peeled and minced
- 2 cups vegetable stock
- ½ cup water
- 2 cups dried lima beans, soaked overnight and drained
- ½ teaspoon salt
- ½ teaspoon ground black pepper
- 2 tablespoons thinly sliced chives

1. Press the Sauté button on the Instant Pot® and heat oil. Add onion and cook until golden brown, about 10 minutes. Add garlic and cook until fragrant, about 30 seconds. Press the Cancel button. 2. Add stock, water, and lima beans. Close lid, set steam release to Sealing, press the Manual button, and set time to 6 minutes. When the timer beeps, let pressure release naturally, about 20 minutes. 3. Open lid and purée soup with an immersion blender or in batches in a blender. Season with salt and pepper, then sprinkle with chives before serving.

Per Serving:

calories: 67 | fat: 2g | protein: 2g | carbs: 9g | fiber: 2g | sodium: 394mg

Puréed Red Lentil Soup

Prep time: 15 minutes | Cook time: 21 minutes | Serves 6

- 2 tablespoons olive oil
- 1 medium yellow onion, peeled and chopped
- 1 medium carrot, peeled and chopped
- 1 medium red bell pepper, seeded and chopped
- 1 clove garlic, peeled and minced
- 1 bay leaf
- ½ teaspoon ground black pepper
- ¼ teaspoon salt
- 1 (15-ounce / 425-g) can diced tomatoes, drained
- 2 cups dried red lentils, rinsed and drained
- 6 cups low-sodium chicken broth

1. Press the Sauté button on the Instant Pot® and heat oil. Add onion, carrot, and bell pepper. Cook until just tender, about 5 minutes. Add garlic, bay leaf, black pepper, and salt, and cook until fragrant, about 30 seconds. Press the Cancel button. 2. Add tomatoes, lentils, and broth, then close lid, set steam release to Sealing, press the Manual button, and set time to 15 minutes. When the timer beeps, let pressure release naturally, about 15 minutes. Open lid, remove and discard bay leaf, and purée with an immersion blender or in batches in a blender. Serve warm.

Per Serving:

calories: 289 | fat: 6g | protein: 18g | carbs: 39g | fiber: 8g | sodium: 438mg

Herbed Polenta

Prep time: 10 minutes | Cook time: 3 to 5 hours | Serves 4

- 1 cup stone-ground polenta
- 4 cups low-sodium vegetable stock or low-sodium chicken stock
- 1 tablespoon extra-virgin olive oil
- 1 small onion, minced
- 2 garlic cloves, minced
- 1 teaspoon sea salt
- 1 teaspoon dried parsley
- 1 teaspoon dried oregano
- 1 teaspoon dried thyme
- ½ teaspoon freshly ground black pepper
- ½ cup grated Parmesan cheese

1. In a slow cooker, combine the polenta, vegetable stock, olive oil, onion, garlic, salt, parsley, oregano, thyme, and pepper. Stir to mix well. 2. Cover the cooker and cook for 3 to 5 hours on Low heat. 3. Stir in the Parmesan cheese for serving.

Per Serving:

calories: 191 | fat: 9g | protein: 11g | carbs: 18g | fiber: 1g | sodium: 796mg

Lentils with Cilantro and Lime

Prep time: 15 minutes | Cook time: 20 minutes | Serves 6

- 2 tablespoons olive oil
- 1 medium yellow onion, peeled and chopped
- 1 medium carrot, peeled and chopped
- ¼ cup chopped fresh cilantro
- ½ teaspoon ground cumin
- ½ teaspoon salt
- 2 cups dried green lentils, rinsed and drained
- 4 cups low-sodium chicken broth
- 2 tablespoons lime juice

1. Press the Sauté button on the Instant Pot® and heat oil. Add onion and carrot, and cook until just tender, about 3 minutes. Add cilantro, cumin, and salt, and cook until fragrant, about 30 seconds. Press the Cancel button. 2. Add lentils and broth to pot. Close lid, set steam release to Sealing, press the Manual button, and set time to 15 minutes. 3. When the timer beeps, let pressure release naturally, about 25 minutes. Open lid and stir in lime juice. Serve warm.

Per Serving:

calories: 316 | fat: 5g | protein: 20g | carbs: 44g | fiber: 21g | sodium: 349mg

Domatorizo (Greek Tomato Rice)

Prep time: 10 minutes | Cook time: 12 minutes | Serves 6

- 2 tablespoons extra-virgin olive oil
- 1 large onion, peeled and diced
- 1 cup Arborio rice
- 1 cup tomato juice
- 3 tablespoons dry white wine
- 2 cups water
- 1 tablespoon tomato paste
- ½ teaspoon salt
- ½ teaspoon ground black pepper
- ½ cup crumbled or cubed feta cheese
- ⅛ teaspoon dried Greek oregano
- 1 scallion, thinly sliced

1. Press the Sauté button on the Instant Pot® and heat oil. Add onion and cook until just tender, about 3 minutes. Stir in rice and cook for 2 minutes. 2. Add tomato juice and wine to rice. Cook, stirring often, until the liquid is absorbed, about 1 minute. 3. In a small bowl, whisk together water and tomato paste. Add to pot along with salt and pepper and stir well. Press the Cancel button. 4. Close lid, set steam release to Sealing, press the Manual button, and set time to 5 minutes. When the timer beeps, let pressure release naturally for 10 minutes, then quick-release any remaining pressure until the float valve drops. 5. Open lid and stir well. Spoon rice into bowls and top with feta, oregano, and scallion. Serve immediately.

Per Serving:

calories: 184 | fat: 9g | protein: 6g | carbs: 20g | fiber: 1g | sodium: 537mg

White Bean Cassoulet

Prep time: 30 minutes | Cook time: 45 minutes | Serves 8

- 1 tablespoon olive oil
- 1 medium onion, peeled and diced
- 2 cups dried cannellini beans, soaked overnight and drained
- 1 medium parsnip, peeled and diced
- 2 medium carrots, peeled and diced
- 2 stalks celery, diced
- 1 medium zucchini, trimmed
- and chopped
- ½ teaspoon fennel seed
- ¼ teaspoon ground nutmeg
- ½ teaspoon garlic powder
- 1 teaspoon sea salt
- ½ teaspoon ground black pepper
- 2 cups vegetable broth
- 1 (14½-ounce / 411-g) can diced tomatoes, including juice
- 2 sprigs rosemary

1. Press the Sauté button on the Instant Pot® and heat oil. Add onion and cook until translucent, about 5 minutes. Add beans and

toss. 2. Add a layer of parsnip, then a layer of carrots, and next a layer of celery. Finally, add a layer of zucchini. Sprinkle in fennel seed, nutmeg, garlic powder, salt, and pepper. Press the Cancel button. 3. Gently pour in broth and canned tomatoes. Top with rosemary. 4. Close lid, set steam release to Sealing, press the Bean button, and cook for the default time of 30 minutes. When the timer beeps, let pressure release naturally for 10 minutes. Quick-release any remaining pressure until the float valve drops and open lid. Press the Cancel button. 5. Press the Sauté button, then press the Adjust button to change the temperature to Less, and simmer bean mixture uncovered for 10 minutes to thicken. Transfer to a serving bowl and carefully toss. Remove and discard rosemary and serve.

Per Serving:

calories: 128 | fat: 2g | protein: 6g | carbs: 21g | fiber: 5g | sodium: 387mg

Moroccan Vegetables and Chickpeas

Prep time: 25 minutes | Cook time: 6 hours | Serves 6

- 1 large carrot, cut into ¼-inch rounds
- 2 large baking potatoes, peeled and cubed
- 1 large bell pepper, any color, chopped
- 6 ounces (170 g) green beans, trimmed and cut into bite-size pieces
- 1 large yellow onion, chopped
- 2 garlic cloves, minced
- 1 teaspoon peeled, grated fresh ginger
- 1 (15-ounce / 425-g) can diced tomatoes, with the juice
- 3 cups canned chickpeas, rinsed and drained
- 1¾ cups vegetable stock
- 1 tablespoon ground coriander
- 1 teaspoon ground cumin
- ¼ teaspoon ground red pepper
- Sea salt
- Black pepper
- 8 ounces (227 g) fresh baby spinach
- ¼ cup diced dried apricots
- ¼ cup diced dried figs
- 1 cup plain greek yogurt

1. Put the carrot, potatoes, bell pepper, green beans, onion, garlic, and ginger in the slow cooker. Stir in the diced tomatoes, chickpeas, and vegetable stock. Sprinkle with coriander, cumin, red pepper, salt, and black pepper. 2. Cover and cook on high for 6 hours or until the vegetables are tender. 3. Add the spinach, apricots, figs, and Greek yogurt, and cook and stir until the spinach wilts, about 4 minutes. Serve hot.

Per Serving:

calories: 307 | fat: 5g | protein: 13g | carbs: 57g | fiber: 12g | sodium: 513mg

Chapter 6 Beef, Pork, and Lamb

Bone-in Pork Chops

Prep time: 5 minutes | Cook time: 10 to 12 minutes | Serves 2

- 1 pound (454 g) bone-in pork chops
- 1 tablespoon avocado oil
- 1 teaspoon smoked paprika
- ½ teaspoon onion powder
- ¼ teaspoon cayenne pepper
- Sea salt and freshly ground black pepper, to taste

1. Brush the pork chops with the avocado oil. In a small dish, mix together the smoked paprika, onion powder, cayenne pepper, and salt and black pepper to taste. Sprinkle the seasonings over both sides of the pork chops. 2. Set the air fryer to 400°F (204°C). Place the chops in the air fryer basket in a single layer, working in batches if necessary. Air fry for 10 to 12 minutes, until an instant-read thermometer reads 145°F (63°C) at the chops' thickest point. 3. Remove the chops from the air fryer and allow them to rest for 5 minutes before serving.

Per Serving:
calories: 356 | fat: 16g | protein: 50g | carbs: 1g | fiber: 1g | sodium: 133mg

Calabrian Braised Beef with Caramelized Onions and Potatoes

Prep time: 10 minutes | Cook time: 4 hours 30 minutes | Serves 6 to 8

- 5 tablespoons olive oil, divided
- 3 medium onions, thinly sliced
- 4 cloves garlic, very thinly sliced
- 1½ teaspoons salt, divided
- 2 pounds (907 g) top sirloin steak
- ½ teaspoon freshly ground black pepper
- 2 tablespoons chopped fresh
- thyme, divided
- 3 medium potatoes, peeled and thinly sliced
- 2 sprigs fresh rosemary, leaves picked and finely chopped, divided
- ¼ cup grated Parmesan cheese, plus 4 tablespoons, divided
- 1 (28-ounce / 794-g) can crushed tomatoes

1. Preheat the oven to 325°F(165°C). 2. Heat 2 tablespoons of olive oil in a large skillet over medium heat. Add the onions and garlic along with ½ teaspoon of salt, reduce the heat to medium-low, and cook, stirring frequently, until they become very soft and golden brown, about 20 minutes. Remove from the heat. 3. Add 1 tablespoon of olive oil to a Dutch oven over medium-high heat. Pat the meat dry with paper towels and sprinkle with the remaining 1 teaspoon of salt and the pepper. Brown the meat on both sides in the Dutch oven, about 10 minutes. 4. Place about half of the cooked onions on top of the meat in an even layer. Sprinkle 1 tablespoon of thyme over the onions, then top with half of the potato slices, arranging them in an even layer. Drizzle with 1 tablespoon of olive oil, and top with half of the rosemary, and 2 tablespoons of cheese. Pour half of the tomatoes over the top. Repeat with the remaining onions, thyme, potatoes, the remaining tablespoon of olive oil, rosemary, 2 tablespoons of cheese, and the tomatoes. Place the lid on the Dutch oven and cook in the preheated oven for about 4 hours, until the meat is very tender. Sprinkle the remaining ¼ cup of cheese over the top and cook under the broiler for a few minutes, until the cheese is melted and golden brown. Serve hot.

Per Serving:
calories: 399 | fat: 23g | protein: 29g | carbs: 19g | fiber: 4g | sodium: 516mg

Beef Brisket with Onions

Prep time: 10 minutes | Cook time: 6 hours | Serves 6

- 1 large yellow onion, thinly sliced
- 2 garlic cloves, smashed and peeled
- 1 first cut of beef brisket (4 pounds / 1.8 kg), trimmed
- of excess fat
- Coarse sea salt
- Black pepper
- 2 cups chicken broth
- 2 tablespoons chopped fresh parsley leaves, for serving

1. Combine the onion and garlic in the slow cooker. 2. Season the brisket with salt and pepper, and place, fat-side up, in the slow cooker. 3. Add the broth to the slow cooker. Cover and cook until the brisket is fork-tender, on high for about 6 hours. 4. Remove the brisket to a cutting board and thinly slice across the grain. 5. Serve with the onion and some cooking liquid, sprinkled with parsley.

Per Serving:
calories: 424 | fat: 16g | protein: 67g | carbs: 4g | fiber: 1g | sodium: 277mg

Pork Casserole with Fennel and Potatoes

Prep time: 20 minutes | Cook time: 6 to 8 hours | Serves 6

- 2 large fennel bulbs
- 3 pounds (1.4 kg) pork tenderloin, cut into 1½-inch pieces
- 2 pounds (907 g) red potatoes, quartered
- 1 cup low-sodium chicken broth
- 4 garlic cloves, minced
- 1½ teaspoons dried thyme
- 1 teaspoon dried parsley
- 1 teaspoon sea salt
- Freshly ground black pepper
- ⅓ cup shredded Parmesan cheese

1. Cut the stalks off the fennel bulbs. Trim a little piece from the bottom of the bulbs to make them stable, then cut straight down through the bulbs to halve them. Cut the halves into quarters. Peel off and discard any wilted outer layers. Cut the fennel pieces crosswise into slices. 2. In a slow cooker, combine the fennel, pork, and potatoes. Stir to mix well. 3. In a small bowl, whisk together the chicken broth, garlic, thyme, parsley, and salt until combined. Season with pepper and whisk again. Pour the sauce over the pork. 4. Cover the cooker and cook for 6 to 8 hours on Low heat. 5. Top with Parmesan cheese for serving.

Per Serving:
calories: 412 | fat: 7g | protein: 55g | carbs: 31g | fiber: 5g | sodium: 592mg

Moroccan Flank Steak with Harissa Couscous

Prep time: 5 minutes | Cook time: 15 minutes | Serves 4

- 1½ teaspoons coriander seeds
- 1¼ teaspoons ground ginger
- ½ teaspoon ground cumin
- ¾ teaspoon ground cinnamon
- ¼ teaspoon ground cloves
- 1½ pounds (680 g) flank steak
- 3 tablespoons olive oil
- ¾ cup chicken broth
- 1 tablespoon harissa
- ½ cup chopped pitted dried dates
- 1 cup uncooked couscous
- Sea salt
- Freshly ground black pepper
- ¼ cup chopped fresh Italian parsley

1. In a small bowl, combine the coriander, ginger, cumin, cinnamon, and cloves. Rub the steak all over with the seasoning mix. 2. In a large sauté pan, heat the olive oil over medium-high heat. Add the steak and cook for 2 to 3 minutes on each side for medium-rare. Transfer the steak to a plate and set aside to rest for 10 minutes. 3. In the same pan, mix together the meat juices with the broth, harissa, and dates. Bring to a boil over medium-high heat. Add the couscous, remove from the heat, cover, and let stand for 5 minutes. Season with salt and pepper. 4. Cut the steak across the grain into thin strips. 5. Serve the steak with the couscous, garnished with parsley.

Per Serving:
calories: 516 | fat: 16g | protein: 43g | carbs: 49g | fiber: 4g | sodium: 137mg

Minty Lamb Meatballs in Spicy Red Pepper Ragu

Prep time: 15 minutes | Cook time: 17 minutes | Makes 16 meatballs

- 1 pound (454 g) ground lamb
- 1 large egg
- ½ cup plus 1 tablespoon chopped fresh mint, divided
- ¼ cup bread crumbs
- 2 tablespoons minced white onion
- ¼ teaspoon salt
- ¼ teaspoon ground black pepper
- 2 tablespoons light olive oil, divided
- 2 medium red bell peppers, seeded and chopped
- 2 cloves garlic, peeled and minced
- ¼ teaspoon crushed red pepper flakes
- 1 tablespoon chopped fresh oregano
- 1 (14½-ounce / 411-g) can diced tomatoes, drained
- ¼ cup water

1. In a medium bowl, combine lamb, egg, ½ cup mint, bread crumbs, onion, salt, and black pepper. Form into 16 golf ball–sized meatballs. Set aside. 2. Press the Sauté button on the Instant Pot® and heat 1 tablespoon oil. Place half of the meatballs around the edges of the Instant Pot®. Sear all sides of meatballs for a total of 4 minutes. Remove first batch and set aside. Add remaining 1 tablespoon oil and meatballs, and sear 4 minutes. Remove meatballs. 3. Add bell peppers to the Instant Pot® and cook until tender, about 5 minutes. Add garlic and red pepper flakes and cook until garlic is fragrant, about 30 seconds. Add oregano, tomatoes, water, and remaining 1 tablespoon mint to the Instant Pot®, and stir well. Press the Cancel button. 4. Top red pepper mixture with browned meatballs. Close lid, set steam release to Sealing, press the Manual button, and set time to 3 minutes. When the timer beeps, quick-release the pressure until the float valve drops and open lid. Transfer meatballs and sauce to bowls and serve warm.

Per Serving:
2 meatballs: calories: 166 | fat: 12g | protein: 12g | carbs: 4g | fiber: 2g | sodium: 204mg

Greek Stuffed Tenderloin

Prep time: 10 minutes | Cook time: 10 minutes | Serves 4

- 1½ pounds (680 g) venison or beef tenderloin, pounded to ¼ inch thick
- 3 teaspoons fine sea salt
- 1 teaspoon ground black pepper
- 2 ounces (57 g) creamy goat cheese
- ½ cup crumbled feta cheese (about 2 ounces / 57 g)
- ¼ cup finely chopped onions
- 2 cloves garlic, minced
- For Garnish/Serving (Optional):
- Prepared yellow mustard
- Halved cherry tomatoes
- Extra-virgin olive oil
- Sprigs of fresh rosemary
- Lavender flowers

1. Spray the air fryer basket with avocado oil. Preheat the air fryer to 400°F (204°C). 2. Season the tenderloin on all sides with the salt and pepper. 3. In a medium-sized mixing bowl, combine the goat cheese, feta, onions, and garlic. Place the mixture in the center of the tenderloin. Starting at the end closest to you, tightly roll the tenderloin like a jelly roll. Tie the rolled tenderloin tightly with kitchen twine. 4. Place the meat in the air fryer basket and air fry for 5 minutes. Flip the meat over and cook for another 5 minutes, or until the internal temperature reaches 135°F (57°C) for medium-rare. 5. To serve, smear a line of prepared yellow mustard on a platter, then place the meat next to it and add halved cherry tomatoes on the side, if desired. Drizzle with olive oil and garnish with rosemary sprigs and lavender flowers, if desired. 6. Best served fresh. Store leftovers in an airtight container in the fridge for 3 days. Reheat in a preheated 350°F (177°C) air fryer for 4 minutes, or until heated through.

Per Serving:
calories: 345 | fat: 17g | protein: 43g | carbs: 2g | fiber: 0g | sodium: 676mg

Saucy Beef Fingers

Prep time: 30 minutes | Cook time: 14 minutes | Serves 4

- 1½ pounds (680 g) sirloin steak
- ¼ cup red wine
- ¼ cup fresh lime juice
- 1 teaspoon garlic powder
- 1 teaspoon shallot powder
- 1 teaspoon celery seeds
- 1 teaspoon mustard seeds
- Coarse sea salt and ground black pepper, to taste
- 1 teaspoon red pepper flakes
- 2 eggs, lightly whisked
- 1 cup Parmesan cheese
- 1 teaspoon paprika

1. Place the steak, red wine, lime juice, garlic powder, shallot powder, celery seeds, mustard seeds, salt, black pepper, and red pepper in a large ceramic bowl; let it marinate for 3 hours. 2. Tenderize the cube steak by pounding with a mallet; cut into 1-inch strips. 3. In a shallow bowl, whisk the eggs. In another bowl, mix the Parmesan cheese and paprika. 4. Dip the beef pieces into the whisked eggs and coat on all sides. Now, dredge the beef pieces in the Parmesan mixture. 5. Cook at 400°F (204°C) for 14 minutes, flipping halfway through the cooking time. 6. Meanwhile, make the sauce by heating the reserved marinade in a saucepan over medium heat; let it simmer until thoroughly warmed. Serve the steak fingers with the sauce on the side. Enjoy!

Per Serving:
calories: 483 | fat: 29g | protein: 49g | carbs: 4g | fiber: 1g | sodium: 141mg

Lamb with Olives and Potatoes

Prep time: 20 minutes | Cook time: 4 hours | Serves 4

- 1¼ pounds (567 g) small potatoes, halved
- 4 large shallots, cut into ½-inch wedges
- 3 cloves garlic, minced
- 1 tablespoon lemon zest
- 3 sprigs fresh rosemary
- Coarse sea salt
- Black pepper
- 4 tablespoons all-purpose flour
- ¾ cup chicken stock
- 3½ pounds (1.6 kg) lamb shanks, cut crosswise into 1½-inch pieces and fat trimmed
- 2 tablespoons extra-virgin olive oil
- ½ cup dry white wine
- 1 cup pitted green olives, halved
- 2 tablespoons lemon juice

1. Combine the potatoes, shallots, garlic, lemon zest, and rosemary sprigs in the slow cooker. Season with salt and pepper. 2. In a small bowl, whisk together 1 tablespoon of the flour and the stock. Add to the slow cooker. 3. Place the remaining 3 tablespoons flour on a plate. Season the lamb with salt and pepper; then coat in the flour, shaking off any excess. 4. In a large skillet over medium-high, heat the olive oil. In batches, cook the lamb until browned on all sides, about 10 minutes. Transfer to the slow cooker. 5. Add the wine to the skillet and cook, stirring with a wooden spoon and scraping up the flavorful browned bits from the bottom of the pan, until reduced by half, about 2 minutes. Then add to the slow cooker. 6. Cover and cook until the lamb is tender, on high for about 3½ hours, or on low for 7 hours. 7. Stir in olive halves, then cover, and cook 20 additional minutes. 8. To serve, transfer the lamb and vegetables to warm plates. 9. Skim the fat from the cooking liquid, then stir in the lemon juice, and season the sauce with salt and pepper. 10. Serve the sauce with the lamb and vegetables.

Per Serving:
calories: 765 | fat: 26g | protein: 93g | carbs: 38g | fiber: 5g | sodium: 596mg

Steak with Bell Pepper

Prep time: 30 minutes | Cook time: 20 to 23 minutes | Serves 6

- ¼ cup avocado oil
- ¼ cup freshly squeezed lime juice
- 2 teaspoons minced garlic
- 1 tablespoon chili powder
- ½ teaspoon ground cumin
- Sea salt and freshly ground black pepper, to taste
- 1 pound (454 g) top sirloin steak or flank steak, thinly sliced against the grain
- 1 red bell pepper, cored, seeded, and cut into ½-inch slices
- 1 green bell pepper, cored, seeded, and cut into ½-inch slices
- 1 large onion, sliced

1. In a small bowl or blender, combine the avocado oil, lime juice, garlic, chili powder, cumin, and salt and pepper to taste. 2. Place the sliced steak in a zip-top bag or shallow dish. Place the bell peppers and onion in a separate zip-top bag or dish. Pour half the marinade over the steak and the other half over the vegetables. Seal both bags and let the steak and vegetables marinate in the refrigerator for at least 1 hour or up to 4 hours. 3. Line the air fryer basket with an air fryer liner or aluminum foil. Remove the vegetables from their bag or dish and shake off any excess marinade. Set the air fryer to 400ºF (204ºC). Place the vegetables in the air fryer basket and cook for 13 minutes. 4. Remove the steak from its bag or dish and shake off any excess marinade. Place the steak on top of the vegetables in the air fryer, and cook for 7 to 10 minutes or until an instant-read thermometer reads 120ºF (49ºC) for medium-rare (or cook to your desired doneness). 5. Serve with desired fixings, such as keto tortillas, lettuce, sour cream, avocado slices, shredded Cheddar cheese, and cilantro.

Per Serving:

calories: 252 | fat: 18g | protein: 17g | carbs: 6g | fiber: 2g | sodium: 81mg

Pepper Steak

Prep time: 30 minutes | Cook time: 16 to 20 minutes | Serves 4

- 1 pound (454 g) cube steak, cut into 1-inch pieces
- 1 cup Italian dressing
- 1½ cups beef broth
- 1 tablespoon soy sauce
- ½ teaspoon salt
- ¼ teaspoon freshly ground
- black pepper
- ¼ cup cornstarch
- 1 cup thinly sliced bell pepper, any color
- 1 cup chopped celery
- 1 tablespoon minced garlic
- 1 to 2 tablespoons oil

1. In a large resealable bag, combine the beef and Italian dressing. Seal the bag and refrigerate to marinate for 8 hours. 2. In a small bowl, whisk the beef broth, soy sauce, salt, and pepper until blended. 3. In another small bowl, whisk ¼ cup water and the cornstarch until dissolved. Stir the cornstarch mixture into the beef broth mixture until blended. 4. Preheat the air fryer to 375ºF (191ºC). 5. Pour the broth mixture into a baking pan. Cook for 4 minutes. Stir and cook for 4 to 5 minutes more. Remove and set aside. 6. Increase the air fryer temperature to 400ºF (204ºC). Line the air fryer basket with parchment paper. 7. Remove the steak from the marinade and place it in a medium bowl. Discard the marinade. Stir in the bell pepper, celery, and garlic. 8. Place the steak and pepper mixture on the parchment. Spritz with oil. 9. Cook for 4 minutes. Shake the basket and cook for 4 to 7 minutes more, until the vegetables are tender and the meat reaches an internal temperature of 145ºF (63ºC). Serve with the gravy.

Per Serving:

calories: 302 | fat: 14g | protein: 27g | carbs: 15g | fiber: 1g | sodium: 635mg

Italian Steak Rolls

Prep time: 30 minutes | Cook time: 9 minutes | Serves 4

- 1 tablespoon vegetable oil
- 2 cloves garlic, minced
- 2 teaspoons dried Italian seasoning
- 1 teaspoon kosher salt
- 1 teaspoon black pepper
- 1 pound (454 g) flank or skirt steak, ¼ to ½ inch thick
- 1 (10-ounce / 283-g) package frozen spinach, thawed and squeezed dry
- ½ cup diced jarred roasted red pepper
- 1 cup shredded Mozzarella cheese

1. In a large bowl, combine the oil, garlic, Italian seasoning, salt, and pepper. Whisk to combine. Add the steak to the bowl, turning to ensure the entire steak is covered with the seasonings. Cover and marinate at room temperature for 30 minutes or in the refrigerator for up to 24 hours. 2. Lay the steak on a flat surface. Spread the spinach evenly over the steak, leaving a ¼-inch border at the edge. Evenly top each steak with the red pepper and cheese. 3. Starting at a long end, roll up the steak as tightly as possible, ending seam side down. Use 2 or 3 wooden toothpicks to hold the roll together. Using a sharp knife, cut the roll in half so that it better fits in the air fryer basket. 4. Place the steak roll, seam side down, in the air fryer basket. Set the air fryer to 400ºF (204ºC) for 9 minutes. Use a meat thermometer to ensure the steak has reached an internal temperature of 145ºF (63ºC). (It is critical to not overcook flank steak, so as to not toughen the meat.) 5. Let the steak rest for 10 minutes before cutting into slices to serve.

Per Serving:

calories: 311 | fat: 15g | protein: 36g | carbs: 7g | fiber: 3g | sodium: 803mg

Spaghetti Zoodles and Meatballs

Prep time: 30 minutes | Cook time: 11 to 13 minutes | Serves 6

- 1 pound (454 g) ground beef
- 1½ teaspoons sea salt, plus more for seasoning
- 1 large egg, beaten
- 1 teaspoon gelatin
- ¾ cup Parmesan cheese
- 2 teaspoons minced garlic
- 1 teaspoon Italian seasoning
- Freshly ground black pepper, to taste
- Avocado oil spray
- Keto-friendly marinara sauce, for serving
- 6 ounces (170 g) zucchini noodles, made using a spiralizer or store-bought

1. Place the ground beef in a large bowl, and season with the salt. 2. Place the egg in a separate bowl and sprinkle with the gelatin. Allow to sit for 5 minutes. 3. Stir the gelatin mixture, then pour it over the ground beef. Add the Parmesan, garlic, and Italian seasoning. Season with salt and pepper. 4. Form the mixture into 1½-inch meatballs and place them on a plate; cover with plastic wrap and refrigerate for at least 1 hour or overnight. 5. Spray the meatballs with oil. Set the air fryer to 400ºF (204ºC) and arrange the meatballs in a single layer in the air fryer basket. Air fry for 4 minutes. Flip the meatballs and spray them with more oil. Air fry for 4 minutes more, until an instant-read thermometer reads 160ºF (71ºC). Transfer the meatballs to a plate and allow them to rest. 6. While the meatballs are resting, heat the marinara in a saucepan on the stove over medium heat. 7. Place the zucchini noodles in the air fryer, and cook at 400ºF (204ºC) for 3 to 5 minutes. 8. To serve, place the zucchini noodles in serving bowls. Top with meatballs and warm marinara.

Per Serving:

calories: 176 | fat: 8g | protein: 23g | carbs: 2g | fiber: 0g | sodium: 689mg

Beef Whirls

Prep time: 30 minutes | Cook time: 18 minutes | Serves 6

- 3 cube steaks (6 ounces / 170 g each)
- 1 (16-ounce / 454-g) bottle Italian dressing
- 1 cup Italian-style bread crumbs
- ½ cup grated Parmesan
- cheese
- 1 teaspoon dried basil
- 1 teaspoon dried oregano
- 1 teaspoon dried parsley
- ¼ cup beef broth
- 1 to 2 tablespoons oil

1. In a large resealable bag, combine the steaks and Italian dressing.

Seal the bag and refrigerate to marinate for 2 hours. 2. In a medium bowl, whisk the bread crumbs, cheese, basil, oregano, and parsley until blended. Stir in the beef broth. 3. Place the steaks on a cutting board and cut each in half so you have 6 equal pieces. Sprinkle with the bread crumb mixture. Roll up the steaks, jelly roll-style, and secure with toothpicks. 4. Preheat the air fryer to 400ºF (204ºC). 5. Place 3 roll-ups in the air fryer basket. 6. Cook for 5 minutes. Flip the roll-ups and spritz with oil. Cook for 4 minutes more until the internal temperature reaches 145ºF (63ºC). Repeat with the remaining roll-ups. Let rest for 5 to 10 minutes before serving.

Per Serving:

calories: 307 | fat: 15g | protein: 24g | carbs: 17g | fiber: 1g | sodium: 236mg

Ground Beef Taco Rolls

Prep time: 20 minutes | Cook time: 10 minutes | Serves 4

- ½ pound (227 g) ground beef
- ⅓ cup water
- 1 tablespoon chili powder
- 2 teaspoons cumin
- ½ teaspoon garlic powder
- ¼ teaspoon dried oregano
- ¼ cup canned diced tomatoes and chiles, drained
- 2 tablespoons chopped
- cilantro
- 1½ cups shredded Mozzarella cheese
- ½ cup blanched finely ground almond flour
- 2 ounces (57 g) full-fat cream cheese
- 1 large egg

1. In a medium skillet over medium heat, brown the ground beef about 7 to 10 minutes. When meat is fully cooked, drain. 2. Add water to skillet and stir in chili powder, cumin, garlic powder, oregano, and tomatoes with chiles. Add cilantro. Bring to a boil, then reduce heat to simmer for 3 minutes. 3. In a large microwave-safe bowl, place Mozzarella, almond flour, cream cheese, and egg. Microwave for 1 minute. Stir the mixture quickly until smooth ball of dough forms. 4. Cut a piece of parchment for your work surface. Press the dough into a large rectangle on the parchment, wetting your hands to prevent the dough from sticking as necessary. Cut the dough into eight rectangles. 5. On each rectangle place a few spoons of the meat mixture. Fold the short ends of each roll toward the center and roll the length as you would a burrito. 6. Cut a piece of parchment to fit your air fryer basket. Place taco rolls onto the parchment and place into the air fryer basket. 7. Adjust the temperature to 360ºF (182ºC) and air fry for 10 minutes. 8. Flip halfway through the cooking time. 9. Allow to cool 10 minutes before serving.

Per Serving:

calories: 411 | fat: 31g | protein: 27g | carbs: 7g | fiber: 3g | sodium: 176mg

Greek-Inspired Beef Kebabs

Prep timePrep Time: 15 minutes | Cook Time: 15 minutes | Serves 2

- 6 ounces (170 g) beef sirloin tip, trimmed of fat and cut into 2-inch pieces
- 3 cups of any mixture of vegetables: mushrooms, zucchini, summer squash, onions, cherry tomatoes, red peppers
- ½ cup olive oil
- ¼ cup freshly squeezed lemon juice
- 2 tablespoons balsamic vinegar
- 2 teaspoons dried oregano
- 1 teaspoon garlic powder
- 1 teaspoon minced fresh rosemary
- 1 teaspoon salt

1. Place the meat in a large shallow container or in a plastic freezer bag. 2. Cut the vegetables into similar-size pieces and place them in a second shallow container or freezer bag. 3. For the marinade, combine the olive oil, lemon juice, balsamic vinegar, oregano, garlic powder, rosemary, and salt in a measuring cup. Whisk well to combine. Pour half of the marinade over the meat, and the other half over the vegetables. 4. Place the meat and vegetables in the refrigerator to marinate for 4 hours. 5. When you are ready to cook, preheat the grill to medium-high (350–400°F) and grease the grill grate. 6. Thread the meat onto skewers and the vegetables onto separate skewers. 7. Grill the meat for 3 minutes on each side. They should only take 10 to 12 minutes to cook, but it will depend on how thick the meat is. 8. Grill the vegetables for about 3 minutes on each side or until they have grill marks and are softened.

Per Serving:
calories: 285 | fat: 18g | protein: 21g | carbs: 9g | fiber: 4g | sodium: 123mg

Mediterranean Pork with Olives

Prep time: 10 minutes | Cook time: 6 to 8 hours | Serves 4

- 1 small onion, sliced
- 4 thick-cut, bone-in pork chops
- 1 cup low-sodium chicken broth
- Juice of 1 lemon
- 2 garlic cloves, minced
- 1 teaspoon sea salt
- 1 teaspoon dried oregano
- 1 teaspoon dried parsley
- ½ teaspoon freshly ground black pepper
- 2 cups whole green olives, pitted
- 1 pint cherry tomatoes

1. Put the onion in a slow cooker and arrange the pork chops on top. 2. In a small bowl, whisk together the chicken broth, lemon juice, garlic, salt, oregano, parsley, and pepper. Pour the sauce over the pork chops. Top with the olives and tomatoes. 3. Cover the cooker

and cook for 6 to 8 hours on Low heat.

Per Serving:
calories: 339 | fat: 14g | protein: 42g | carbs: 6g | fiber: 4g | sodium: 708mg

Lamb and Onion Tagine

Prep time: 10 minutes | Cook time: 2 hours 15 minutes | Serves 4

- 2 tablespoons finely chopped fresh flat-leaf parsley
- 2 tablespoons finely chopped fresh cilantro
- 2 cloves garlic, minced
- ½ teaspoon ground turmeric
- ½ teaspoon ground ginger
- 1 teaspoon ground cinnamon, divided
- 1 teaspoon plus a pinch kosher salt
- ½ teaspoon ground black pepper
- 2 tablespoons plus ⅓ cup water
- 3 tablespoons extra-virgin olive oil
- 4 bone-in leg of lamb steaks, ½' thick (about 2½ pounds / 1.1 kg)
- 1 can (28 ounces / 794-g) whole peeled plum tomatoes, drained
- 2 large red onions, 1 finely chopped, the other sliced in ⅛' rounds
- 2 teaspoons honey, divided
- 1 tablespoon toasted sesame seeds

1. In a large bowl, combine the parsley, cilantro, garlic, turmeric, ginger, ¼ teaspoon of the cinnamon, 1 teaspoon of the salt, and the pepper. Add 2 tablespoons of the water and the oil and mix. Add the lamb steaks and turn to coat each one. Cover and refrigerate, turning the steaks occasionally, for at least 1 hour. 2. Make a small cut into each tomato and squeeze out the seeds and excess juices. 3. In a 12' tagine or a deep heavy-bottom skillet, scatter the chopped onion. Arrange the lamb steaks snugly in a single layer. Drizzle the remaining marinade over the top. Add the tomatoes around the lamb. Drizzle 1 teaspoon of the honey and ¼ teaspoon of the cinnamon over the top. 4. Lay the onion rounds on top of the lamb. Drizzle the remaining 1 teaspoon honey. Sprinkle the remaining ½ teaspoon cinnamon and the pinch of salt. Turn the heat on to medium (medium-low if using a pot) and cook, uncovered, nudging the lamb occasionally, until the chopped onion below is translucent, about 15 minutes. 5. Pour in the ⅓ cup water around the outer edges of the food. Cover with a lid, slightly askew to keep air flowing in and out of the tagine or skillet. Reduce the heat to low and simmer gently, nudging the lamb occasionally to prevent sticking. Cook until the lamb is very tender, adding water as needed to keep the sauce moist, about 2 hours. 6. Sprinkle with the sesame seeds and serve.

Per Serving:
calories: 537 | fat: 25g | protein: 63g | carbs: 19g | fiber: 6g | sodium: 791mg

Kofta with Vegetables in Tomato Sauce

Prep time: 15 minutes | Cook time: 6 to 8 hours | Serves 4

- 1 pound (454 g) raw ground beef
- 1 small white or yellow onion, finely diced
- 2 garlic cloves, minced
- 1 tablespoon dried parsley
- 2 teaspoons ground coriander
- 1 teaspoon ground cumin
- ½ teaspoon sea salt
- ½ teaspoon freshly ground black pepper
- ¼ teaspoon ground nutmeg
- ¼ teaspoon dried mint
- ¼ teaspoon paprika
- 1 (28-ounce/ 794-g) can no-salt-added diced tomatoes
- 2 or 3 zucchini, cut into 1½-inch-thick rounds
- 4 ounces (113 g) mushrooms
- 1 large red onion, chopped
- 1 green bell pepper, seeded and chopped

1. In large bowl, mix together the ground beef, white or yellow onion, garlic, parsley, coriander, cumin, salt, pepper, nutmeg, mint, and paprika until well combined and all of the spices and onion are well blended into the meat. Form the meat mixture into 10 to 12 oval patties. Set aside. 2. In a slow cooker, combine the tomatoes, zucchini, mushrooms, red onion, and bell pepper. Stir to mix well. 3. Place the kofta patties on top of the tomato mixture. 4. Cover the cooker and cook for 6 to 8 hours on Low heat.

Per Serving:

calories: 263 | fat: 9g | protein: 27g | carbs: 23g | fiber: 7g | sodium: 480mg

Beesteya (Moroccan-Style Lamb Pie)

Prep time: 15 minutes | Cook time: 1 hour | Serves 8

- 2 tablespoons olive oil
- 1 medium onion, chopped (about 1¼ cups)
- 3 carrots, finely chopped (about 1 cup)
- 1 teaspoon ground turmeric
- 2 garlic cloves, minced
- 1 pound (454 g) ground lamb, turkey, or lean beef
- ⅓ cup golden raisins
- ½ cup pistachios, toasted
- ¼ cup chopped fresh cilantro
- 1 teaspoon ground cinnamon
- 6 eggs
- 1 (5-ounce / 142-g) container 2% Greek yogurt
- Olive oil cooking spray or other nonstick cooking spray
- 12 sheets frozen phyllo dough, thawed

1. Preheat the oven to 375°F (190°C). 2. In a large skillet, heat 1 tablespoon of the olive oil over medium heat. Add the onion and carrots and cook, stirring occasionally for 5 to 6 minutes, until the onion is translucent. Stir in the turmeric and garlic; cook for 1 minute. Add the remaining 1 tablespoon olive oil and the ground lamb to the skillet. Cook, breaking up the meat with a wooden spoon as it cooks, for 6 to 8 minutes, until the lamb is browned. 3. Stir in the raisins, pistachios, cilantro, and cinnamon until well combined; set aside. 4. In a medium bowl, whisk the eggs and yogurt together; set aside. 5. Spray a 9-inch springform pan with olive oil cooking spray or other cooking spray. On a clean work surface, stack 4 phyllo sheets, spray both sides with cooking spray, and place in the stack in the prepared pan, extending the edges of the stack up the sides of the pan. Repeat with a second stack of 4 phyllo sheets; place them crosswise over the first stack, extending the edges over the top edge of the pan. 6. Fill the phyllo crust with the lamb mixture, then pour in the egg mixture. Spray the remaining 4 phyllo sheets with cooking spray and cut in half. Place them over the filling to cover it completely. Fold the phyllo toward the center over the filling. Spray with additional cooking spray. 7. Bake for 45 to 50 minutes, until golden brown. Let stand for 15 minutes before serving.

Per Serving:

1 cup: calories: 362 | fat: 19g | protein: 22g | carbs: 28g | fiber: 3g | sodium: 241mg

Smoky Herb Lamb Chops and Lemon-Rosemary Dressing

Prep time: 1 hour 35 minutes | Cook time: 10 minutes | Serves 6

- 4 large cloves garlic
- 1 cup lemon juice
- ⅓ cup fresh rosemary
- 1 cup extra-virgin olive oil
- 1½ teaspoons salt
- 1 teaspoon freshly ground black pepper
- 6 (1-inch-thick) lamb chops

1. In a food processor or blender, blend the garlic, lemon juice, rosemary, olive oil, salt, and black pepper for 15 seconds. Set aside. 2. Put the lamb chops in a large plastic zip-top bag or container. Cover the lamb with two-thirds of the rosemary dressing, making sure that all of the lamb chops are coated with the dressing. Let the lamb marinate in the fridge for 1 hour. 3. When you are almost ready to eat, take the lamb chops out of the fridge and let them sit on the counter-top for 20 minutes. Preheat a grill, grill pan, or lightly oiled skillet to high heat. 4. Cook the lamb chops for 3 minutes on each side. To serve, drizzle the lamb with the remaining dressing.

Per Serving:

calories: 484 | fat: 42g | protein: 24g | carbs: 5g | fiber: 1g | sodium: 655mg

Italian Braised Pork

Prep time: 10 minutes | Cook time: 4⅓ hours | Serves 4

- 2½ pounds (1.1 kg) boneless pork shoulder
- Coarse sea salt
- Black pepper
- 2 tablespoons olive oil
- 1 large yellow onion, finely diced
- 3 cloves garlic, minced
- 1 stalk celery, finely diced
- ¾ teaspoon fennel seeds
- ½ cup dry red wine
- 1 (28-ounce / 794-g) can crushed tomatoes
- 4 cups prepared hot couscous, for serving

1. Season the pork with salt and pepper. 2. In a large skillet, heat the olive oil over medium-high heat. Cook the pork, turning occasionally, until browned on all sides, about 8 minutes. Transfer the pork to the slow cooker. 3. Reduce the heat under the skillet to medium, and add the onion, garlic, celery, and fennel seeds. Cook, stirring often, until the onion is softened, about 4 minutes. 4. Add the wine and cook, stirring with a wooden spoon and scraping up the flavorful browned bits from the bottom of the pan, until the liquid is reduced by half, about 2 minutes. Add the wine mixture to the slow cooker, and stir in the tomatoes. 5. Cover and cook on high for 4 hours, or until the pork is very tender, or on low for 8 hours. 6. Transfer the pork to a cutting board. Shred the meat into bite-size pieces. Discard any pieces of fat. 7. Skim the fat off the sauce in the slow cooker and discard. Return the shredded pork to the slow cooker and stir to combine. Cook the pork and sauce for 5 minutes to reheat. 8. Serve hot over the couscous.

Per Serving:

calories: 669 | fat: 17g | protein: 72g | carbs: 49g | fiber: 7g | sodium: 187mg

Meatballs in Creamy Almond Sauce

Prep time: 15 minutes | Cook time: 35 minutes | Serves 4 to 6

- 8 ounces (227 g) ground veal or pork
- 8 ounces (227 g) ground beef
- ½ cup finely minced onion, divided
- 1 large egg, beaten
- ¼ cup almond flour
- 1½ teaspoons salt, divided
- 1 teaspoon garlic powder
- ½ teaspoon freshly ground black pepper
- ½ teaspoon ground nutmeg
- 2 teaspoons chopped fresh flat-leaf Italian parsley, plus ¼ cup, divided
- ½ cup extra-virgin olive oil, divided
- ¼ cup slivered almonds
- 1 cup dry white wine or chicken broth
- ¼ cup unsweetened almond butter

1. In a large bowl, combine the veal, beef, ¼ cup onion, and the egg and mix well with a fork. In a small bowl, whisk together the almond flour, 1 teaspoon salt, garlic powder, pepper, and nutmeg. Add to the meat mixture along with 2 teaspoons chopped parsley and incorporate well. Form the mixture into small meatballs, about 1 inch in diameter, and place on a plate. Let sit for 10 minutes at room temperature. 2. In a large skillet, heat ¼ cup oil over medium-high heat. Add the meatballs to the hot oil and brown on all sides, cooking in batches if necessary, 2 to 3 minutes per side. Remove from skillet and keep warm. 3. In the hot skillet, sauté the remaining ¼ cup minced onion in the remaining ¼ cup olive oil for 5 minutes. Reduce the heat to medium-low and add the slivered almonds. Sauté until the almonds are golden, another 3 to 5 minutes. 4. In a small bowl, whisk together the white wine, almond butter, and remaining ½ teaspoon salt. Add to the skillet and bring to a boil, stirring constantly. Reduce the heat to low, return the meatballs to skillet, and cover. Cook until the meatballs are cooked through, another 8 to 10 minutes. 5. Remove from the heat, stir in the remaining ¼ cup chopped parsley, and serve the meatballs warm and drizzled with almond sauce.

Per Serving:

calories: 447 | fat: 36g | protein: 20g | carbs: 7g | fiber: 2g | sodium: 659mg

Greek Meatball Soup

Prep time: 20 minutes | Cook time: 45 minutes | Serves 5

- 1 pound (454 g) ground beef
- ⅓ cup orzo
- 4 large eggs
- 1 onion, finely chopped
- 2 garlic cloves, minced
- 2 tablespoons finely chopped fresh Italian parsley
- Sea salt
- Freshly ground black pepper
- ½ cup all-purpose flour
- 5 to 6 cups chicken broth
- Juice of 2 lemons

1. In a large bowl, combine the ground beef, orzo, 1 egg, the onion, garlic, and parsley and stir until well mixed. Season with salt and pepper and mix again. 2. Place the flour in a small bowl. 3. Roll the meat mixture into a ball about the size of a golf ball and dredge it in the flour to coat, shaking off any excess. Place the meatball in a stockpot and repeat with the remaining meat mixture. 4. Pour enough broth into the pot to cover the meatballs by about 1 inch. Bring the broth to a boil over high heat. Reduce the heat to low, cover, and simmer for 30 to 45 minutes, until the meatballs are cooked through. 5. While the meatballs are simmering, in a small bowl, whisk the 3 remaining eggs until frothy. Add the lemon juice and whisk well. 6. When the meatballs are cooked, while whisking continuously, slowly pour 1½ cups of the hot broth into the egg mixture. Pour the egg mixture back into the pot and mix well. Bring back to a simmer, then remove from the heat and serve.

Per Serving:

calories: 297 | fat: 9g | protein: 27g | carbs: 28g | fiber: 1g | sodium: 155mg

Beef Meatballs in Garlic Cream Sauce

Prep time: 15 minutes | Cook time: 6 to 8 hours | Serves 4

For the Sauce:
- 1 cup low-sodium vegetable broth or low-sodium chicken broth
- 1 tablespoon extra-virgin olive oil
- 2 garlic cloves, minced
- 1 tablespoon dried onion flakes

For the Meatballs:
- 1 pound (454 g) raw ground beef
- 1 large egg
- 2 tablespoons bread crumbs
- 1 teaspoon ground cumin
- 1 teaspoon salt

- 1 teaspoon dried rosemary
- 2 tablespoons freshly squeezed lemon juice
- Pinch sea salt
- Pinch freshly ground black pepper

- ½ teaspoon freshly ground black pepper

To Finish
- 2 cups plain Greek yogurt
- 2 tablespoons chopped fresh parsley

Make the Sauce: 1. In a medium bowl, whisk together the vegetable broth, olive oil, garlic, onion flakes, rosemary, lemon juice, salt, and pepper until combined. Make the Meatballs: 2. In a large bowl, mix together the ground beef, egg, bread crumbs, cumin, salt, and pepper until combined. Shape the meat mixture into 10 to 12 (2½-inch) meatballs. 3. Pour the sauce into the slow cooker. 4. Add the meatballs to the slow cooker. 5. Cover the cooker and cook for 6 to 8 hours on Low heat. 6. Stir in the yogurt. Replace the cover on the cooker and cook for 15 to 30 minutes on Low heat, or until the sauce has thickened. 7. Garnish with fresh parsley for serving.

Per Serving:

calories: 345 | fat: 20g | protein: 29g | carbs: 13g | fiber: 1g | sodium: 842mg

Chapter 7 Fish and Seafood

Trout Cooked in Parchment

Prep time: 10 minutes | Cook time: 10 minutes | Serves 4

- 4 (4 ounces / 113 g each) trout fillets
- 3 cloves garlic, finely chopped
- 8 fresh sage leaves, finely chopped
- ½ cup finely chopped fresh parsley
- Zest and juice of 1 lemon
- ⅓ cup extra-virgin olive oil
- 1 teaspoon unrefined sea salt or salt
- Freshly ground pepper
- Lemon wedges

1. Preheat the oven to 425ºF (220ºC). Combine the garlic, sage, parsley, lemon zest and juice, olive oil, salt, and pepper in a small bowl. Cut four pieces of parchment paper—each more than double the size of the trout. 2. Place 1 trout on top of each piece of parchment and equally distribute ¼ of garlic herb mixture on each fish. Brush any remaining garlic herb mixture over the fish and fold the parchment over the fish. Fold and crimp the edges to seal tightly and place in a baking dish. 3. Bake about 10 minutes, until fish is cooked through. Remove from the oven, and serve with lemon wedges, allowing guests to open their own individual packages at the table.

Per Serving:

calories: 339 | fat: 26g | protein: 24g | carbs: 3g | fiber: 1g | sodium: 646mg

Seasoned Steamed Crab

Prep time: 10 minutes | Cook time: 3 minutes | Serves 2

- 1 tablespoon extra-virgin olive oil
- ½ teaspoon Old Bay seafood seasoning
- ½ teaspoon smoked paprika
- ¼ teaspoon cayenne pepper
- 2 cloves garlic, peeled and minced
- 2 (2-pound / 907-g) Dungeness crabs
- 1 cup water

1. In a medium bowl, combine oil, seafood seasoning, smoked paprika, cayenne pepper, and garlic. Mix well. Coat crabs in seasoning mixture and place in the steamer basket. 2. Add water to the Instant Pot® and place steamer basket inside. Close lid, set steam release to Sealing, press the Manual button, and set time to 3 minutes. 3. When the timer beeps, quick-release the pressure until the float valve drops. Press the Cancel button and open lid. Transfer crabs to a serving platter. Serve hot.

Per Serving:

calories: 185 | fat: 8g | protein: 25g | carbs: 1g | fiber: 0g | sodium: 434mg

South Indian Fried Fish

Prep time: 20 minutes | Cook time: 8 minutes | Serves 4

- 2 tablespoons olive oil
- 2 tablespoons fresh lime or lemon juice
- 1 teaspoon minced fresh ginger
- 1 clove garlic, minced
- 1 teaspoon ground turmeric
- ½ teaspoon kosher salt
- ¼ to ½ teaspoon cayenne pepper
- 1 pound (454 g) tilapia fillets (2 to 3 fillets)
- Olive oil spray
- Lime or lemon wedges (optional)

1. In a large bowl, combine the oil, lime juice, ginger, garlic, turmeric, salt, and cayenne. Stir until well combined; set aside. 2. Cut each tilapia fillet into three or four equal-size pieces. Add the fish to the bowl and gently mix until all of the fish is coated in the marinade. Marinate for 10 to 15 minutes at room temperature. (Don't marinate any longer or the acid in the lime juice will "cook" the fish.) 3. Spray the air fryer basket with olive oil spray. Place the fish in the basket and spray the fish. Set the air fryer to 325ºF (163ºC) for 3 minutes to partially cook the fish. Set the air fryer to 400ºF (204ºC) for 5 minutes to finish cooking and crisp up the fish. (Thinner pieces of fish will cook faster so you may want to check at the 3-minute mark of the second cooking time and remove those that are cooked through, and then add them back toward the end of the second cooking time to crisp.) 4. Carefully remove the fish from the basket. Serve hot, with lemon wedges if desired.

Per Serving:

calories: 175 | fat: 9g | protein: 23g | carbs: 2g | fiber: 0g | sodium: 350mg

Mediterranean Grilled Shrimp

Prep time: 20 minutes | Cook time: 5 minutes | Serves 4 to 6

- 2 tablespoons garlic, minced
- ½ cup lemon juice
- 3 tablespoons fresh Italian parsley, finely chopped
- ¼ cup extra-virgin olive oil
- 1 teaspoon salt
- 2 pounds (907 g) jumbo shrimp (21-25), peeled and deveined

1. In a large bowl, mix the garlic, lemon juice, parsley, olive oil, and salt. 2. Add the shrimp to the bowl and toss to make sure all the pieces are coated with the marinade. Let the shrimp sit for 15 minutes. 3. Preheat a grill, grill pan, or lightly oiled skillet to high heat. While heating, thread about 5 to 6 pieces of shrimp onto each skewer. 4. Place the skewers on the grill, grill pan, or skillet and cook for 2 to 3 minutes on each side until cooked through. Serve warm.

Per Serving:

calories: 217 | fat: 10g | protein: 31g | carbs: 2g | fiber: 0g | sodium: 569mg

Layered Bacalhau and Potato Casserole

Prep time : 15 minutes | Cook time: 1 hour 15 minutes | Serves 6

- 2 pounds (907 g) salt cod
- 6 tablespoons olive oil, plus extra for greasing and drizzling
- 4 medium waxy potatoes, sliced ¼-inch thick
- ½ teaspoon salt
- 2 large yellow onions, sliced
- 4 cloves garlic, minced
- Pinch of nutmeg
- White pepper

1. Rinse the salt cod and then place it in a large, non-reactive pot. Add cold water to cover and refrigerate for 24 hours, changing the water 2 or 3 times. 2. Preheat the oven to 400°F(205°C) and brush a 9-by-13-inch baking dish and a large baking sheet generously with olive oil. 3. Put the potatoes in a saucepan and cover them with water. Add the salt. Bring the water to a boil, reduce the heat to low, and simmer until the potatoes are just tender, about 10 minutes. Drain. 4. Drain the soaking water from the fish, add more clean water to cover, and bring to a boil over medium-high heat. Reduce the heat to medium-low and simmer for about 10 minutes, until the fish is tender. Drain. 5. While the fish is simmering, heat 3 tablespoons of olive oil in a large skillet set over medium heat. Add the onions and cook, stirring frequently, for about 6 minutes, until they are just beginning to brown. Stir in the garlic and remove from the heat. 6. Place the fish in a large bowl and flake it with a fork. Discard the skin and bones. Stir the onion mixture into the fish, along with the nutmeg, the remaining 3 tablespoons olive oil, and season with white pepper. Transfer the mixture to the prepared baking dish, packing it in in a tight, even layer. Top with the potato slices. 7. Place the prepared baking sheet over the baking dish and invert the baking dish but do not remove it. Bake in the preheated oven for about 30 minutes, then carefully remove the baking dish and continue to bake for another 10 to 15 minutes, until the fish is lightly browned. Serve hot, garnished with parsley.

Per Serving:

calories: 417 | fat: 16g | protein: 39g | carbs: 30g | fiber: 4g | sodium: 10mg

Poached Octopus

Prep time: 10 minutes | Cook time: 16 minutes | Serves 8

- 2 pounds (907 g) potatoes (about 6 medium)
- 3 teaspoons salt, divided
- 1 (2-pound / 907-g) frozen octopus, thawed, cleaned, and rinsed
- 3 cloves garlic, peeled, divided
- 1 bay leaf
- 2 teaspoons whole peppercorns
- ½ cup olive oil
- ¼ cup white wine vinegar
- ½ teaspoon ground black pepper
- ½ cup chopped fresh parsley

1. Place potatoes in the Instant Pot® with 2 teaspoons salt and enough water to just cover the potatoes halfway. Close lid, set steam release to Sealing, press the Manual button, and set time to 6 minutes. When the timer beeps, quick-release the pressure until the float valve drops and open lid. Press the Cancel button. 2. Remove potatoes with tongs (reserve the cooking water), and peel them as soon as you can handle them. Dice potatoes into bite-sized pieces. Set aside. 3. Add octopus to potato cooking water in the pot and add more water to cover if needed. Add 1 garlic clove, bay leaf, and peppercorns. Close lid, set steam release to Sealing, press the Manual button, and set time to 10 minutes. When the timer beeps, quick-release the pressure until the float valve drops and open lid. Remove and discard bay leaf. 4. Check octopus for tenderness by seeing if a fork will sink easily into the thickest part of the flesh. If not, close the top and bring it to pressure for another minute or two and check again. 5. Remove octopus and drain. Chop head and tentacles into small, bite-sized chunks. 6. Crush remaining 2 garlic cloves and place in a small jar or plastic container. Add olive oil, vinegar, remaining 1 teaspoon salt, and pepper. Close the lid and shake well. 7. In a large serving bowl, mix potatoes with octopus, cover with vinaigrette, and sprinkle with parsley.

Per Serving:

calories: 301 | fat: 15g | protein: 15g | carbs: 30g | fiber: 2g | sodium: 883mg

Catfish in Creole Sauce

Prep time: 10 minutes | Cook time: 5 minutes | Serves 4

- 1 (1½-pound / 680-g) catfish fillet, rinsed in cold water, patted dry, cut into bite-sized pieces
- 1 (14½-ounce / 411-g) can diced tomatoes
- 2 teaspoons dried minced onion
- ¼ teaspoon onion powder
- 1 teaspoon dried minced garlic
- ¼ teaspoon garlic powder
- 1 teaspoon hot paprika
- ¼ teaspoon dried tarragon
- 1 medium green bell pepper, seeded and diced
- 1 stalk celery, finely diced
- ¼ teaspoon sugar
- ½ cup chili sauce
- ½ teaspoon salt
- ½ teaspoon ground black pepper

1. Add all ingredients to the Instant Pot® and stir to mix. 2. Close lid, set steam release to Sealing, press the Manual button, and set time to 5 minutes. When the timer beeps, quick-release the pressure until the float valve drops and open lid. Gently stir and serve.

Per Serving:
calories: 284 | fat: 9g | protein: 31g | carbs: 7g | fiber: 3g | sodium: 696mg

Cod with Warm Beet and Arugula Salad

Prep time: 15 minutes | Cook time: 8 minutes | Serves 4

- ¼ cup extra-virgin olive oil, divided, plus extra for drizzling
- 1 shallot, sliced thin
- 2 garlic cloves, minced
- 1½ pounds (680 g) small beets, scrubbed, trimmed, and cut into ½-inch wedges
- ½ cup chicken or vegetable broth
- 1 tablespoon dukkah, plus extra for sprinkling
- ¼ teaspoon table salt
- 4 (6-ounce / 170-g) skinless cod fillets, 1½ inches thick
- 1 tablespoon lemon juice
- 2 ounces (57 g) baby arugula

1. Using highest sauté function, heat 1 tablespoon oil in Instant Pot until shimmering. Add shallot and cook until softened, about 2 minutes. Stir in garlic and cook until fragrant, about 30 seconds. Stir in beets and broth. Lock lid in place and close pressure release valve. Select high pressure cook function and cook for 3 minutes. Turn off Instant Pot and quick-release pressure. Carefully remove lid, allowing steam to escape away from you. 2. Fold sheet of aluminum foil into 16 by 6-inch sling. Combine 2 tablespoons oil, dukkah, and salt in bowl, then brush cod with oil mixture. Arrange cod skinned side down in center of sling. Using sling, lower cod into Instant Pot; allow narrow edges of sling to rest along sides of insert. Lock lid in place and close pressure release valve. Select high pressure cook function and cook for 2 minutes. 3. Turn off Instant Pot and quick-release pressure. Carefully remove lid, allowing steam to escape away from you. Using sling, transfer cod to large plate. Tent with foil and let rest while finishing beet salad. 4. Combine lemon juice and remaining 1 tablespoon oil in large bowl. Using slotted spoon, transfer beets to bowl with oil mixture. Add arugula and gently toss to combine. Season with salt and pepper to taste. 5 Serve cod with salad, sprinkling individual portions with extra dukkah and drizzling with extra oil.

Per Serving:
calories: 340 | fat: 16g | protein: 33g | carbs: 14g | fiber: 4g | sodium: 460mg

One-Pot Shrimp Fried Rice

Prep time: 10 minutes | Cook time: 25 minutes | Serves 4

Shrimp:
- 1 teaspoon cornstarch
- ½ teaspoon kosher salt
- ¼ teaspoon black pepper

Rice:
- 2 cups cold cooked rice
- 1 cup frozen peas and carrots, thawed
- ¼ cup chopped green onions (white and green parts)

Eggs:
- 2 large eggs, beaten
- ¼ teaspoon kosher salt

- 1 pound (454 g) jumbo raw shrimp (21 to 25 count), peeled and deveined
- 3 tablespoons toasted sesame oil
- 1 tablespoon soy sauce
- ½ teaspoon kosher salt
- 1 teaspoon black pepper
- ¼ teaspoon black pepper

1. For the shrimp: In a small bowl, whisk together the cornstarch, salt, and pepper until well combined. Place the shrimp in a large bowl and sprinkle the seasoned cornstarch over. Toss until well coated; set aside. 2. For the rice: In a baking pan, combine the rice, peas and carrots, green onions, sesame oil, soy sauce, salt, and pepper. Toss and stir until well combined. 3. Place the pan in the air fryer basket. Set the air fryer to 350°F (177°C) for 15 minutes, stirring and tossing the rice halfway through the cooking time. 4. Place the shrimp on top of the rice. Set the air fryer to 350°F (177°C) for 5 minutes. 5. Meanwhile, for the eggs: In a medium bowl, beat the eggs with the salt and pepper. 6. Open the air fryer and pour the eggs over the shrimp and rice mixture. Set the air fryer to 350°F (177°C) for 5 minutes. 7. Remove the pan from the air fryer. Stir to break up the rice and mix in the eggs and shrimp.

Per Serving:
calories: 364 | fat: 15g | protein: 30g | carbs: 28g | fiber: 3g | sodium: 794mg

Crispy Fish Sticks

Prep time: 15 minutes | Cook time: 10 minutes | Serves 4

- 1 ounce (28 g) pork rinds, finely ground
- ¼ cup blanched finely ground almond flour
- ½ teaspoon Old Bay seasoning
- 1 tablespoon coconut oil
- 1 large egg
- 1 pound (454 g) cod fillet, cut into ¾-inch strips

1. Place ground pork rinds, almond flour, Old Bay seasoning, and coconut oil into a large bowl and mix together. In a medium bowl, whisk egg. 2. Dip each fish stick into the egg and then gently press into the flour mixture, coating as fully and evenly as possible. Place fish sticks into the air fryer basket. 3. Adjust the temperature to 400ºF (204ºC) and air fry for 10 minutes or until golden. 4. Serve immediately.

Per Serving:

calories: 223 | fat: 14g | protein: 21g | carbs: 2g | fiber: 1g | sodium: 390mg

Fish Chili

Prep time: 10 minutes | Cook time: 5 to 7 hours | Serves 6

- 1 (28-ounce / 794-g) can no-salt-added diced tomatoes
- 1 (15-ounce / 425-g) can reduced sodium white beans, drained and rinsed
- 1 (10-ounce / 283-g) can no-salt-added diced tomatoes with green chiles
- 1 (8-ounce / 227-g) can no-salt-added tomato sauce
- 3 garlic cloves, minced
- 1 small onion, diced
- 1 bell pepper, any color, seeded and diced
- 2 tablespoons chili powder
- 2 teaspoons ground cumin
- 1½ teaspoons paprika
- 1 teaspoon sea salt
- 1 teaspoon dried oregano
- 2 pounds (907 g) fresh or frozen fish fillets of your choice, cut into 2-inch pieces

1. In a slow cooker, combine the tomatoes, beans, tomatoes with green chiles, tomato sauce, garlic, onion, bell pepper, chili powder, cumin, paprika, salt, and oregano. Stir to mix well. 2. Cover the cooker and cook for 5 to 7 hours on Low heat. 3. Stir in the fish, replace the cover on the cooker, and cook for 30 minutes on Low heat.

Per Serving:

calories: 292 | fat: 2g | protein: 41g | carbs: 27g | fiber: 9g | sodium: 611mg

Parchment-Baked Halibut with Fennel and Carrots

Prep time: 10 minutes | Cook time: 25 minutes | Serves 4

- 1 bulb fennel, cored, thinly sliced, and fronds reserved
- 1 bunch young carrots, quartered and tops removed
- 1 small shallot, sliced
- 4 skinless halibut fillets (6 ounces / 170 geach)
- ½ teaspoon kosher salt
- ¼ teaspoon ground black pepper
- 4 slices orange
- 8 sprigs thyme
- 4 leaves fresh sage, sliced
- ½ cup white wine

1. Preheat the oven to 425ºF(220ºC). Tear 4 squares of parchment paper, about 15' × 15'. 2. In the middle of a piece of parchment, set ¼ of the fennel, carrots, and shallot, topped by 1 piece of fish. Sprinkle with ⅛ teaspoon of the salt and a pinch of the pepper. Lay 1 slice of the orange, 2 sprigs of the thyme, ¼ of the sage, and a bit of fennel frond on top. Drizzle 2 tablespoons of the wine around the fish. 3. Bring up the opposite sides of the parchment and fold them together, like you're folding the top of a paper bag, to seal all the edges. Set the packet on a baking sheet, and repeat with the remaining ingredients. 4. Bake until the packets are slightly browned and puffed, about 13 minutes. Allow to rest for 2 to 3 minutes. Set individual packets on plates and with kitchen shears or a small knife, carefully cut open at the table. (Caution: The escaping steam will be hot.)

Per Serving:

calories: 253 | fat: 3g | protein: 34g | carbs: 18g | fiber: 5g | sodium: 455mg

Paprika-Spiced Fish

Prep time: 5 minutes | Cook time: 10 minutes | Serves 4

- 4 (5-ounce / 142-g) sea bass fillets
- ½ teaspoon salt
- 1 tablespoon smoked paprika
- 3 tablespoons unsalted butter
- Lemon wedges

1. Season the fish on both sides with the salt. Repeat with the paprika. 2. Preheat a skillet over high heat. Melt the butter. 3. Once the butter is melted, add the fish and cook for 4 minutes on each side. 4. Once the fish is done cooking, move to a serving dish and squeeze lemon over the top.

Per Serving:

calories: 257 | fat: 34g | protein: 34g | carbs: 1g | fiber: 1g | sodium: 416mg

Sesame-Crusted Tuna Steak

Prep time: 5 minutes | Cook time: 8 minutes | Serves 2

- 2 (6 ounces / 170 g) tuna steaks
- 1 tablespoon coconut oil, melted
- ½ teaspoon garlic powder
- 2 teaspoons white sesame seeds
- 2 teaspoons black sesame seeds

1. Brush each tuna steak with coconut oil and sprinkle with garlic powder. 2. In a large bowl, mix sesame seeds and then press each tuna steak into them, covering the steak as completely as possible. Place tuna steaks into the air fryer basket. 3. Adjust the temperature to 400ºF (204ºC) and air fry for 8 minutes. 4. Flip the steaks halfway through the cooking time. Steaks will be well-done at 145ºF (63ºC) internal temperature. Serve warm.

Per Serving:

calories: 281 | fat: 11g | protein: 43g | carbs: 1g | fiber: 1g | sodium: 80mg

Fish Tagine

Prep time: 25 minutes | Cook time: 12 minutes | Serves 4

- 2 tablespoons extra-virgin olive oil, plus extra for drizzling
- 1 large onion, halved and sliced ¼ inch thick
- 1 pound (454 g) carrots, peeled, halved lengthwise, and sliced ¼ inch thick
- 2 (2-inch) strips orange zest, plus 1 teaspoon grated zest
- ¾ teaspoon table salt, divided
- 2 tablespoons tomato paste
- 4 garlic cloves, minced, divided
- 1¼ teaspoons paprika
- 1 teaspoon ground cumin
- ¼ teaspoon red pepper flakes
- ¼ teaspoon saffron threads, crumbled
- 1 (8-ounce / 227-g) bottle clam juice
- 1½ pounds (680 g) skinless halibut fillets, 1½ inches thick, cut into 2-inch pieces
- ¼ cup pitted oil-cured black olives, quartered
- 2 tablespoons chopped fresh parsley
- 1 teaspoon sherry vinegar

1. Using highest sauté function, heat oil in Instant Pot until shimmering. Add onion, carrots, orange zest strips, and ¼ teaspoon salt, and cook until vegetables are softened and lightly browned, 10 to 12 minutes. Stir in tomato paste, three-quarters of garlic, paprika, cumin, pepper flakes, and saffron and cook until fragrant, about 30 seconds. Stir in clam juice, scraping up any browned bits. 2. Sprinkle halibut with remaining ½ teaspoon salt. Nestle halibut into onion mixture and spoon some of cooking liquid on top of

pieces. Lock lid in place and close pressure release valve. Select high pressure cook function and set cook time for 0 minutes. Once Instant Pot has reached pressure, immediately turn off pot and quick-release pressure. 3. Discard orange zest. Gently stir in olives, parsley, vinegar, grated orange zest, and remaining garlic. Season with salt and pepper to taste. Drizzle extra oil over individual portions before serving.

Per Serving:

calories: 310 | fat: 15g | protein: 34g | carbs: 18g | fiber: 4g | sodium: 820mg

Citrus Mediterranean Salmon with Lemon Caper Sauce

Prep time: 15 minutes | Cook time: 22 minutes | Serves 2

- 2 tablespoons fresh lemon juice
- ⅓ cup orange juice
- 1 tablespoon extra virgin olive oil
- ⅛ teaspoon freshly ground black pepper
- 2 (6-ounce / 170-g) salmon fillets
- Lemon Caper Sauce:
- 2 tablespoons extra virgin
- olive oil
- 1 tablespoon finely chopped red onion
- 1 garlic clove, minced
- 2 tablespoons fresh lemon juice
- 5 ounces (142) dry white wine
- 2 tablespoons capers, rinsed
- ⅛ teaspoon freshly ground black pepper

1. Preheat the oven to 350°F (180°C). 2. In a small bowl, combine the lemon juice, orange juice, olive oil, and black pepper. Whisk until blended, then pour the mixture into a zipper-lock bag. Place the fillets in the bag, shake gently, and transfer the salmon to the refrigerator to marinate for 10 minutes. 3. When the salmon is done marinating, transfer the fillets and marinade to a medium baking dish. Bake for 10–15 minutes or until the salmon is cooked through and the internal temperature reaches 165°F (74°C). Remove the salmon from the oven and cover loosely with foil. Set aside to rest. 4. While the salmon is resting, make the lemon caper sauce by heating the olive oil in a medium pan over medium heat. When the olive oil begins to shimmer, add the onions and sauté for 3 minutes, stirring frequently, then add the garlic and sauté for another 30 seconds. 5. Add the lemon juice and wine. Bring the mixture to a boil and cook until the sauce becomes thick, about 2–3 minutes, then remove the pan from the heat. Add the capers and black pepper, and stir. 6. Transfer the fillets to 2 plates, and spoon 1½ tablespoons of the sauce over each fillet. Store covered in the refrigerator for up to 3 days.

Per Serving:

calories: 485 | fat: 28g | protein: 36g | carbs: 11g | fiber: 1g | sodium: 331mg

Garlicky Broiled Sardines

Prep time: 5 minutes | Cook time: 3 minutes | Serves 4

- 4 (3¼-ounce / 92-g) cans sardines (about 16 sardines), packed in water or olive oil
- 2 tablespoons extra-virgin olive oil (if sardines are packed in water)
- 4 garlic cloves, minced
- ½ teaspoon red pepper flakes
- ½ teaspoon salt
- ¼ teaspoon freshly ground black pepper

1. Preheat the broiler. Line a baking dish with aluminum foil. Arrange the sardines in a single layer on the foil. 2. Combine the olive oil (if using), garlic, and red pepper flakes in a small bowl and spoon over each sardine. Season with salt and pepper. 3. Broil just until sizzling, 2 to 3 minutes. 4. To serve, place 4 sardines on each plate and top with any remaining garlic mixture that has collected in the baking dish.

Per Serving:

calories: 197 | fat: 11g | protein: 23g | carbs: 1g | fiber: 0g | sodium: 574mg

Salmon Cakes with Bell Pepper and Lemon Yogurt

Prep time: 15 minutes | Cook time: 15 minutes | Serves 4

- ¼ cup whole-wheat bread crumbs
- ¼ cup mayonnaise
- 1 large egg, beaten
- 1 tablespoon chives, chopped
- 1 tablespoon fresh parsley, chopped
- Zest of 1 lemon
- ¾ teaspoon kosher salt, divided
- ¼ teaspoon freshly ground
- black pepper
- 2 (5- to 6-ounce / 142- to 170-g) cans no-salt boneless/skinless salmon, drained and finely flaked
- ½ bell pepper, diced small
- 2 tablespoons extra-virgin olive oil, divided
- 1 cup plain Greek yogurt
- Juice of 1 lemon

1. In a large bowl, combine the bread crumbs, mayonnaise, egg, chives, parsley, lemon zest, ½ teaspoon of the salt, and black pepper and mix well. Add the salmon and the bell pepper and stir gently until well combined. Shape the mixture into 8 patties. 2. Heat 1 tablespoon of the olive oil in a large skillet over medium-high heat. Cook half the cakes until the bottoms are golden brown, 4 to 5 minutes. Adjust the heat to medium if the bottoms start to burn. Flip the cakes and cook until golden brown, an additional 4 to 5 minutes. Repeat with the remaining 1 tablespoon olive oil and the rest of the cakes. 3. In a small bowl, combine the yogurt, lemon juice, and the remaining ¼ teaspoon salt and mix well. Serve with the salmon cakes.

Per Serving:

calories: 330 | fat: 23g | protein: 21g | carbs: 9g | fiber: 1g | sodium: 385mg

Italian Halibut with Grapes and Olive Oil

Prep time: 15 minutes | Cook time: 20 minutes | Serves 4

- ¼ cup extra-virgin olive oil
- 4 boneless halibut fillets, 4 ounces (113 g) each
- 4 cloves garlic, roughly chopped
- 1 small red chile pepper, finely chopped
- 2 cups seedless green grapes
- A handful of fresh basil leaves, roughly torn
- ½ teaspoon unrefined sea salt or salt
- Freshly ground black pepper

1. Heat the olive oil in a large, heavy-bottomed skillet over medium-high heat. Add the halibut, followed by the garlic, chile pepper, grapes, basil, and the salt and pepper. Pour in 1¾ cups of water, turn the heat down to medium-low, cover, and cook the fish until opaque, or for 7 minutes on each side. 2. Remove the fish from the pan and place on a large serving dish. Raise the heat, cook the sauce for 30 seconds to concentrate the flavors slightly. Taste and adjust salt and pepper. Pour sauce over the fish.

Per Serving:

calories: 389 | fat: 29g | protein: 17g | carbs: 15g | fiber: 1g | sodium: 384mg

Lime Lobster Tails

Prep time: 10 minutes | Cook time: 6 minutes | Serves 4

- 4 lobster tails, peeled
- 2 tablespoons lime juice
- ½ teaspoon dried basil
- ½ teaspoon coconut oil, melted

1. Mix lobster tails with lime juice, dried basil, and coconut oil. 2. Put the lobster tails in the air fryer and cook at 380°F (193°C) for 6 minutes.

Per Serving:

calories: 123 | fat: 2g | protein: 25g | carbs: 1g | fiber: 0g | sodium: 635mg

Tuna Nuggets in Hoisin Sauce

Prep time: 15 minutes | Cook time: 5 to 7 minutes | Serves 4

- ½ cup hoisin sauce
- 2 tablespoons rice wine vinegar
- 2 teaspoons sesame oil
- 1 teaspoon garlic powder
- 2 teaspoons dried lemongrass
- ¼ teaspoon red pepper flakes
- ½ small onion, quartered and thinly sliced
- 8 ounces (227 g) fresh tuna, cut into 1-inch cubes
- Cooking spray
- 3 cups cooked jasmine rice

1. Mix the hoisin sauce, vinegar, sesame oil, and seasonings together. 2. Stir in the onions and tuna nuggets. 3. Spray a baking pan with nonstick spray and pour in tuna mixture. 4. Roast at 390°F (199°C) for 3 minutes. Stir gently. 5. Cook 2 minutes and stir again, checking for doneness. Tuna should be barely cooked through, just beginning to flake and still very moist. If necessary, continue cooking and stirring in 1-minute intervals until done. 6. Serve warm over hot jasmine rice.

Per Serving:

calories: 342 | fat: 7g | protein: 18g | carbs: 49g | fiber: 4g | sodium: 548mg

Wild Cod Oreganata

Prep time: 10 minutes | Cook time: 20 minutes | Serves 2

- 10 ounces (283 g) wild cod (1 large piece or 2 smaller ones)
- ⅓ cup panko bread crumbs
- 1 tablespoon dried oregano
- Zest of 1 lemon
- ½ teaspoon salt
- Pinch freshly ground black pepper
- 1 tablespoon olive oil
- 2 tablespoons freshly squeezed lemon juice
- 2 tablespoons white wine
- 1 tablespoon minced fresh parsley

1. Preheat the oven to 350°F(180°C). Place the cod in a baking dish and pat it dry with a paper towel. 2. In a small bowl, combine the panko, oregano, lemon zest, salt, pepper, and olive oil and mix well. Pat the panko mixture onto the fish. 3. Combine the lemon juice and wine in a small bowl and pour it around the fish. 4. Bake the fish for 20 minutes, or until it flakes apart easily and reaches an internal temperature of 145°F(63°C). 5. Garnish with fresh minced parsley.

Per Serving:

calories: 203 | fat: 8g | protein: 23g | carbs: 9g | fiber: 2g | sodium: 149mg

Cod with Parsley Pistou

Prep time: 15 minutes | Cook time: 10 minutes | Serves 4

- 1 cup packed roughly chopped fresh flat-leaf Italian parsley
- 1 to 2 small garlic cloves, minced
- Zest and juice of 1 lemon
- 1 teaspoon salt
- ½ teaspoon freshly ground black pepper
- 1 cup extra-virgin olive oil, divided
- 1 pound (454 g) cod fillets, cut into 4 equal-sized pieces

1. In a food processor, combine the parsley, garlic, lemon zest and juice, salt, and pepper. Pulse to chop well. 2. While the food processor is running, slowly stream in ¾ cup olive oil until well combined. Set aside. 3. In a large skillet, heat the remaining ¼ cup olive oil over medium-high heat. Add the cod fillets, cover, and cook 4 to 5 minutes on each side, or until cooked through. Thicker fillets may require a bit more cooking time. Remove from the heat and keep warm. 4. Add the pistou to the skillet and heat over medium-low heat. Return the cooked fish to the skillet, flipping to coat in the sauce. Serve warm, covered with pistou.

Per Serving:

calories: 580 | fat: 55g | protein: 21g | carbs: 2g | fiber: 1g | sodium: 591mg

Spicy Steamed Chili Crab

Prep time: 10 minutes | Cook time: 3 minutes | Serves 2

- 2 tablespoons garlic chili sauce
- 1 tablespoon hoisin sauce
- 1 tablespoon minced fresh ginger
- 1 teaspoon fish sauce
- 2 cloves garlic, peeled and minced
- 2 small bird's eye chilies, minced
- 2 (2-pound / 907-g) Dungeness crabs
- 1 cup water

1. In a medium bowl, combine garlic chili sauce, hoisin sauce, ginger, fish sauce, garlic, and chilies. Mix well. Coat crabs in chili mixture. 2. Add water to the Instant Pot® and insert steamer basket. Add crabs to basket. Close lid, set steam release to Sealing, press the Manual button, and set time to 3 minutes. 3. When the timer beeps, quick-release the pressure until the float valve drops. Press the Cancel button and open lid. Transfer crabs to a serving platter. Serve hot.

Per Serving:

calories: 128 | fat: 1g | protein: 25g | carbs: 1g | fiber: 0g | sodium: 619mg

Salmon with Provolone Cheese

Prep time: 5 minutes | Cook time: 15 minutes | Serves 4

- 1 pound (454 g) salmon fillet, chopped
- 2 ounces (57 g) Provolone, grated
- 1 teaspoon avocado oil
- ¼ teaspoon ground paprika

1. Sprinkle the salmon fillets with avocado oil and put in the air fryer. 2. Then sprinkle the fish with ground paprika and top with Provolone cheese. 3. Cook the fish at 360ºF (182ºC) for 15 minutes.

Per Serving:

calories: 204 | fat: 10g | protein: 27g | carbs: 0g | fiber: 0g | sodium: 209mg

Olive Oil–Poached Fish over Citrus Salad

Prep time: 10 minutes | Cook time: 25 minutes | Serves 4

Fish
- 4 skinless white fish fillets (1¼ to 1½ pounds / 567 to 680 g total), such as halibut, sole, or cod, ¾'–1' thick
- ¼ teaspoon kosher salt
Salad
- ¼ cup white wine vinegar
- 1 Earl Grey tea bag
- 2 blood oranges or tangerines
- 1 ruby red grapefruit or pomelo
- 6 kumquats, thinly sliced, or 2 clementines, peeled and sectioned
- 4 cups baby arugula
- ¼ teaspoon ground black pepper
- 5–7 cups olive oil
- 1 lemon, thinly sliced
- ½ cup pomegranate seeds
- ¼ cup extra-virgin olive oil
- 2 teaspoons minced shallot
- ½ teaspoon kosher salt
- ¼ teaspoon ground black pepper
- ¼ cup mint leaves, coarsely chopped

1. Make the fish: Season the fish with the salt and pepper and set aside for 30 minutes. 2. Preheat the oven to 225°F. 3. In a large high-sided ovenproof skillet or roasting pan over medium heat, warm 1' to 1½' of the oil and the lemon slices until the temperature reaches 120°F (use a candy thermometer). Add the fish fillets to the oil, without overlapping, making sure they're completely submerged. 4. Transfer the skillet or pan to the oven, uncovered. Bake for 25 minutes. Transfer the fish to a rack to drain for 5 minutes. 5. Make the salad: In a small saucepan, heat the vinegar until almost boiling. Add the tea bag and set aside to steep for 10 minutes. 6. Meanwhile, with a paring knife, cut off enough of the top and bottom of 1 of the oranges or tangerines to reveal the flesh. Cut along the inside of the peel, between the pith and the flesh, taking off as much pith as possible. Over a large bowl, hold the orange in 1 hand. With the paring knife, cut along the membranes between each section, allowing the fruit to fall into the bowl. Once all the fruit segments have been released, squeeze the remaining membranes over a small bowl. Repeat with the second orange and the grapefruit or pomelo. 7. In the large bowl with the segmented fruit, add the kumquats or clementines, arugula, and pomegranate seeds. Gently toss to distribute. 8. Remove the tea bag from the vinegar and squeeze out as much liquid as possible. Discard the bag and add the vinegar to the small bowl with the citrus juice. Slowly whisk in the oil, shallot, salt, and pepper. Drizzle 3 to 4 tablespoons over the salad and gently toss. (Store the remaining vinaigrette in the refrigerator for up to 1 week.) 9. Sprinkle the salad with the mint and serve with the fish.

Per Serving:

calories: 280 | fat: 7g | protein: 29g | carbs: 25g | fiber: 6g | sodium: 249mg

Caramelized Fennel and Sardines with Penne

Prep time: 15 minutes | Cook time: 30 minutes | Serves 4

- 8 ounces (227 g) whole-wheat penne
- 2 tablespoons extra-virgin olive oil
- 1 bulb fennel, cored and thinly sliced, plus ¼ cup fronds
- 2 celery stalks, thinly sliced, plus ½ cup leaves
- 4 garlic cloves, sliced
- ¾ teaspoon kosher salt
- ¼ teaspoon freshly ground black pepper
- Zest of 1 lemon
- Juice of 1 lemon
- 2 (4.4-ounce / 125-g) cans boneless/skinless sardines packed in olive oil, undrained

1. Cook the penne according to the package directions. Drain, reserving 1 cup pasta water. 2. Heat the olive oil in a large skillet or sauté pan over medium heat. Add the fennel and celery and cook, stirring often, until tender and golden, about 10 to 12 minutes. Add the garlic and cook for 1 minute. 3. Add the penne, reserved pasta water, salt, and black pepper. Increase the heat to medium-high and cook for 1 to 2 minutes. 4. Remove the pan from the heat and stir in the lemon zest, lemon juice, fennel fronds, and celery leaves. Break the sardines into bite-size pieces and gently mix in, along with the oil they were packed in.

Per Serving:

calories: 400 | fat: 15g | protein: 22g | carbs: 46g | fiber: 6g | sodium: 530mg

Mediterranean Cod Stew

Prep time: 10 minutes |Cook time: 20 minutes| Serves: 6

- 2 tablespoons extra-virgin olive oil
- 2 cups chopped onion (about 1 medium onion)
- 2 garlic cloves, minced (about 1 teaspoon)
- ¾ teaspoon smoked paprika
- 1 (14½-ounce / 411-g) can diced tomatoes, undrained
- 1 (12-ounce / 340-g) jar roasted red peppers, drained
- and chopped
- 1 cup sliced olives, green or black
- ⅓ cup dry red wine
- ¼ teaspoon freshly ground black pepper
- ¼ teaspoon kosher or sea salt
- 1½ pounds (680 g) cod fillets, cut into 1-inch pieces
- 3 cups sliced mushrooms (about 8 ounces / 227 g)

1. In a large stockpot over medium heat, heat the oil. Add the onion and cook for 4 minutes, stirring occasionally. Add the garlic and smoked paprika and cook for 1 minute, stirring often. 2. Mix in the tomatoes with their juices, roasted peppers, olives, wine, pepper, and salt, and turn the heat up to medium-high. Bring to a boil. Add the cod and mushrooms, and reduce the heat to medium. 3. Cover and cook for about 10 minutes, stirring a few times, until the cod is cooked through and flakes easily, and serve.

Per Serving:

calories: 209 | fat: 8g | protein: 23g | carbs: 12g | fiber: 4g | sodium: 334mg

Halibut Fillets with Vegetables

Prep time: 20 minutes | Cook time: 5 minutes | Serves 2

- 1 cup chopped broccoli
- 1 large potato, peeled and diced
- 1 large carrot, peeled and grated
- 1 small zucchini, trimmed and grated
- 4 ounces (113 g) mushrooms, sliced
- ¼ teaspoon dried thyme
- ¼ teaspoon grated lemon zest
- 1 (½-pound / 227-g) halibut fillet
- ½ cup white wine
- ½ cup lemon juice
- 1 teaspoon dried parsley
- ¼ teaspoon salt
- ¼ teaspoon ground black pepper
- ⅛ teaspoon ground nutmeg

1. Place the rack and steamer basket in the Instant Pot®. Place broccoli, potato, carrot, zucchini, and mushrooms in layers in the basket. Sprinkle thyme and lemon zest over vegetables. 2. Place fish over vegetables. Pour wine and lemon juice over fish. Sprinkle parsley, salt, and pepper over the fish and vegetables. 3. Close lid, set steam release to Sealing, press the Manual button, and set time to 5 minutes. When the timer beeps, quick-release the pressure until the float valve drops and open lid. Divide fish and vegetables between two plates. Sprinkle nutmeg over each serving.

Per Serving:

calories: 278 | fat: 3g | protein: 31g | carbs: 23g | fiber: 5g | sodium: 409mg

Escabeche

Prep time: 10 minutes | Cook time: 20 minutes | Serves 4

- 1 pound (454 g) wild-caught Spanish mackerel fillets, cut into four pieces
- 1 teaspoon salt
- ½ teaspoon freshly ground black pepper
- 8 tablespoons extra-virgin olive oil, divided
- 1 bunch asparagus, trimmed
- and cut into 2-inch pieces
- 1 (13¾-ounce / 390-g) can artichoke hearts, drained and quartered
- 4 large garlic cloves, peeled and crushed
- 2 bay leaves
- ¼ cup red wine vinegar
- ½ teaspoon smoked paprika

1. Sprinkle the fillets with salt and pepper and let sit at room temperature for 5 minutes. 2. In a large skillet, heat 2 tablespoons olive oil over medium-high heat. Add the fish, skin-side up, and cook 5 minutes. Flip and cook 5 minutes on the other side, until browned and cooked through. Transfer to a serving dish, pour the cooking oil over the fish, and cover to keep warm. 3. Heat the remaining 6 tablespoons olive oil in the same skillet over medium heat. Add the asparagus, artichokes, garlic, and bay leaves and sauté until the vegetables are tender, 6 to 8 minutes. 4. Using a slotted spoon, top the fish with the cooked vegetables, reserving the oil in the skillet. Add the vinegar and paprika to the oil and whisk to combine well. Pour the vinaigrette over the fish and vegetables and let sit at room temperature for at least 15 minutes, or marinate in the refrigerator up to 24 hours for a deeper flavor. Remove the bay leaf before serving.

Per Serving:

calories: 459 | fat: 34g | protein: 26g | carbs: 13g | fiber: 6g | sodium: 597mg

Chapter 8 Vegetables and Sides

Sautéed Kale with Tomato and Garlic

Prep time: 5 minutes | Cook time: 10 minutes | Serves 4

- 1 tablespoon extra-virgin olive oil
- 4 garlic cloves, sliced
- ¼ teaspoon red pepper flakes
- 2 bunches kale, stemmed and
- chopped or torn into pieces
- 1 (14½-ounce / 411-g) can no-salt-added diced tomatoes
- ½ teaspoon kosher salt

1. Heat the olive oil in a wok or large skillet over medium-high heat. Add the garlic and red pepper flakes, and sauté until fragrant, about 30 seconds. Add the kale and sauté, about 3 to 5 minutes, until the kale shrinks down a bit. 2. Add the tomatoes and the salt, stir together, and cook for 3 to 5 minutes, or until the liquid reduces and the kale cooks down further and becomes tender.

Per Serving:
calories: 110 | fat: 5g | protein: 6g | carbs: 15g | fiber: 6g | sodium: 222mg

Sicilian-Style Roasted Cauliflower with Capers, Currants, and Crispy Breadcrumbs

Prep time: 10 minutes | Cook time: 55 minutes | Serves 4

- 1 large head of cauliflower (2 pounds / 907 g), cut into 2-inch florets
- 6 tablespoons olive oil, divided
- 1 teaspoon salt
- ½ teaspoon freshly ground black pepper
- 3 garlic cloves, thinly sliced
- 2 tablespoons salt-packed capers, soaked, rinsed, and
- patted dry
- ¾ cup fresh whole-wheat breadcrumbs
- ½ cup chicken broth
- 1 teaspoon anchovy paste
- ⅓ cup golden raisins
- 1 tablespoon white wine vinegar
- 2 tablespoons chopped flat-leaf parsley

1. Preheat the oven to 425°F(220ºC). 2. In a medium bowl, toss the cauliflower florets with 3 tablespoons olive oil, and the salt and pepper. Spread the cauliflower out in a single layer on a large, rimmed baking sheet and roast in the preheated oven, stirring occasionally, for about 45 minutes, until the cauliflower is golden brown and crispy at the edges. 3. While the cauliflower is roasting, put the remaining 3 tablespoons of olive oil in a small saucepan and heat over medium-low heat. Add the garlic and cook, stirring, for about 5 minutes, until the garlic begins to turn golden. Stir in the capers and cook for 3 minutes more. Add the breadcrumbs, stir to mix well, and cook until the breadcrumbs turn golden brown and are crisp. Use a slotted spoon to transfer the breadcrumbs to a bowl or plate. 4. In the same saucepan, stir together the broth and anchovy paste and bring to a boil over medium-high heat. Stir in the raisins and vinegar and cook, stirring occasionally, for 5 minutes, until the liquid has mostly been absorbed. 5. When the cauliflower is done, transfer it to a large serving bowl. Add the raisin mixture and toss to mix. Top with the breadcrumbs and serve immediately, garnished with parsley.

Per Serving:
calories: 364 | fat: 22g | protein: 8g | carbs: 37g | fiber: 6g | sodium: 657mg

Greek Fasolakia (Green Beans)

Prep time: 10 minutes | Cook time: 6 to 8 hours | Serves 6

- 2 pounds (907 g) green beans, trimmed
- 1 (15-ounce / 425-g) can no-salt-added diced tomatoes, with juice
- 1 large onion, chopped
- 4 garlic cloves, chopped
- Juice of 1 lemon
- 1 teaspoon dried dill
- 1 teaspoon ground cumin
- 1 teaspoon dried oregano
- 1 teaspoon sea salt
- ½ teaspoon freshly ground black pepper
- ¼ cup feta cheese, crumbled

1. In a slow cooker, combine the green beans, tomatoes and their juice, onion, garlic, lemon juice, dill, cumin, oregano, salt, and pepper. Stir to mix well. 2. Cover the cooker and cook for 6 to 8 hours on Low heat. 3. Top with feta cheese for serving.

Per Serving:
calories: 94 | fat: 2g | protein: 5g | carbs: 18g | fiber: 7g | sodium: 497mg

Roasted Cherry Tomato Caprese

Prep time: 15 minutes | Cook time: 30 minutes | Serves 4

- 2 pints (about 20 ounces / 567 g) cherry tomatoes
- 6 thyme sprigs
- 6 garlic cloves, smashed
- 2 tablespoons extra-virgin olive oil
- ½ teaspoon kosher salt
- 8 ounces (227 g) fresh, unsalted Mozzarella, cut into bite-size slices
- ¼ cup basil, chopped or cut into ribbons
- Loaf of crusty whole-wheat bread, for serving

1. Preheat the oven to 350ºF (180ºC). Line a baking sheet with parchment paper or foil. 2. Put the tomatoes, thyme, garlic, olive oil, and salt into a large bowl and mix together. Place on the prepared baking sheet in a single layer. Roast for 30 minutes, or until the tomatoes are bursting and juicy. 3. Place the Mozzarella on a platter or in a bowl. Pour all the tomato mixture, including the juices, over the Mozzarella. Garnish with the basil. 4. Serve with crusty bread.

Per Serving:

calories: 250 | fat: 17g | protein: 17g | carbs: 9g | fiber: 2g | sodium: 157mg

Air-Fried Okra

Prep time: 10 minutes | Cook time: 10 minutes | Serves 4

- 1 egg
- ½ cup almond milk
- ½ cup crushed pork rinds
- ¼ cup grated Parmesan cheese
- ¼ cup almond flour
- 1 teaspoon garlic powder
- ¼ teaspoon freshly ground black pepper
- ½ pound (227 g) fresh okra, stems removed and chopped into 1-inch slices

1. Preheat the air fryer to 400ºF (204ºC). 2. In a shallow bowl, whisk together the egg and milk. 3. In a second shallow bowl, combine the pork rinds, Parmesan, almond flour, garlic powder, and black pepper. 4. Working with a few slices at a time, dip the okra into the egg mixture followed by the crumb mixture. Press lightly to ensure an even coating. 5. Working in batches if necessary, arrange the okra in a single layer in the air fryer basket and spray lightly with olive oil. Pausing halfway through the cooking time to turn the okra, air fry for 10 minutes until tender and golden brown. Serve warm.

Per Serving:

calories: 200 | fat: 16g | protein: 6g | carbs: 8g | fiber: 2g | sodium: 228mg

Caramelized Root Vegetables

Prep time: 20 minutes | Cook time: 40 minutes | Serves 6

- 2 medium carrots, peeled and cut into chunks
- 2 medium red or gold beets, cut into chunks
- 2 turnips, peeled and cut into chunks
- 2 tablespoons olive oil
- 1 teaspoon cumin
- 1 teaspoon sweet paprika
- Sea salt and freshly ground pepper, to taste
- Juice of 1 lemon
- 1 small bunch flat-leaf parsley, chopped

1. Preheat oven to 400ºF (205ºC). 2. Toss the vegetables with the olive oil and seasonings. 3. Lay in a single layer on a sheet pan, cover with lemon juice, and roast for 30–40 minutes, until veggies are slightly browned and crisp. 4. Serve warm, topped with the chopped parsley.

Per Serving:

calories: 79 | fat: 5g | protein: 1g | carbs: 9g | fiber: 3g | sodium: 69mg

Stuffed Artichokes

Prep time: 20 minutes | Cook time: 5 to 7 hours | Serves 4 to 6

- 4 to 6 fresh large artichokes
- ½ cup bread crumbs
- ½ cup grated Parmesan cheese or Romano cheese
- 4 garlic cloves, minced
- ½ teaspoon sea salt
- ½ teaspoon freshly ground
- black pepper
- ¼ cup water
- 2 tablespoons extra-virgin olive oil
- 2 tablespoons chopped fresh parsley for garnish (optional)

1. To trim and prepare the artichokes, cut off the bottom along with 1 inch from the top of each artichoke. Pull off and discard the lowest leaves nearest the stem end. Trim off any pointy tips of artichoke leaves that are poking out. Set aside. 2. In a small bowl, stir together the bread crumbs, Parmesan cheese, garlic, salt, and pepper. 3. Spread apart the artichoke leaves and stuff the bread-crumb mixture into the spaces, down to the base. 4. Pour the water into a slow cooker. 5. Place the artichokes in the slow cooker in a single layer. Drizzle the olive oil over the artichokes. 6. Cover the cooker and cook for 5 to 7 hours on Low heat, or until the artichokes are tender. 7. Garnish with fresh parsley if desired.

Per Serving:

calories: 224 | fat: 12g | protein: 12g | carbs: 23g | fiber: 8g | sodium: 883mg

Glazed Carrots

Prep time: 10 minutes | Cook time: 8 to 10 minutes | Serves 4

- 2 teaspoons honey
- 1 teaspoon orange juice
- ½ teaspoon grated orange rind
- ⅛ teaspoon ginger
- 1 pound (454 g) baby carrots
- 2 teaspoons olive oil
- ¼ teaspoon salt

1. Combine honey, orange juice, grated rind, and ginger in a small bowl and set aside. 2. Toss the carrots, oil, and salt together to coat well and pour them into the air fryer basket. 3. Roast at 390°F (199°C) for 5 minutes. Shake basket to stir a little and cook for 2 to 4 minutes more, until carrots are barely tender. 4. Pour carrots into a baking pan. 5. Stir the honey mixture to combine well, pour glaze over carrots, and stir to coat. 6. Roast at 360°F (182°C) for 1 minute or just until heated through.

Per Serving:

calories: 71 | fat: 2g | protein: 1g | carbs: 12g | fiber: 3g | sodium: 234mg

Mediterranean Lentil Sloppy Joes

Prep time: 5 minutes |Cook time: 15 minutes| Serves: 4

- 1 tablespoon extra-virgin olive oil
- 1 cup chopped onion (about ½ medium onion)
- 1 cup chopped bell pepper, any color (about 1 medium bell pepper)
- 2 garlic cloves, minced (about 1 teaspoon)
- 1 (15-ounce / 425-g) can lentils, drained and rinsed
- 1 (14½-ounce / 411-g) can low-sodium or no-salt-
- added diced tomatoes, undrained
- 1 teaspoon ground cumin
- 1 teaspoon dried thyme
- ¼ teaspoon kosher or sea salt
- 4 whole-wheat pita breads, split open
- 1½ cups chopped seedless cucumber (1 medium cucumber)
- 1 cup chopped romaine lettuce

1. In a medium saucepan over medium-high heat, heat the oil. Add the onion and bell pepper and cook for 4 minutes, stirring frequently. Add the garlic and cook for 1 minute, stirring frequently. Add the lentils, tomatoes (with their liquid), cumin, thyme, and salt. Turn the heat to medium and cook, stirring occasionally, for 10 minutes, or until most of the liquid has evaporated. 2. Stuff the lentil mixture inside each pita. Lay the cucumbers and lettuce on top of the lentil mixture and serve.

Per Serving:

calories: 530 | fat: 6g | protein: 31g | carbs: 93g | fiber: 17g | sodium: 292mg

Herbed Shiitake Mushrooms

Prep time: 10 minutes | Cook time: 5 minutes | Serves 4

- 8 ounces (227 g) shiitake mushrooms, stems removed and caps roughly chopped
- 1 tablespoon olive oil
- ½ teaspoon salt
- Freshly ground black pepper, to taste
- 1 teaspoon chopped fresh thyme leaves
- 1 teaspoon chopped fresh oregano
- 1 tablespoon chopped fresh parsley

1. Preheat the air fryer to 400°F (204°C). 2. Toss the mushrooms with the olive oil, salt, pepper, thyme and oregano. Air fry for 5 minutes, shaking the basket once or twice during the cooking process. The mushrooms will still be somewhat chewy with a meaty texture. If you'd like them a little more tender, add a couple of minutes to this cooking time. 3. Once cooked, add the parsley to the mushrooms and toss. Season again to taste and serve.

Per Serving:

calories: 50 | fat: 4g | protein: 1g | carbs: 4g | fiber: 2g | sodium: 296mg

Garlicky Sautéed Zucchini with Mint

Prep time: 5 minutes | Cook time: 10 minutes | Serves 4

- 3 large green zucchini
- 3 tablespoons extra-virgin olive oil
- 1 large onion, chopped
- 3 cloves garlic, minced
- 1 teaspoon salt
- 1 teaspoon dried mint

1. Cut the zucchini into ½-inch cubes. 2. In a large skillet over medium heat, cook the olive oil, onions, and garlic for 3 minutes, stirring constantly. 3. Add the zucchini and salt to the skillet and toss to combine with the onions and garlic, cooking for 5 minutes. 4. Add the mint to the skillet, tossing to combine. Cook for another 2 minutes. Serve warm.

Per Serving:

calories: 147 | fat: 11g | protein: 4g | carbs: 12g | fiber: 3g | sodium: 607mg

Greek Bean Soup

Prep time: 10 minutes | Cook time: 45 minutes | Serves 4

- 2 tablespoons olive oil
- 1 large onion, chopped
- 1 (15-ounce / 425-g) can diced tomatoes
- 1 (15-ounce / 425-g) can great northern beans, drained and rinsed
- 2 celery stalks, chopped
- 2 carrots, cut into long ribbons
- ⅓ teaspoon chopped fresh thyme
- ¼ cup chopped fresh Italian parsley
- 1 bay leaf
- Sea salt
- Freshly ground black pepper

1. In a Dutch oven, heat the olive oil over medium-high heat. Add the onion and sauté for 4 minutes, or until softened. Add the tomatoes, beans, celery, carrots, thyme, parsley, and bay leaf, then add water to cover by about 2 inches. 2. Bring the soup to a boil, reduce the heat to low, cover, and simmer for 30 minutes, or until the vegetables are tender. 3. Remove the bay leaf, season with salt and pepper, and serve.

Per Serving:
calories: 185 | fat: 7g | protein: 7g | carbs: 25g | fiber: 8g | sodium: 155mg

Green Veg & Macadamia Smash

Prep time: 25 minutes | Cook time: 15 minutes | Serves 6

- ⅔ cup macadamia nuts
- Enough water to cover and soak the macadamias
- 7 ounces (198 g) cavolo nero or kale, stalks removed and chopped
- 1 medium head broccoli, cut into florets, or broccolini
- 2 cloves garlic, crushed
- ¼ cup extra-virgin olive oil
- 2 tablespoons fresh lemon juice
- 4 medium spring onions, sliced
- ¼ cup chopped fresh herbs, such as parsley, dill, basil, or mint
- Salt and black pepper, to taste

1. Place the macadamias in a small bowl and add enough water to cover them. Soak for about 2 hours, then drain. Discard the water. 2. Fill a large pot with about 1½ cups (360 ml) of water, then insert a steamer colander. Bring to a boil over high heat, then reduce to medium-high. Add the cavolo nero and cook for 6 minutes. Add the broccoli and cook for 8 minutes or until fork-tender. Remove the lid, let the steam escape, and let cool slightly. 3. Place the cooked vegetables in a blender or a food processor. Add the soaked macadamias, garlic, olive oil, lemon juice, spring onions, and fresh herbs (you can reserve some for topping). 4. Process to the desired

consistency (smooth or chunky). Season with salt and pepper to taste and serve. To store, let cool completely and store in a sealed container in the fridge for up to 5 days.

Per Serving:
calories: 250 | fat: 22g | protein: 5g | carbs: 12g | fiber: 5g | sodium: 44mg

Cucumbers with Feta, Mint, and Sumac

Prep time: 15 minutes | Cook time: 0 minutes | Serves 4

- 1 tablespoon extra-virgin olive oil
- 1 tablespoon lemon juice
- 2 teaspoons ground sumac
- ½ teaspoon kosher salt
- 2 hothouse or English cucumbers, diced
- ¼ cup crumbled feta cheese
- 1 tablespoon fresh mint, chopped
- 1 tablespoon fresh parsley, chopped
- ⅛ teaspoon red pepper flakes

1. In a large bowl, whisk together the olive oil, lemon juice, sumac, and salt. Add the cucumber and feta cheese and toss well. 2. Transfer to a serving dish and sprinkle with the mint, parsley, and red pepper flakes.

Per Serving:
calories: 85 | fat: 6g | protein: 3g | carbs: 8g | fiber: 1g | sodium: 230mg

Sautéed Garlic Spinach

Prep time: 5 minutes | Cook time: 10 minutes | Serves 4

- ¼ cup extra-virgin olive oil
- 1 large onion, thinly sliced
- 3 cloves garlic, minced
- 6 (1-pound / 454-g) bags of
- baby spinach, washed
- ½ teaspoon salt
- 1 lemon, cut into wedges

1. Cook the olive oil, onion, and garlic in a large skillet for 2 minutes over medium heat. 2. Add one bag of spinach and ½ teaspoon of salt. Cover the skillet and let the spinach wilt for 30 seconds. Repeat (omitting the salt), adding 1 bag of spinach at a time. 3. Once all the spinach has been added, remove the cover and cook for 3 minutes, letting some of the moisture evaporate. 4. Serve warm with a generous squeeze of lemon over the top.

Per Serving:
calories: 301 | fat: 14g | protein: 17g | carbs: 29g | fiber: 17g | sodium: 812mg

Cauliflower with Lime Juice

Prep time: 10 minutes | Cook time: 7 minutes | Serves 4

- 2 cups chopped cauliflower florets
- 2 tablespoons coconut oil, melted
- 2 teaspoons chili powder
- ½ teaspoon garlic powder
- 1 medium lime
- 2 tablespoons chopped cilantro

1. In a large bowl, toss cauliflower with coconut oil. Sprinkle with chili powder and garlic powder. Place seasoned cauliflower into the air fryer basket. 2. Adjust the temperature to 350°F (177°C) and set the timer for 7 minutes. 3. Cauliflower will be tender and begin to turn golden at the edges. Place into a serving bowl. 4. Cut the lime into quarters and squeeze juice over cauliflower. Garnish with cilantro.

Per Serving:

calories: 80 | fat: 7g | protein: 1g | carbs: 5g | fiber: 2g | sodium: 55mg

Zucchini Pomodoro

Prep time: 15 minutes | Cook time: 12 minutes | Serves 4

- 1 tablespoon vegetable oil
- 1 large onion, peeled and diced
- 3 cloves garlic, peeled and minced
- 1 (28-ounce / 794-g) can diced tomatoes, including juice
- ½ cup water
- 1 tablespoon Italian seasoning
- ½ teaspoon salt
- ½ teaspoon ground black pepper
- 2 medium zucchini, trimmed and spiralized

1. Press the Sauté button on the Instant Pot® and heat oil. Add onion and cook until translucent, about 5 minutes. Add garlic and cook for an additional 30 seconds. Add tomatoes, water, Italian seasoning, salt, and pepper. Add zucchini and toss to combine. Press the Cancel button. 2. Close lid, set steam release to Sealing, press the Manual button, and set time to 1 minute. When the timer beeps, let pressure release naturally for 5 minutes. Quick-release any remaining pressure until the float valve drops and open lid. Press the Cancel button. 3. Transfer zucchini to four bowls. Press the Sauté button, then press the Adjust button to change the temperature to Less, and simmer sauce in the Instant Pot® uncovered for 5 minutes. Ladle over zucchini and serve immediately.

Per Serving:

calories: 72 | fat: 4g | protein: 2g | carbs: 9g | fiber: 2g | sodium: 476mg

Roasted Broccoli with Tahini Yogurt Sauce

Prep time: 15 minutes | Cook time: 30 minutes | Serves 4

For the Broccoli:
- 1½ to 2 pounds (680 to 907 g) broccoli, stalk trimmed and cut into slices, head cut into florets
- 1 lemon, sliced into ¼-inch-thick rounds
- 3 tablespoons extra-virgin olive oil
- ½ teaspoon kosher salt
- ¼ teaspoon freshly ground black pepper

For the Tahini Yogurt Sauce:
- ½ cup plain Greek yogurt
- 2 tablespoons tahini
- 1 tablespoon lemon juice
- ¼ teaspoon kosher salt
- 1 teaspoon sesame seeds, for garnish (optional)

Make the Broccoli: 1. Preheat the oven to 425°F (220°C). Line a baking sheet with parchment paper or foil. 2. In a large bowl, gently toss the broccoli, lemon slices, olive oil, salt, and black pepper to combine. Arrange the broccoli in a single layer on the prepared baking sheet. Roast 15 minutes, stir, and roast another 15 minutes, until golden brown. Make the Tahini Yogurt Sauce: 3. In a medium bowl, combine the yogurt, tahini, lemon juice, and salt; mix well. 4. Spread the tahini yogurt sauce on a platter or large plate and top with the broccoli and lemon slices. Garnish with the sesame seeds (if desired).

Per Serving:

calories: 245 | fat: 16g | protein: 12g | carbs: 20g | fiber: 7g | sodium: 305mg

Garlic and Herb Roasted Grape Tomatoes

Prep time: 10 minutes | Cook time: 45 minutes | Serves 2

- 1 pint grape tomatoes
- 10 whole garlic cloves, skins removed
- ¼ cup olive oil
- ½ teaspoon salt
- 1 fresh rosemary sprig
- 1 fresh thyme sprig

1. Preheat oven to 350°F(180°C). 2. Toss tomatoes, garlic cloves, oil, salt, and herb sprigs in a baking dish. 3. Roast tomatoes until they are soft and begin to caramelize, about 45 minutes. 4. Remove herbs before serving.

Per Serving:

calories: 271 | fat: 26g | protein: 3g | carbs: 12g | fiber: 3g | sodium: 593mg

Roasted Asparagus and Fingerling Potatoes with Thyme

Prep time: 5 minutes | Cook time: 20 minutes | Serves 4

- 1 pound (454 g) asparagus, trimmed
- 1 pound (454 g) fingerling potatoes, cut into thin rounds
- 2 scallions, thinly sliced
- 3 tablespoons olive oil
- ¾ teaspoon salt
- ¼ teaspoon freshly ground black pepper
- 1 tablespoon fresh thyme leaves

1. Preheat the oven to 450ºF (235ºC). 2. In a large baking dish, combine the asparagus, potatoes, and scallions and toss to mix. Add the olive oil, salt, and pepper and toss again to coat all of the vegetables in the oil. Spread the vegetables out in as thin a layer as possible and roast in the preheated oven, stirring once, until the vegetables are tender and nicely browned, about 20 minutes. Just before serving, sprinkle with the thyme leaves. Serve hot.

Per Serving:
calories: 197 | fat: 11g | protein: 5g | carbs: 24g | fiber: 5g | sodium: 449mg

Roasted Brussels Sprouts with Delicata Squash and Balsamic Glaze

Prep time: 10 minutes | Cook time: 30 minutes | Serves 2

- ½ pound (227 g) Brussels sprouts, ends trimmed and outer leaves removed
- 1 medium delicata squash, halved lengthwise, seeded, and cut into 1-inch pieces
- 1 cup fresh cranberries
- 2 teaspoons olive oil
- Salt
- Freshly ground black pepper
- ½ cup balsamic vinegar
- 2 tablespoons roasted pumpkin seeds
- 2 tablespoons fresh pomegranate arils (seeds)

1. Preheat oven to 400°F (205ºC) and set the rack to the middle position. Line a sheet pan with parchment paper. 2. Combine the Brussels sprouts, squash, and cranberries in a large bowl. Drizzle with olive oil, and season liberally with salt and pepper. Toss well to coat and arrange in a single layer on the sheet pan. 3. Roast for 30 minutes, turning vegetables halfway through, or until Brussels sprouts turn brown and crisp in spots and squash has golden-brown spots. 4. While vegetables are roasting, prepare the balsamic glaze by simmering the vinegar for 10 to 12 minutes, or until mixture has reduced to about ¼ cup and turns a syrupy consistency. 5. Remove the vegetables from the oven, drizzle with balsamic syrup, and sprinkle with pumpkin seeds and pomegranate arils before serving.

Per Serving:
calories: 201 | fat: 7g | protein: 6g | carbs: 21g | fiber: 8g | sodium: 34mg

Garlic Roasted Broccoli

Prep time: 8 minutes | Cook time: 10 to 14 minutes | Serves 6

- 1 head broccoli, cut into bite-size florets
- 1 tablespoon avocado oil
- 2 teaspoons minced garlic
- ⅛ teaspoon red pepper flakes
- Sea salt and freshly ground black pepper, to taste
- 1 tablespoon freshly squeezed lemon juice
- ½ teaspoon lemon zest

1. In a large bowl, toss together the broccoli, avocado oil, garlic, red pepper flakes, salt, and pepper. 2. Set the air fryer to 375ºF (191ºC). Arrange the broccoli in a single layer in the air fryer basket, working in batches if necessary. Roast for 10 to 14 minutes, until the broccoli is lightly charred. 3. Place the florets in a medium bowl and toss with the lemon juice and lemon zest. Serve.

Per Serving:
calories: 58 | fat: 3g | protein: 3g | carbs: 7g | fiber: 3g | sodium: 34mg

Rustic Cauliflower and Carrot Hash

Prep time: 10 minutes | Cook time: 10 minutes | Serves 4

- 3 tablespoons extra-virgin olive oil
- 1 large onion, chopped
- 1 tablespoon garlic, minced
- 2 cups carrots, diced
- 4 cups cauliflower pieces, washed
- 1 teaspoon salt
- ½ teaspoon ground cumin

1. In a large skillet over medium heat, cook the olive oil, onion, garlic, and carrots for 3 minutes. 2. Cut the cauliflower into 1-inch or bite-size pieces. Add the cauliflower, salt, and cumin to the skillet and toss to combine with the carrots and onions. 3. Cover and cook for 3 minutes. 4. Toss the vegetables and continue to cook uncovered for an additional 3 to 4 minutes. 5. Serve warm.

Per Serving:
calories: 159 | fat: 11g | protein: 3g | carbs: 15g | fiber: 5g | sodium: 657mg

Garlic Cauliflower with Tahini

Prep time: 10 minutes | Cook time: 20 minutes | Serves 4

Cauliflower:
- 5 cups cauliflower florets (about 1 large head)
- 6 garlic cloves, smashed and cut into thirds

Sauce:
- 2 tablespoons tahini (sesame paste)
- 2 tablespoons hot water
- 1 tablespoon fresh lemon

- 3 tablespoons vegetable oil
- ½ teaspoon ground cumin
- ½ teaspoon ground coriander
- ½ teaspoon kosher salt

  juice
- 1 teaspoon minced garlic
- ½ teaspoon kosher salt

1. For the cauliflower: In a large bowl, combine the cauliflower florets and garlic. Drizzle with the vegetable oil. Sprinkle with the cumin, coriander, and salt. Toss until well coated. 2. Place the cauliflower in the air fryer basket. Set the air fryer to 400°F (204°C) for 20 minutes, turning the cauliflower halfway through the cooking time. 3. Meanwhile, for the sauce: In a small bowl, combine the tahini, water, lemon juice, garlic, and salt. (The sauce will appear curdled at first, but keep stirring until you have a thick, creamy, smooth mixture.) 4. Transfer the cauliflower to a large serving bowl. Pour the sauce over and toss gently to coat. Serve immediately.

Per Serving:
calories: 176 | fat: 15g | protein: 4g | carbs: 10g | fiber: 4g | sodium: 632mg

Warm Beets with Hazelnuts and Spiced Yogurt

Prep time: 5 minutes | Cook time: 40 minutes | Serves 4

- 4 or 5 beets, peeled
- ¼ cup hazelnuts
- ½ cup low-fat plain Greek yogurt
- 1 tablespoon honey
- 1 tablespoon chopped fresh

  mint
- 1 teaspoon ground cinnamon
- ¼ teaspoon ground cumin
- ⅛ teaspoon ground black pepper

1. Place racks in the upper and lower thirds of the oven. Preheat the oven to 400°F(205°C). 2. Place the beets on a 12' × 12' piece of foil. Fold the foil over the beets, and seal the sides. Bake until the beets are tender enough to be pierced by a fork, about 40 minutes. Remove from the oven, carefully open the packet, and let cool slightly. When cool enough to handle, slice the beets into ¼'-thick rounds. 3. Meanwhile, toast the hazelnuts on a small baking sheet until browned and fragrant, about 5 minutes. Using a paper towel or kitchen towel, rub the skins off. Coarsely chop the nuts and set aside. 4. In a medium bowl, stir together the yogurt, honey, mint, cinnamon, cumin, and pepper. 5. Serve the beets with a dollop of the spiced yogurt and a sprinkle of the nuts.

Per Serving:
calories: 126 | fat: 6g | protein: 5g | carbs: 15g | fiber: 4g | sodium: 74mg

Green Beans with Tomatoes and Potatoes

Prep time: 15 minutes | Cook time: 5 minutes | Serves 8

- 1 pound (454 g) small new potatoes
- 1 cup water
- 1 teaspoon salt
- 2 pounds (907 g) fresh green beans, trimmed
- 2 medium tomatoes, seeded and diced
- 2 tablespoons olive oil

- 1 tablespoon red wine vinegar
- 1 clove garlic, peeled and minced
- ½ teaspoon dry mustard powder
- ¼ teaspoon smoked paprika
- ¼ teaspoon ground black pepper

1. Place potatoes in a steamer basket. Place the rack in the Instant Pot®, add water, and then top with the steamer basket. Close lid, set steam release to Sealing, press the Manual button, and set time to 4 minutes. When the timer beeps, quick-release the pressure until the float valve drops. Press the Cancel button and open lid. 2. Add salt, green beans, and tomatoes to the Instant Pot®. Close lid, set steam release to Sealing, press the Manual button, and set time to 1 minute. When the timer beeps, quick-release the pressure until the float valve drops, press the Cancel button, and open lid. Transfer mixture to a serving platter or large bowl. 3. In a small bowl, whisk oil, vinegar, garlic, mustard, paprika, and pepper. Pour dressing over vegetables and gently toss to coat. Serve hot.

Per Serving:
calories: 112 | fat: 4g | protein: 2g | carbs: 20g | fiber: 5g | sodium: 368mg

Potato Vegetable Hash

Prep time: 20 minutes | Cook time: 5 to 7 hours | Serves 4

- 1½ pounds (680 g) red potatoes, diced
- 8 ounces (227 g) green beans, trimmed and cut into ½-inch pieces
- 4 ounces (113 g) mushrooms, chopped
- 1 large tomato, chopped
- 1 large zucchini, diced
- 1 small onion, diced
- 1 red bell pepper, seeded and chopped
- ⅓ cup low-sodium vegetable broth
- 1 teaspoon sea salt
- ½ teaspoon garlic powder
- ½ teaspoon freshly ground black pepper
- ¼ teaspoon red pepper flakes
- ¼ cup shredded cheese of your choice (optional)

1. In a slow cooker, combine the potatoes, green beans, mushrooms, tomato, zucchini, onion, bell pepper, vegetable broth, salt, garlic powder, black pepper, and red pepper flakes. Stir to mix well. 2. Cover the cooker and cook for 5 to 7 hours on Low heat. 3. Garnish with cheese for serving (if using).

Per Serving:

calories: 183 | fat: 1g | protein: 7g | carbs: 41g | fiber: 8g | sodium: 642mg

Herb Vinaigrette Potato Salad

Prep time: 10 minutes | Cook time: 4 minutes | Serves 10

- ¼ cup olive oil
- 3 tablespoons red wine vinegar
- ¼ cup chopped fresh flat-leaf parsley
- 2 tablespoons chopped fresh dill
- 2 tablespoons chopped fresh chives
- 1 clove garlic, peeled and minced
- ½ teaspoon dry mustard powder
- ¼ teaspoon ground black pepper
- 2 pounds (907 g) baby Yukon Gold potatoes
- 1 cup water
- 1 teaspoon salt

1. Whisk together oil, vinegar, parsley, dill, chives, garlic, mustard, and pepper in a small bowl. Set aside. 2. Place potatoes in a steamer basket. Place the rack in the Instant Pot®, add water and salt, then top with the steamer basket. Close lid, set steam release to Sealing, press the Manual button, and set time to 4 minutes. When the timer beeps, quick-release the pressure until the float valve drops. Press the Cancel button and open lid. 3. Transfer hot potatoes to a serving bowl. Pour dressing over potatoes and gently toss to coat. Serve warm or at room temperature.

Per Serving:

calories: 116 | fat: 6g | protein: 2g | carbs: 16g | fiber: 1g | sodium: 239mg

One-Pan Herb-Roasted Tomatoes, Green Beans, and Baby Potatoes

Prep time: 10 minutes | Cook time: 30 minutes | Serves 6

- ¼ cup chopped mixed fresh herbs, such as flat-leaf parsley, oregano, mint, and dill
- 3 tablespoons olive oil
- ½ teaspoon kosher salt
- ½ teaspoon ground black pepper
- 1 pound (454 g) baby potatoes, halved
- 1 pound (454 g) green beans, trimmed and halved
- 2 large shallots, cut into wedges
- 2 pints cherry tomatoes

1. Preheat the oven to 400°F (205°C). 2. In a small bowl, whisk together the herbs, oil, salt, and pepper. Place the potatoes, string beans, and shallots on a large rimmed baking sheet. Drizzle the herb mixture over the vegetables and toss thoroughly to coat. 3. Roast the vegetables until the potatoes are just tender, about 15 minutes. Remove from the oven and toss in the tomatoes. Roast until the tomatoes blister and the potatoes are completely tender, about 15 minutes.

Per Serving:

calories: 173 | fat: 8g | protein: 5g | carbs: 26g | fiber: 5g | sodium: 185mg

Chapter 9 Vegetarian Mains

Tortellini in Red Pepper Sauce

Prep time: 15 minutes | Cook time: 10 minutes | Serves 4

- 1 (16-ounce / 454-g) container fresh cheese tortellini (usually green and white pasta)
- 1 (16-ounce / 454-g) jar roasted red peppers, drained
- 1 teaspoon garlic powder
- ¼ cup tahini
- 1 tablespoon red pepper oil (optional)

1. Bring a large pot of water to a boil and cook the tortellini according to package directions. 2. In a blender, combine the red peppers with the garlic powder and process until smooth. Once blended, add the tahini until the sauce is thickened. If the sauce gets too thick, add up to 1 tablespoon red pepper oil (if using). 3. Once tortellini are cooked, drain and leave pasta in colander. Add the sauce to the bottom of the empty pot and heat for 2 minutes. Then, add the tortellini back into the pot and cook for 2 more minutes. Serve and enjoy!

Per Serving:
calories: 350 | fat: 11g | protein: 12g | carbs: 46g | fiber: 4g | sodium: 192mg

Pistachio Mint Pesto Pasta

Prep time: 10 minutes | Cook time: 10 minutes | Serves 4

- 8 ounces (227 g) whole-wheat pasta
- 1 cup fresh mint
- ½ cup fresh basil
- ⅓ cup unsalted pistachios, shelled
- 1 garlic clove, peeled
- ½ teaspoon kosher salt
- Juice of ½ lime
- ⅓ cup extra-virgin olive oil

1. Cook the pasta according to the package directions. Drain, reserving ½ cup of the pasta water, and set aside. 2. In a food processor, add the mint, basil, pistachios, garlic, salt, and lime juice. Process until the pistachios are coarsely ground. Add the olive oil in a slow, steady stream and process until incorporated. 3. In a large bowl, mix the pasta with the pistachio pesto; toss well to incorporate. If a thinner, more saucy consistency is desired, add some of the reserved pasta water and toss well.

Per Serving:
calories: 420 | fat: 3g | protein: 11g | carbs: 48g | fiber: 2g | sodium: 150mg

Sheet Pan Roasted Chickpeas and Vegetables with Harissa Yogurt

Prep time: 10 minutes | Cook time: 30 minutes | Serves 2

- 4 cups cauliflower florets (about ½ small head)
- 2 medium carrots, peeled, halved, and then sliced into quarters lengthwise
- 2 tablespoons olive oil, divided
- ½ teaspoon garlic powder, divided
- ½ teaspoon salt, divided
- 2 teaspoons za'atar spice mix, divided
- 1 (15-ounce / 425-g) can chickpeas, drained, rinsed, and patted dry
- ¾ cup plain Greek yogurt
- 1 teaspoon harissa spice paste

1. Preheat the oven to 400°F (205°C) and set the rack to the middle position. Line a sheet pan with foil or parchment paper. 2. Place the cauliflower and carrots in a large bowl. Drizzle with 1 tablespoon olive oil and sprinkle with ¼ teaspoon of garlic powder, ¼ teaspoon of salt, and 1 teaspoon of za'atar. Toss well to combine. 3. Spread the vegetables onto one half of the sheet pan in a single layer. 4. Place the chickpeas in the same bowl and season with the remaining 1 tablespoon of oil, ¼ teaspoon of garlic powder, and ¼ teaspoon of salt, and the remaining za'atar. Toss well to combine. 5. Spread the chickpeas onto the other half of the sheet pan. 6. Roast for 30 minutes, or until the vegetables are tender and the chickpeas start to turn golden. Flip the vegetables halfway through the cooking time, and give the chickpeas a stir so they cook evenly. 7. The chickpeas may need an extra few minutes if you like them crispy. If so, remove the vegetables and leave the chickpeas in until they're cooked to desired crispiness. 8. While the vegetables are roasting, combine the yogurt and harissa in a small bowl. Taste, and add additional harissa as desired.

Per Serving:
calories: 467 | fat: 23g | protein: 18g | carbs: 54g | fiber: 15g | sodium: 632mg

Stuffed Pepper Stew

Prep time: 20 minutes | Cook time: 50 minutes | Serves 2

- 2 tablespoons olive oil
- 2 sweet peppers, diced (about 2 cups)
- ½ large onion, minced
- 1 garlic clove, minced
- 1 teaspoon oregano
- 1 tablespoon gluten-free vegetarian Worcestershire
- sauce
- 1 cup low-sodium vegetable stock
- 1 cup low-sodium tomato juice
- ¼ cup brown lentils
- ¼ cup brown rice
- Salt

1. Heat olive oil in a Dutch oven over medium-high heat. Add the sweet peppers and onion and sauté for 10 minutes, or until the peppers are wilted and the onion starts to turn golden. 2. Add the garlic, oregano, and Worcestershire sauce, and cook for another 30 seconds. Add the vegetable stock, tomato juice, lentils, and rice. 3. Bring the mixture to a boil. Cover, and reduce the heat to medium-low. Simmer for 45 minutes, or until the rice is cooked and the lentils are softened. Season with salt.

Per Serving:

calories: 379 | fat: 16g | protein: 11g | carbs: 53g | fiber: 7g | sodium: 392mg

Roasted Portobello Mushrooms with Kale and Red Onion

Prep time: 15 minutes | Cook time: 30 minutes | Serves 4

- ¼ cup white wine vinegar
- 3 tablespoons extra-virgin olive oil, divided
- ½ teaspoon honey
- ¾ teaspoon kosher salt, divided
- ¼ teaspoon freshly ground black pepper
- 4 large (4 to 5 ounces / 113 to 142 g each) portobello
- mushrooms, stems removed
- 1 red onion, julienned
- 2 garlic cloves, minced
- 1 (8-ounce / 227-g) bunch kale, stemmed and chopped small
- ¼ teaspoon red pepper flakes
- ¼ cup grated Parmesan or Romano cheese

1. Line a baking sheet with parchment paper or foil. In a medium bowl, whisk together the vinegar, 1½ tablespoons of the olive oil, honey, ¼ teaspoon of the salt, and the black pepper. Arrange the mushrooms on the baking sheet and pour the marinade over them. Marinate for 15 to 30 minutes. 2. Meanwhile, preheat the oven to 400°F (205°C). 3. Bake the mushrooms for 20 minutes, turning over halfway through. 4. Heat the remaining 1½ tablespoons olive oil in a large skillet or ovenproof sauté pan over medium-high heat. Add the onion and the remaining ½ teaspoon salt and sauté until golden brown, 5 to 6 minutes. Add the garlic and sauté for 30 seconds. Add the kale and red pepper flakes and sauté until the kale cooks down, about 5 minutes. 5. Remove the mushrooms from the oven and increase the temperature to broil. 6. Carefully pour the liquid from the baking sheet into the pan with the kale mixture; mix well. 7. Turn the mushrooms over so that the stem side is facing up. Spoon some of the kale mixture on top of each mushroom. Sprinkle 1 tablespoon Parmesan cheese on top of each. 8. Broil until golden brown, 3 to 4 minutes.

Per Serving:

calories: 200 | fat: 13g | protein: 8g | carbs: 16g | fiber: 4g | sodium: 365mg

Baked Tofu with Sun-Dried Tomatoes and Artichokes

Prep time: 15 minutes | Cook time: 30 minutes | Serves 4

- 1 (16-ounce / 454-g) package extra-firm tofu, drained and patted dry, cut into 1-inch cubes
- 2 tablespoons extra-virgin olive oil, divided
- 2 tablespoons lemon juice, divided
- 1 tablespoon low-sodium soy sauce or gluten-free tamari
- 1 onion, diced
- ½ teaspoon kosher salt
- 2 garlic cloves, minced
- 1 (14-ounce / 397-g) can artichoke hearts, drained
- 8 sun-dried tomato halves packed in oil, drained and chopped
- ¼ teaspoon freshly ground black pepper
- 1 tablespoon white wine vinegar
- Zest of 1 lemon
- ¼ cup fresh parsley, chopped

1. Preheat the oven to 400°F (205°C). Line a baking sheet with foil or parchment paper. 2. In a bowl, combine the tofu, 1 tablespoon of the olive oil, 1 tablespoon of the lemon juice, and the soy sauce. Allow to sit and marinate for 15 to 30 minutes. Arrange the tofu in a single layer on the prepared baking sheet and bake for 20 minutes, turning once, until light golden brown. 3. Heat the remaining 1 tablespoon olive oil in a large skillet or sauté pan over medium heat. Add the onion and salt; sauté until translucent, 5 to 6 minutes. Add the garlic and sauté for 30 seconds. Add the artichoke hearts, sun-dried tomatoes, and black pepper and sauté for 5 minutes. Add the white wine vinegar and the remaining 1 tablespoon lemon juice and deglaze the pan, scraping up any brown bits. Remove the pan from the heat and stir in the lemon zest and parsley. Gently mix in the baked tofu.

Per Serving:

calories: 230 | fat: 14g | protein: 14g | carbs: 13g | fiber: 5g | sodium: 500mg

Cheese Stuffed Zucchini

Prep time: 20 minutes | Cook time: 8 minutes | Serves 4

- 1 large zucchini, cut into four pieces
- 2 tablespoons olive oil
- 1 cup Ricotta cheese, room temperature
- 2 tablespoons scallions, chopped
- 1 heaping tablespoon fresh parsley, roughly chopped
- 1 heaping tablespoon coriander, minced
- 2 ounces (57 g) Cheddar cheese, preferably freshly grated
- 1 teaspoon celery seeds
- ½ teaspoon salt
- ½ teaspoon garlic pepper

1. Cook your zucchini in the air fryer basket for approximately 10 minutes at 350ºF (177ºC). Check for doneness and cook for 2-3 minutes longer if needed. 2. Meanwhile, make the stuffing by mixing the other items. 3. When your zucchini is thoroughly cooked, open them up. Divide the stuffing among all zucchini pieces and bake an additional 5 minutes.

Per Serving:
calories: 242 | fat: 20g | protein: 12g | carbs: 5g | fiber: 1g | sodium: 443mg

Quinoa Lentil "Meatballs" with Quick Tomato Sauce

Prep time: 25 minutes | Cook time: 45 minutes | Serves 4

For the Meatballs:
- Olive oil cooking spray
- 2 large eggs, beaten
- 1 tablespoon no-salt-added tomato paste
- ½ teaspoon kosher salt
- ½ cup grated Parmesan

For the Tomato Sauce:
- 1 tablespoon extra-virgin olive oil
- 1 onion, minced
- ½ teaspoon dried oregano
- ½ teaspoon kosher salt

- cheese
- ½ onion, roughly chopped
- ¼ cup fresh parsley
- 1 garlic clove, peeled
- 1½ cups cooked lentils
- 1 cup cooked quinoa

- 2 garlic cloves, minced
- 1 (28-ounce / 794-g) can no-salt-added crushed tomatoes
- ½ teaspoon honey
- ¼ cup fresh basil, chopped

Make the Meatballs: 1. Preheat the oven to 400ºF (205ºC). Lightly grease a 12-cup muffin pan with olive oil cooking spray. 2. In a large bowl, whisk together the eggs, tomato paste, and salt until fully combined. Mix in the Parmesan cheese. 3. In a food processor, add the onion, parsley, and garlic. Process until minced. Add to the egg mixture and stir together. Add the lentils to the food processor

and process until puréed into a thick paste. Add to the large bowl and mix together. Add the quinoa and mix well. 4. Form balls, slightly larger than a golf ball, with ¼ cup of the quinoa mixture. Place each ball in a muffin pan cup. Note: The mixture will be somewhat soft but should hold together. 5. Bake 25 to 30 minutes, until golden brown. Make the Tomato Sauce: 6. Heat the olive oil in a large saucepan over medium heat. Add the onion, oregano, and salt and sauté until light golden brown, about 5 minutes. Add the garlic and cook for 30 seconds. 7. Stir in the tomatoes and honey. Increase the heat to high and cook, stirring often, until simmering, then decrease the heat to medium-low and cook for 10 minutes. Remove from the heat and stir in the basil. Serve with the meatballs.

Per Serving:
3 meatballs: calories: 360 | fat: 10g | protein: 20g | carbs: 48g | fiber: 14g | sodium: 520mg

Moroccan Vegetable Tagine

Prep time: 20 minutes | Cook time: 1 hour | Serves 6

- ½ cup extra-virgin olive oil
- 2 medium yellow onions, sliced
- 6 celery stalks, sliced into ¼-inch crescents
- 6 garlic cloves, minced
- 1 teaspoon ground cumin
- 1 teaspoon ginger powder
- 1 teaspoon salt
- ½ teaspoon paprika
- ½ teaspoon ground cinnamon
- ¼ teaspoon freshly ground black pepper
- 2 cups vegetable stock
- 1 medium eggplant, cut into

- 1-inch cubes
- 2 medium zucchini, cut into ½-inch-thick semicircles
- 2 cups cauliflower florets
- 1 (13¾-ounce / 390-g) can artichoke hearts, drained and quartered
- 1 cup halved and pitted green olives
- ½ cup chopped fresh flat-leaf parsley, for garnish
- ½ cup chopped fresh cilantro leaves, for garnish
- Greek yogurt, for garnish (optional)

1. In a large, thick soup pot or Dutch oven, heat the olive oil over medium-high heat. Add the onion and celery and sauté until softened, 6 to 8 minutes. Add the garlic, cumin, ginger, salt, paprika, cinnamon, and pepper and sauté for another 2 minutes. 2. Add the stock and bring to a boil. Reduce the heat to low and add the eggplant, zucchini, and cauliflower. Simmer on low heat, covered, until the vegetables are tender, 30 to 35 minutes. Add the artichoke hearts and olives, cover, and simmer for another 15 minutes. 3. Serve garnished with parsley, cilantro, and Greek yogurt (if using).

Per Serving:
calories: 265 | fat: 21g | protein: 5g | carbs: 19g | fiber: 9g | sodium: 858mg

Broccoli-Cheese Fritters

Prep time: 5 minutes | Cook time: 20 to 25 minutes | Serves 4

- 1 cup broccoli florets
- 1 cup shredded Mozzarella cheese
- ¾ cup almond flour
- ½ cup flaxseed meal, divided
- 2 teaspoons baking powder
- 1 teaspoon garlic powder
- Salt and freshly ground black pepper, to taste
- 2 eggs, lightly beaten
- ½ cup ranch dressing

1. Preheat the air fryer to 400ºF (204ºC). 2. In a food processor fitted with a metal blade, pulse the broccoli until very finely chopped. 3. Transfer the broccoli to a large bowl and add the Mozzarella, almond flour, ¼ cup of the flaxseed meal, baking powder, and garlic powder. Stir until thoroughly combined. Season to taste with salt and black pepper. Add the eggs and stir again to form a sticky dough. Shape the dough into 1¼-inch fritters. 4. Place the remaining ¼ cup flaxseed meal in a shallow bowl and roll the fritters in the meal to form an even coating. 5. Working in batches if necessary, arrange the fritters in a single layer in the basket of the air fryer and spray generously with olive oil. Pausing halfway through the cooking time to shake the basket, air fry for 20 to 25 minutes until the fritters are golden brown and crispy. Serve with the ranch dressing for dipping.

Per Serving:
calories: 388 | fat: 30g | protein: 19g | carbs: 14g | fiber: 7g | sodium: 526mg

Grilled Eggplant Stacks

Prep time: 20 minutes | Cook time: 10 minutes | Serves 2

- 1 medium eggplant, cut crosswise into 8 slices
- ¼ teaspoon salt
- 1 teaspoon Italian herb seasoning mix
- 2 tablespoons olive oil
- 1 large tomato, cut into 4 slices
- 4 (1-ounce / 28-g) slices of buffalo mozzarella
- Fresh basil, for garnish

1. Place the eggplant slices in a colander set in the sink or over a bowl. Sprinkle both sides with the salt. Let the eggplant sit for 15 minutes. 2. While the eggplant is resting, heat the grill to medium-high heat (about 350ºF / 180ºC). 3. Pat the eggplant dry with paper towels and place it in a mixing bowl. Sprinkle it with the Italian herb seasoning mix and olive oil. Toss well to coat. 4. Grill the eggplant for 5 minutes, or until it has grill marks and is lightly charred. Flip each eggplant slice over, and grill on the second side for another 5 minutes. 5. Flip the eggplant slices back over and top

four of the slices with a slice of tomato and a slice of mozzarella. Top each stack with one of the remaining four slices of eggplant. 6. Turn the grill down to low and cover it to let the cheese melt. Check after 30 seconds and remove when the cheese is soft and mostly melted. 7. Sprinkle with fresh basil slices.

Per Serving:
calories: 354 | fat: 29g | protein: 13g | carbs: 19g | fiber: 9g | sodium: 340mg

Crustless Spinach Cheese Pie

Prep time: 10 minutes | Cook time: 20 minutes | Serves 4

- 6 large eggs
- ¼ cup heavy whipping cream
- 1 cup frozen chopped spinach, drained
- 1 cup shredded sharp Cheddar cheese
- ¼ cup diced yellow onion

1. In a medium bowl, whisk eggs and add cream. Add remaining ingredients to bowl. 2. Pour into a round baking dish. Place into the air fryer basket. 3. Adjust the temperature to 320ºF (160ºC) and bake for 20 minutes. 4. Eggs will be firm and slightly browned when cooked. Serve immediately.

Per Serving:
calories: 263 | fat: 20g | protein: 18g | carbs: 4g | fiber: 1g | sodium: 321mg

Vegetable Burgers

Prep time: 10 minutes | Cook time: 12 minutes | Serves 4

- 8 ounces (227 g) cremini mushrooms
- 2 large egg yolks
- ½ medium zucchini, trimmed and chopped
- ¼ cup peeled and chopped
- yellow onion
- 1 clove garlic, peeled and finely minced
- ½ teaspoon salt
- ¼ teaspoon ground black pepper

1. Place all ingredients into a food processor and pulse twenty times until finely chopped and combined. 2. Separate mixture into four equal sections and press each into a burger shape. Place burgers into ungreased air fryer basket. Adjust the temperature to 375ºF (191ºC) and air fry for 12 minutes, turning burgers halfway through cooking. Burgers will be browned and firm when done. 3. Place burgers on a large plate and let cool 5 minutes before serving.

Per Serving:
calories: 50 | fat: 3g | protein: 3g | carbs: 4g | fiber: 1g | sodium: 299mg

Crustless Spanakopita

Prep time: 15 minutes | Cook time: 45 minutes | Serves 6

- 12 tablespoons extra-virgin olive oil, divided
- 1 small yellow onion, diced
- 1 (32-ounce / 907-g) bag frozen chopped spinach, thawed, fully drained, and patted dry (about 4 cups)
- 4 garlic cloves, minced
- ½ teaspoon salt
- ½ teaspoon freshly ground black pepper
- 1 cup whole-milk ricotta cheese
- 4 large eggs
- ¾ cup crumbled traditional feta cheese
- ¼ cup pine nuts

1. Preheat the oven to 375°F (190°C). 2. In a large skillet, heat 4 tablespoons olive oil over medium-high heat. Add the onion and sauté until softened, 6 to 8 minutes. 3. Add the spinach, garlic, salt, and pepper and sauté another 5 minutes. Remove from the heat and allow to cool slightly. 4. In a medium bowl, whisk together the ricotta and eggs. Add to the cooled spinach and stir to combine. 5. Pour 4 tablespoons olive oil in the bottom of a 9-by-13-inch glass baking dish and swirl to coat the bottom and sides. Add the spinach-ricotta mixture and spread into an even layer. 6. Bake for 20 minutes or until the mixture begins to set. Remove from the oven and crumble the feta evenly across the top of the spinach. Add the pine nuts and drizzle with the remaining 4 tablespoons olive oil. Return to the oven and bake for an additional 15 to 20 minutes, or until the spinach is fully set and the top is starting to turn golden brown. Allow to cool slightly before cutting to serve.

Per Serving:
calories: 497 | fat: 44g | protein: 18g | carbs: 11g | fiber: 5g | sodium: 561mg

Farro with Roasted Tomatoes and Mushrooms

Prep time: 20 minutes | Cook time: 1 hour | Serves 4

For the Tomatoes:
- 2 pints cherry tomatoes
- 1 teaspoon extra-virgin olive

For the Farro:
- 3 to 4 cups water
- ½ cup farro

For the Mushrooms:
- 2 tablespoons extra-virgin olive oil
- 1 onion, julienned
- ½ teaspoon kosher salt
- ¼ teaspoon freshly ground black pepper

- oil
- ¼ teaspoon kosher salt

- ¼ teaspoon kosher salt

- 10 ounces (283 g) baby bella (crimini) mushrooms, stemmed and thinly sliced
- ½ cup no-salt-added vegetable stock
- 1 (15-ounce / 425-g) can no-salt-added or low-sodium cannellini beans, drained and rinsed
- 1 cup baby spinach
- 2 tablespoons fresh basil, cut into ribbons
- ¼ cup pine nuts, toasted
- Aged balsamic vinegar (optional)

Make the Tomatoes: 1. Preheat the oven to 400°F (205°C). Line a baking sheet with parchment paper or foil. Toss the tomatoes, olive oil, and salt together on the baking sheet and roast for 30 minutes. Make the Farro: 2. Bring the water, farro, and salt to a boil in a medium saucepan or pot over high heat. Cover, reduce the heat to low, and simmer, and cook for 30 minutes, or until the farro is al dente. Drain and set aside. Make the Mushrooms: 3. Heat the olive oil in a large skillet or sauté pan over medium-low heat. Add the onions, salt, and black pepper and sauté until golden brown and starting to caramelize, about 15 minutes. Add the mushrooms, increase the heat to medium, and sauté until the liquid has evaporated and the mushrooms brown, about 10 minutes. Add the vegetable stock and deglaze the pan, scraping up any brown bits, and reduce the liquid for about 5 minutes. Add the beans and warm through, about 3 minutes. 4. Remove from the heat and mix in the spinach, basil, pine nuts, roasted tomatoes, and farro. Garnish with a drizzle of balsamic vinegar, if desired.

Per Serving:
calories: 375 | fat: 15g | protein: 14g | carbs: 48g | fiber: 10g | sodium: 305mg

Herbed Ricotta–Stuffed Mushrooms

Prep time: 10 minutes | Cook time: 30 minutes | Serves 4

- 6 tablespoons extra-virgin olive oil, divided
- 4 portobello mushroom caps, cleaned and gills removed
- 1 cup whole-milk ricotta cheese
- ⅓ cup chopped fresh herbs
- (such as basil, parsley, rosemary, oregano, or thyme)
- 2 garlic cloves, finely minced
- ½ teaspoon salt
- ¼ teaspoon freshly ground black pepper

1. Preheat the oven to 400°F (205°C). 2. Line a baking sheet with parchment or foil and drizzle with 2 tablespoons olive oil, spreading evenly. Place the mushroom caps on the baking sheet, gill-side up. 3. In a medium bowl, mix together the ricotta, herbs, 2 tablespoons olive oil, garlic, salt, and pepper. Stuff each mushroom cap with one-quarter of the cheese mixture, pressing down if needed. Drizzle with remaining 2 tablespoons olive oil and bake until golden brown and the mushrooms are soft, 30 to 35 minutes, depending on the size of the mushrooms.

Per Serving:
calories: 308 | fat: 29g | protein: 9g | carbs: 6g | fiber: 1g | sodium: 351mg

Spinach-Artichoke Stuffed Mushrooms

Prep time: 10 minutes | Cook time: 10 to 14 minutes | Serves 4

- 2 tablespoons olive oil
- 4 large portobello mushrooms, stems removed and gills scraped out
- ½ teaspoon salt
- ¼ teaspoon freshly ground pepper
- 4 ounces (113 g) goat cheese, crumbled
- ½ cup chopped marinated artichoke hearts
- 1 cup frozen spinach, thawed and squeezed dry
- ½ cup grated Parmesan cheese
- 2 tablespoons chopped fresh parsley

1. Preheat the air fryer to 400ºF (204ºC). 2. Rub the olive oil over the portobello mushrooms until thoroughly coated. Sprinkle both sides with the salt and black pepper. Place top-side down on a clean work surface. 3. In a small bowl, combine the goat cheese, artichoke hearts, and spinach. Mash with the back of a fork until thoroughly combined. Divide the cheese mixture among the mushrooms and sprinkle with the Parmesan cheese. 4. Air fry for 10 to 14 minutes until the mushrooms are tender and the cheese has begun to brown. Top with the fresh parsley just before serving.

Per Serving:

calories: 284 | fat: 21g | protein: 16g | carbs: 10g | fiber: 4g | sodium: 686mg

Mediterranean Pan Pizza

Prep time: 5 minutes | Cook time: 8 minutes | Serves 2

- 1 cup shredded Mozzarella cheese
- ¼ medium red bell pepper, seeded and chopped
- ½ cup chopped fresh spinach
- leaves
- 2 tablespoons chopped black olives
- 2 tablespoons crumbled feta cheese

1. Sprinkle Mozzarella into an ungreased round nonstick baking dish in an even layer. Add remaining ingredients on top. 2. Place dish into air fryer basket. Adjust the temperature to 350ºF (177ºC) and bake for 8 minutes, checking halfway through to avoid burning. Top of pizza will be golden brown and the cheese melted when done. 3. Remove dish from fryer and let cool 5 minutes before slicing and serving.

Per Serving:

calories: 108 | fat: 1g | protein: 20g | carbs: 5g | fiber: 3g | sodium: 521mg

Cauliflower Steaks with Olive Citrus Sauce

Prep time: 15 minutes | Cook time: 30 minutes | Serves 4

- 1 or 2 large heads cauliflower (at least 2 pounds / 907 g, enough for 4 portions)
- ⅓ cup extra-virgin olive oil
- ¼ teaspoon kosher salt
- ⅛ teaspoon ground black pepper
- Juice of 1 orange
- Zest of 1 orange
- ¼ cup black olives, pitted and chopped
- 1 tablespoon Dijon or grainy mustard
- 1 tablespoon red wine vinegar
- ½ teaspoon ground coriander

1. Preheat the oven to 400ºF (205ºC). Line a baking sheet with parchment paper or foil. 2. Cut off the stem of the cauliflower so it will sit upright. Slice it vertically into four thick slabs. Place the cauliflower on the prepared baking sheet. Drizzle with the olive oil, salt, and black pepper. Bake for about 30 minutes, turning over once, until tender and golden brown. 3. In a medium bowl, combine the orange juice, orange zest, olives, mustard, vinegar, and coriander; mix well. 4. Serve the cauliflower warm or at room temperature with the sauce.

Per Serving:

calories: 265 | fat: 21g | protein: 5g | carbs: 19g | fiber: 4g | sodium: 310mg

Caprese Eggplant Stacks

Prep time: 5 minutes | Cook time: 12 minutes | Serves 4

- 1 medium eggplant, cut into ¼-inch slices
- 2 large tomatoes, cut into ¼-inch slices
- 4 ounces (113 g) fresh
- Mozzarella, cut into ½-ounce / 14-g slices
- 2 tablespoons olive oil
- ¼ cup fresh basil, sliced

1. In a baking dish, place four slices of eggplant on the bottom. Place a slice of tomato on top of each eggplant round, then Mozzarella, then eggplant. Repeat as necessary. 2. Drizzle with olive oil. Cover dish with foil and place dish into the air fryer basket. 3. Adjust the temperature to 350ºF (177ºC) and bake for 12 minutes. 4. When done, eggplant will be tender. Garnish with fresh basil to serve.

Per Serving:

calories: 97 | fat: 7g | protein: 2g | carbs: 8g | fiber: 4g | sodium: 11mg

Chapter 10 Desserts

Blueberry Pomegranate Granita

Prep time: 5 minutes | Cook time: 10 minutes | Serves 2

- 1 cup frozen wild blueberries
- 1 cup pomegranate or pomegranate blueberry juice
- ¼ cup sugar
- ¼ cup water

1. Combine the frozen blueberries and pomegranate juice in a saucepan and bring to a boil. Reduce the heat and simmer for 5 minutes, or until the blueberries start to break down. 2. While the juice and berries are cooking, combine the sugar and water in a small microwave-safe bowl. Microwave for 60 seconds, or until it comes to a rolling boil. Stir to make sure all of the sugar is dissolved and set the syrup aside. 3. Combine the blueberry mixture and the sugar syrup in a blender and blend for 1 minute, or until the fruit is completely puréed. 4. Pour the mixture into an 8-by-8-inch baking pan or a similar sized bowl. The liquid should come about ½ inch up the sides. Let the mixture cool for 30 minutes, and then put it into the freezer. 5. Every 30 minutes for the next 2 hours, scrape the granita with a fork to keep it from freezing solid. 6. Serve it after 2 hours, or store it in a covered container in the freezer.

Per Serving:
calories: 214 | fat: 0g | protein: 1g | carbs: 54g | fiber: 2g | sodium: 15mg

Greek Island Almond Cocoa Bites

Prep time: 5 minutes | Cook time: 0 minutes | Serves 6

- ½ cup roasted, unsalted whole almonds (with skins)
- 3 tablespoons granulated sugar, divided
- 1½ teaspoons unsweetened cocoa powder
- 1¼ tablespoons unseasoned breadcrumbs
- ¾ teaspoon pure vanilla extract
- 1½ teaspoons orange juice

1. Place the almonds in a food processor and process until you have a coarse ground texture. 2. In a medium bowl, combine the ground almonds, 2 tablespoons sugar, the cocoa powder, and the breadcrumbs. Mix well. 3. In a small bowl, combine the vanilla extract and orange juice. Stir and then add the mixture to the almond mixture. Mix well. 4. Measure out a teaspoon of the mixture. Squeeze the mixture with your hand to make the dough stick together, then mold the dough into a small ball. 5. Add the remaining tablespoon of the sugar to a shallow bowl. Roll the balls in the sugar until covered, then transfer the bites to an airtight container. Store covered at room temperature for up to 1 week.

Per Serving:
calories: 102 | fat: 6g | protein: 3g | carbs: 10g | fiber: 2g | sodium: 11mg

Pumpkin-Ricotta Cheesecake

Prep time: 25 minutes | Cook time: 45 minutes | Serves 10 to 12

- 1 cup almond flour
- ½ cup butter, melted
- 1 (14½-ounce / 411-g) can pumpkin purée
- 8 ounces (227 g) cream cheese, at room temperature
- ½ cup whole-milk ricotta cheese
- ½ to ¾ cup sugar-free sweetener
- 4 large eggs
- 2 teaspoons vanilla extract
- 2 teaspoons pumpkin pie spice
- Whipped cream, for garnish (optional)

1. Preheat the oven to 350°F(180°C). Line the bottom of a 9-inch springform pan with parchment paper. 2. In a small bowl, combine the almond flour and melted butter with a fork until well combined. Using your fingers, press the mixture into the bottom of the prepared pan. 3. In a large bowl, beat together the pumpkin purée, cream cheese, ricotta, and sweetener using an electric mixer on medium. 4. Add the eggs, one at a time, beating after each addition. Stir in the vanilla and pumpkin pie spice until just combined. 5. Pour the mixture over the crust and bake until set, 40 to 45 minutes. 6. Allow to cool to room temperature. Refrigerate for at least 6 hours before serving. 7. Serve chilled, garnishing with whipped cream, if desired.

Per Serving:
calories: 230 | fat: 21g | protein: 6g | carbs: 5g | fiber: 1g | sodium: 103mg

Chocolate Turtle Hummus

Prep time: 15 minutes | Cook time: 0 minutes | Serves 2

For the Caramel:
- 2 tablespoons coconut oil
- 1 tablespoon maple syrup
- 1 tablespoon almond butter
- Pinch salt

For the Hummus:
- ½ cup chickpeas, drained and rinsed
- 2 tablespoons unsweetened cocoa powder
- 1 tablespoon maple syrup,
- plus more to taste
- 2 tablespoons almond milk, or more as needed, to thin
- Pinch salt
- 2 tablespoons pecans

Make the caramel 1. put the coconut oil in a small microwave-safe bowl. If it's solid, microwave it for about 15 seconds to melt it. 2. Stir in the maple syrup, almond butter, and salt. 3. Place the caramel in the refrigerator for 5 to 10 minutes to thicken. Make the hummus 1. In a food processor, combine the chickpeas, cocoa powder, maple syrup, almond milk, and pinch of salt, and process until smooth. Scrape down the sides to make sure everything is incorporated. 2. If the hummus seems too thick, add another tablespoon of almond milk. 3. Add the pecans and pulse 6 times to roughly chop them. 4. Transfer the hummus to a serving bowl and when the caramel is thickened, swirl it into the hummus. Gently fold it in, but don't mix it in completely. 5. Serve with fresh fruit or pretzels.

Per Serving:
calories: 321 | fat: 22g | protein: 7g | carbs: 30g | fiber: 6g | sodium: 100mg

Chocolate-Dipped Fruit Bites

Prep time: 10 minutes | Cook time: 0 minutes | Serves 4 to 6

- ½ cup semisweet chocolate chips
- ¼ cup low-fat milk
- ½ teaspoon pure vanilla extract
- ½ teaspoon ground nutmeg
- ¼ teaspoon salt
- 2 kiwis, peeled and sliced
- 1 cup honeydew melon chunks (about 2-inch chunks)
- 1 pound (454 g) whole strawberries

1. Place the chocolate chips in a small bowl. 2. In another small bowl, microwave the milk until hot, about 30 seconds. Pour the milk over the chocolate chips and let sit for 1 minute, then whisk until the chocolate is melted and smooth. Stir in the vanilla, nutmeg, and salt and allow to cool for 5 minutes. 3. Line a baking sheet with wax paper. Dip each piece of fruit halfway into the chocolate, tap gently to remove excess chocolate, and place the fruit on the baking sheet. 4. Once all the fruit has been dipped, allow it to sit until dry, about 30 minutes. Arrange on a platter and serve.

Per Serving:
calories: 125 | fat: 5g | protein: 2g | carbs: 21g | fiber: 3g | sodium: 110mg

Fruit with Mint and Crème Fraîche

Prep time: 10 minutes | Cook time: 0 minutes | Serves 4

- 4 cups chopped fresh fruit (such as strawberries, honeydew, cantaloupe, watermelon, and blueberries)
- 1 cup crème fraîche
- 1 teaspoon sugar (optional)
- ¼ cup chopped fresh mint leaves, plus mint sprigs for garnish

1. Evenly divide the fruit among four bowls. 2. In a small bowl, mix the crème fraîche and sugar, if desired. Top the fruit with a generous spoonful or two of the crème fraîche. 3. Sprinkle the mint over each bowl, garnish with 1 to 2 whole sprigs of mint, and serve.

Per Serving:
calories: 164 | fat: 12g | protein: 2g | carbs: 14g | fiber: 3g | sodium: 29mg

Red Grapefruit Granita

Prep time: 5 minutes | Cook time: 0 minutes | Serves 4 to 6

- 3 cups red grapefruit sections
- 1 cup freshly squeezed red grapefruit juice
- ¼ cup honey
- 1 tablespoon freshly squeezed lime juice
- Fresh basil leaves for garnish

1. Remove as much pith (white part) and membrane as possible from the grapefruit segments. 2. Combine all ingredients except the basil in a blender or food processor and pulse just until smooth. 3. Pour the mixture into a shallow glass baking dish and place in the freezer for 1 hour. Stir with a fork and freeze for another 30 minutes, then repeat. To serve, scoop into small dessert glasses and garnish with fresh basil leaves.

Per Serving:
calories: 94 | fat: 0g | protein: 1g | carbs: 24g | fiber: 1g | sodium: 1mg

S'mores

Prep time: 5 minutes | Cook time: 30 seconds | Makes 8 s'mores

- Oil, for spraying
- 8 graham cracker squares
- 2 (1½-ounce / 43-g) chocolate bars
- 4 large marshmallows

1. Line the air fryer basket with parchment and spray lightly with oil. 2. Place 4 graham cracker squares in the prepared basket. 3. Break the chocolate bars in half and place 1 piece on top of each graham cracker. Top with 1 marshmallow. 4. Air fry at 370°F (188°C) for 30 seconds, or until the marshmallows are puffed and golden brown and slightly melted. 5. Top with the remaining graham cracker squares and serve.

Per Serving:

calories: 154 | fat: 7g | protein: 2g | carbs: 22g | fiber: 2g | sodium: 75mg

Lemon Coconut Cake

Prep time: 5 minutes | Cook time: 40 minutes | Serves 9

Base:
- 6 large eggs, separated
- ⅓ cup melted ghee or virgin coconut oil
- 1 tablespoon fresh lemon juice
- Zest of 2 lemons
- 2 cups almond flour
- ½ cup coconut flour

- ¼ cup collagen powder
- 1 teaspoon baking soda
- 1 teaspoon vanilla powder or 1 tablespoon unsweetened vanilla extract
- Optional: low-carb sweetener, to taste

Topping:
- ½ cup unsweetened large coconut flakes
- 1 cup heavy whipping cream or coconut cream
- ¼ cup mascarpone, more

- heavy whipping cream, or coconut cream
- ½ teaspoon vanilla powder or 1½ teaspoons unsweetened vanilla extract

1. Preheat the oven to 285°F (140°C) fan assisted or 320°F (160°C) conventional. Line a baking tray with parchment paper (or use a silicone tray). A square 8 × 8–inch (20 × 20 cm) or a rectangular tray of similar size will work best. 2. To make the base: Whisk the egg whites in a bowl until stiff peaks form. In a separate bowl, whisk the egg yolks, melted ghee, lemon juice, and lemon zest. In a third bowl, mix the almond flour, coconut flour, collagen, baking soda, vanilla and optional sweetener. 3. Add the whisked egg yolk–ghee mixture into the dry mixture and combine well. Gently fold in the egg whites, trying not to deflate them. 4. Pour into the baking tray. Bake for 35 to 40 minutes, until lightly golden on top and set inside. Remove from the oven and let cool completely before adding the topping. 5. To make the topping: Preheat the oven to 350°F (175°C) fan assisted or 380°F (195°C) conventional. Place the coconut flakes on a baking tray and bake for 2 to 3 minutes. Remove from the oven and set aside to cool. 6. Once the cake is cool, place the cream, mascarpone, and vanilla in a bowl. Whip until soft peaks form. Spread on top of the cooled cake and top with the toasted coconut flakes. 7. To store, refrigerate for up to 5 days or freeze for up to 3 months. Coconut flakes will soften in the fridge. If you want to keep them crunchy, sprinkle on top of each slice before serving.

Per Serving:

calories: 342 | fat: 31g | protein: 9g | carbs: 10g | fiber: 4g | sodium: 208mg

Apricot and Mint No-Bake Parfait

Prep time: 10 minutes | Cook time: 0 minutes | Serves 6

- 4 ounces (113 g) Neufchâtel or other light cream cheese
- 1 (7-ounce / 198-g) container 2% Greek yogurt
- ½ cup plus 2 tablespoons sugar
- 2 teaspoons vanilla extract
- 1 tablespoon fresh lemon

- juice
- 1 pound (454 g) apricots, rinsed, pitted, and cut into bite-size pieces
- 2 tablespoons finely chopped fresh mint, plus whole leaves for garnish if desired

1. In the bowl of a stand mixer fitted with the paddle attachment, beat the Neufchâtel cheese and yogurt on low speed until well combined, about 2 minutes, scraping down the bowl as needed. Add ½ cup of the sugar, the vanilla, and the lemon juice. Mix until smooth and free of lumps, 2 to 3 minutes; set aside. 2. In a medium bowl, combine the apricots, mint, and remaining 2 tablespoons sugar. Stir occasionally, waiting to serve until after the apricots have released their juices and have softened. 3. Line up six 6-to 8-ounce (170-to 227-g) glasses. Using an ice cream scoop, spoon 3 to 4 tablespoons of the cheesecake mixture evenly into the bottom of each glass. (Alternatively, transfer the cheesecake mixture to a piping bag or a small zip-top bag with one corner snipped and pipe the mixture into the glasses.) Add a layer of the same amount of apricots to each glass. Repeat so you have two layers of cheesecake mixture and two layers of the apricots, ending with the apricots.) Garnish with the mint, if desired, and serve.

Per Serving:

calories: 132 | fat: 2g | protein: 5g | carbs: 23g | fiber: 2g | sodium: 35mg

Creamy Spiced Almond Milk

Prep time: 5 minutes | Cook time: 1 minute | Serves 6

- 1 cup raw almonds
- 5 cups filtered water, divided
- 1 teaspoon vanilla bean paste
- ½ teaspoon pumpkin pie spice

1. Add almonds and 1 cup water to the Instant Pot®. Close lid, set steam release to Sealing, press the Manual button, and set time to 1 minute. 2. When the timer beeps, quick-release the pressure until the float valve drops. Press the Cancel button and open lid. Strain almonds and rinse under cool water. Transfer to a high-powered blender with remaining 3.cups water. Purée for 2 minutes on high speed. 4. Pour mixture into a nut milk bag set over a large bowl. Squeeze bag to extract all liquid. Stir in vanilla and pumpkin pie spice. Transfer to a Mason jar or sealed jug and refrigerate for 8 hours. Stir or shake gently before serving.

Per Serving:

calories: 86 | fat: 8g | protein: 3g | carbs: 3g | fiber: 2g | sodium: 0mg

Karithopita (Greek Juicy Walnut Cake)

Prep time: 10 minutes | Cook time: 30 minutes | Serves 8

- ¼ cup extra virgin olive oil plus 1 teaspoon for brushing
- ½ cup walnut halves
- ¼ cup granulated sugar
- ¼ cup brown sugar
- 1 egg
- 1 tablespoon pure vanilla
Syrup:
- ⅓ cup water
- ¼ cup granulated sugar
- extract
- ¼ cup orange juice, strained
- ½ cup all-purpose flour
- ¼ cup whole-wheat flour
- ¼ teaspoon baking powder
- ¼ teaspoon baking soda
- ¼ teaspoon ground cinnamon
- 1 cinnamon stick
- 1 tablespoon orange juice

1. Preheat the oven to 350°F (180°C). Brush an 8 × 4-inch loaf pan with 1 teaspoon of the olive oil, and then line the pan with parchment paper. 2. Prepare the syrup by combining the water, sugar, and cinnamon stick in a small pan placed over medium heat. Bring to a boil and then boil for 2 minutes, then remove the pan from the heat. Remove the cinnamon stick, add the orange juice, then stir and set aside to cool. 3. Pulse the walnuts in a food processor until you achieve a cornmeal-like consistency. (Do not over-grind.) 4. In a large bowl, combine ¼ cup of the olive oil, the granulated sugar, and the brown sugar. Stir until the sugar is dissolved, then add the egg. Add the vanilla extract and orange juice. Mix well. 5. In a small bowl, combine the all-purpose flour and whole-wheat flour with the baking powder, baking soda, and cinnamon. 6. Add the flour mixture to the olive oil mixture and mix just until the flour has been incorporated. Add ¼ cup of the ground walnuts and mix until they are distributed throughout the batter. 7. Pour the batter into the prepared pan. Bake for 25–30 minutes or until a toothpick inserted into the cake comes out clean. 8. Use a toothpick to poke 8 holes across the top of the cake and then pour the syrup over the entire surface of the cake. Sprinkle the remaining ground walnuts over the top, and then set the cake aside to rest for 30 minutes before cutting it in equal-sized 1-inch slices. Store in an airtight container in the refrigerator for up to 5 days.

Per Serving:

calories: 240 | fat: 12g | protein: 3g | carbs: 30g | fiber: 1g | sodium: 52mg

Honey-Vanilla Apple Pie with Olive Oil Crust

Prep time: 10 minutes | Cook time: 45 minutes | Serves 8

For the crust:
- ¼ cup olive oil
- 1½ cups whole-wheat flour
For the filling:
- 4 large apples of your choice, peeled, cored, and sliced
- Juice of 1 lemon
- 1 tablespoon pure vanilla
- ½ teaspoon sea salt
- 2 tablespoons ice water
- extract
- 1 tablespoon honey
- ½ teaspoon sea salt
- Olive oil

Make the crust: 1. Put the olive oil, flour, and sea salt in a food processor and process until dough forms. 2. Slowly add the water and pulse until you have a stiff dough. 3. Form the dough into 2 equal-sized balls, wrap in plastic wrap, and put in the refrigerator while you make the filling. Make the filling: 1. Combine the apples, lemon juice, vanilla, honey, and sea salt in a large bowl. 2. Stir and allow to sit for at least 10 minutes. Preheat oven to 400°F (205°C). 3. Roll 1 crust out on a lightly floured surface. Transfer to a 9-inch pie plate and top with filling. 4. Roll the other ball of dough out and put on top of the pie. Cut a few slices in the top to vent the pie, and lightly brush the top of the pie with olive oil. 5. Bake for 45 minutes, or until top is browned and apples are bubbly. 6. Allow to cool completely before slicing and serving with your favorite frozen yogurt.

Per Serving:

calories: 208 | fat: 8g | protein: 3g | carbs: 34g | fiber: 5g | sodium: 293mg

Creamy Rice Pudding

Prep time: 5 minutes | Cook time: 45 minutes | Serves 6

- 1¼ cups long-grain rice
- 5 cups whole milk
- 1 cup sugar
- 1 tablespoon rose water or orange blossom water
- 1 teaspoon cinnamon

1. Rinse the rice under cold water for 30 seconds. 2. Put the rice, milk, and sugar in a large pot. Bring to a gentle boil while continually stirring. 3. Turn the heat down to low and let simmer for 40 to 45 minutes, stirring every 3 to 4 minutes so that the rice does not stick to the bottom of the pot. 4. Add the rose water at the end and simmer for 5 minutes. 5. Divide the pudding into 6 bowls. Sprinkle the top with cinnamon. Cool for at least 1 hour before serving. Store in the fridge.

Per Serving:
calories: 394 | fat: 7g | protein: 9g | carbs: 75g | fiber: 1g | sodium: 102mg

Crispy Apple Phyllo Tart

Prep time: 15 minutes | Cook time: 30 minutes | Serves 4

- 5 teaspoons extra virgin olive oil
- 2 teaspoons fresh lemon juice
- ¼ teaspoon ground cinnamon
- 1½ teaspoons granulated sugar, divided
- 1 large apple (any variety), peeled and cut into ⅛-inch thick slices
- 5 phyllo sheets, defrosted
- 1 teaspoon all-purpose flour
- 1½ teaspoons apricot jam

1. Preheat the oven to 350°F (180°C). Line a baking sheet with parchment paper, and pour the olive oil into a small dish. Set aside. 2. In a separate small bowl, combine the lemon juice, cinnamon, 1 teaspoon of the sugar, and the apple slices. Mix well to ensure the apple slices are coated in the seasonings. Set aside. 3. On a clean working surface, stack the phyllo sheets one on top of the other. Place a large bowl with an approximate diameter of 15 inches on top of the sheets, then draw a sharp knife around the edge of the bowl to cut out a circle through all 5 sheets. Discard the remaining phyllo. 4. Working quickly, place the first sheet on the lined baking sheet and then brush with the olive oil. Repeat the process by placing a second sheet on top of the first sheet, then brushing the second sheet with olive oil. Repeat until all the phyllo sheets are in a single stack. 5. Sprinkle the flour and remaining sugar over the top of the sheets. Arrange the apples in overlapping circles 4 inches from the edge of the phyllo. 6. Fold the edges of the phyllo in and then twist them all around the apple filling to form a crust edge. Brush the edge with the remaining olive oil. Bake for 30 minutes or

until the crust is golden and the apples are browned on the edges. 7. While the tart is baking, heat the apricot jam in a small sauce pan over low heat until it's melted. 8. When the tart is done baking, brush the apples with the jam sauce. Slice the tart into 4 equal servings and serve warm. Store at room temperature, covered in plastic wrap, for up to 2 days.

Per Serving:
calories: 165 | fat: 7g | protein: 2g | carbs: 24g | fiber: 2g | sodium: 116mg

Cherry-Stuffed Apples

Prep time: 15 minutes | Cook time: 4 hours | Serves 2

- 3 apples
- 1 tablespoon freshly squeezed lemon juice
- ⅓ cup dried cherries
- 2 tablespoons apple cider
- 2 tablespoons honey
- ¼ cup water

1. Cut about half an inch off the top of each of the apples, and peel a small strip of the skin away around the top. 2. Using a small serrated spoon or melon baller, core the apples, making sure not to go through the bottom. Drizzle with the lemon juice. 3. Fill the apples with the dried cherries. Carefully spoon the cider and honey into the apples. 4. Place the apples in the slow cooker. Pour the water around the apples. 5. Cover and cook on low for 4 hours, or until the apples are soft, and serve.

Per Serving:
calories: 227 | fat: 1g | protein: 1g | carbs: 60g | fiber: 7g | sodium: 6mg

Grilled Pineapple and Melon

Prep time: 10 minutes | Cook time: 7 minutes | Serves 4

- 8 fresh pineapple rings, rind removed
- 8 watermelon triangles, with rind
- 1 tablespoon honey
- ½ teaspoon freshly ground black pepper

1. Preheat an outdoor grill or a grill pan over high heat. 2. Drizzle the fruit slices with honey and sprinkle one side of each piece with pepper. Grill for 5 minutes, turn, and grill for another 2 minutes. Serve.

Per Serving:
calories: 244 | fat: 1g | protein: 4g | carbs: 62g | fiber: 4g | sodium: 7mg

Strawberry Panna Cotta

Prep time: 10 minutes | Cook time: 10 minutes | Serves 4

- 2 tablespoons warm water
- 2 teaspoons gelatin powder
- 2 cups heavy cream
- 1 cup sliced strawberries, plus more for garnish
- 1 to 2 tablespoons sugar-free sweetener of choice (optional)
- 1½ teaspoons pure vanilla extract
- 4 to 6 fresh mint leaves, for garnish (optional)

1. Pour the warm water into a small bowl. Sprinkle the gelatin over the water and stir well to dissolve. Allow the mixture to sit for 10 minutes. 2. In a blender or a large bowl, if using an immersion blender, combine the cream, strawberries, sweetener (if using), and vanilla. Blend until the mixture is smooth and the strawberries are well puréed. 3. Transfer the mixture to a saucepan and heat over medium-low heat until just below a simmer. Remove from the heat and cool for 5 minutes. 4. Whisking constantly, add in the gelatin mixture until smooth. Divide the custard between ramekins or small glass bowls, cover and refrigerate until set, 4 to 6 hours. 5. Serve chilled, garnishing with additional sliced strawberries or mint leaves (if using).

Per Serving:

calories: 229 | fat: 22g | protein: 3g | carbs: 5g | fiber: 1g | sodium: 26mg

Poached Pears with Greek Yogurt and Pistachio

Prep time: 10 minutes | Cook time: 3 minutes | Serves 8

- 2 cups water
- 1¾ cups apple cider
- ¼ cup lemon juice
- 1 cinnamon stick
- 1 teaspoon vanilla bean paste
- 4 large Bartlett pears, peeled
- 1 cup low-fat plain Greek yogurt
- ½ cup unsalted roasted pistachio meats

1. Add water, apple cider, lemon juice, cinnamon, vanilla, and pears to the Instant Pot®. Close lid, set steam release to Sealing, press the Manual button, and set time to 3 minutes. 2. When the timer beeps, quick-release the pressure until the float valve drops. Press the Cancel button and open lid. With a slotted spoon remove pears to a plate and allow to cool to room temperature. 3. To serve, carefully slice pears in half with a sharp paring knife and scoop out core with a melon baller. Lay pear halves on dessert plates or in shallow bowls. Top with yogurt and garnish with pistachios. Serve immediately.

Per Serving:

calories: 181 | fat: 7g | protein: 7g | carbs: 23g | fiber: 4g | sodium: 11mg

Fruit Compote

Prep time: 15 minutes | Cook time: 11 minutes | Serves 6

- 1 cup apple juice
- 1 cup dry white wine
- 2 tablespoons honey
- 1 cinnamon stick
- ¼ teaspoon ground nutmeg
- 1 tablespoon grated lemon zest
- 1½ tablespoons grated orange zest
- 3 large apples, peeled, cored, and chopped
- 3 large pears, peeled, cored, and chopped
- ½ cup dried cherries

1. Place all ingredients in the Instant Pot® and stir well. Close lid, set steam release to Sealing, press the Manual button, and set time to 1 minute. When the timer beeps, quick-release the pressure until the float valve drops. Press the Cancel button and open lid. 2. Use a slotted spoon to transfer fruit to a serving bowl. Remove and discard cinnamon stick. Press the Sauté button and bring juice in the pot to a boil. Cook, stirring constantly, until reduced to a syrup that will coat the back of a spoon, about 10 minutes. 3. Stir syrup into fruit mixture. Allow to cool slightly, then cover with plastic wrap and refrigerate overnight.

Per Serving:

calories: 211 | fat: 1g | protein: 2g | carbs: 44g | fiber: 5g | sodium: 7mg

Frozen Raspberry Delight

Prep time: 10 minutes | Cook time: 0 minutes | Serves 2

- 3 cups frozen raspberries
- 1 peach, peeled and pitted
- 1 mango, peeled and pitted
- 1 teaspoon honey

1. Add all ingredients to a blender and purée, only adding enough water to keep the mixture moving and your blender from overworking itself. 2. Freeze for 10 minutes to firm up if desired.

Per Serving:

calories: 237 | fat: 2g | protein: 4g | carbs: 57g | fiber: 16g | sodium: 4mg

Strawberry-Pomegranate Molasses Sauce

Prep time: 10 minutes | Cook time: 5 minutes | Serves 6

- 3 tablespoons olive oil
- ¼ cup honey
- 2 pints strawberries, hulled and halved
- 1 to 2 tablespoons pomegranate molasses
- 2 tablespoons chopped fresh mint
- Greek yogurt, for serving

1. In a medium saucepan, heat the olive oil over medium heat. Add the strawberries; cook until their juices are released. Stir in the honey and cook for 1 to 2 minutes. Stir in the molasses and mint. Serve warm over Greek yogurt.

Per Serving:

calories: 189 | fat: 7g | protein: 4g | carbs: 24g | fiber: 3g | sodium: 12mg

Chapter 11 Salads

Sicilian Salad

Prep time: 5 minutes | Cook time: 0 minutes | Serves 2

- 2 tablespoons extra virgin olive oil
- 1 tablespoon red wine vinegar
- 2 medium tomatoes (preferably beefsteak variety), sliced
- ½ medium red onion, thinly sliced
- 2 tablespoons capers, drained
- 6 green olives, halved
- 1 teaspoon dried oregano
- Pinch of fine sea salt

1. Make the dressing by combining the olive oil and vinegar in a small bowl. Use a fork to whisk until the mixture thickens slightly. Set aside. 2. Arrange the sliced tomatoes on a large plate and then scatter the onions, capers, and olives over the tomatoes. 3. Sprinkle the oregano and sea salt over the top, then drizzle the dressing over the salad. Serve promptly. (This salad is best served fresh, but can be stored covered in the refrigerator for up to 1 day.)

Per Serving:

calories: 169 | fat: 15g | protein: 2g | carbs: 8g | fiber: 3g | sodium: 336mg

Tossed Green Mediterranean Salad

Prep time: 15 minutes | Cook time: 0 minutes | Serves 4

- 1 medium head romaine lettuce, washed, dried, and chopped into bite-sized pieces
- 2 medium cucumbers, peeled and sliced
- 3 spring onions (white parts only), sliced
- ½ cup finely chopped fresh dill
- ⅓ cup extra virgin olive oil
- 2 tablespoons fresh lemon juice
- ¼ teaspoon fine sea salt
- 4 ounces (113 g) crumbled feta
- 7 Kalamata olives, pitted

1. Add the lettuce, cucumber, spring onions, and dill to a large bowl. Toss to combine. 2. In a small bowl, whisk together the olive oil and lemon juice. Pour the dressing over the salad, toss, then sprinkle the sea salt over the top. 3. Sprinkle the feta and olives over the top and then gently toss the salad one more time. Serve promptly. (This recipe is best served fresh.)

Per Serving:

calories: 284 | fat: 25g | protein: 7g | carbs: 10g | fiber: 5g | sodium: 496mg

Italian Summer Vegetable Barley Salad

Prep time: 1 minutes | Cook time: 25 to 45 minutes | Serves 4

- 1 cup uncooked barley (hulled or pearl)
- 3 cups water
- ¾ teaspoon fine sea salt, divided
- 1 teaspoon plus 3 tablespoons extra virgin olive oil, divided
- 3 tablespoons fresh lemon juice
- 2 medium zucchini, washed and chopped
- 15 Kalamata olives, pitted and sliced or chopped
- ¼ cup chopped fresh parsley
- ¼ cup chopped fresh basil
- 1 cup cherry tomatoes, halved
- ½ teaspoon freshly ground black pepper

1. Place the barley in a medium pot and add 3 cups of water and ¼ teaspoon of the sea salt. Bring to a boil over high heat, then reduce the heat to low. Simmer for 25–40 minutes, depending on the type of barley you're using, adding small amounts of hot water if the barley appears to be drying out. Cook until the barley is soft but still chewy, then transfer to a mesh strainer and rinse with cold water. 2. Empty the rinsed barley into a large bowl, drizzle 1 teaspoon of the olive oil over the top, fluff with a fork, and then set aside. 3. In a small bowl, combine the remaining 3 tablespoons of olive oil and the lemon juice. Whisk until the dressing thickens. 4. In a large bowl, combine the barley, zucchini, olives, parsley, and basil. Toss and then add the cherry tomatoes, remaining ½ teaspoon of sea salt, and black pepper. Toss gently, drizzle the dressing over the top, and continue tossing until the ingredients are coated with the dressing. Serve promptly. Store covered in the refrigerator for up to 3 days.

Per Serving:

calories: 308 | fat: 13g | protein: 7g | carbs: 45g | fiber: 10g | sodium: 614mg

Tuna Niçoise

Prep time: 15 minutes | Cook time: 20 minutes | Serves 4

- 1 pound (454 g) small red or fingerling potatoes, halved
- 1 pound (454 g) green beans or haricots verts, trimmed
- 1 head romaine lettuce, chopped or torn into bite-size pieces
- ½ pint cherry tomatoes, halved
- 8 radishes, thinly sliced
- ½ cup olives, pitted (any kind you like)
- 2 (5-ounce / 142-g) cans no-salt-added tuna packed in olive oil, drained
- 8 anchovies (optional)

1. Fill a large pot fitted with a steamer basket with 2 to 3 inches of water. Put the potatoes in the steamer basket and lay the green beans on top of the potatoes. Bring the water to a boil over high heat, lower the heat to low and simmer, cover, and cook for 7 minutes, or until the green beans are tender but crisp. Remove the green beans and continue to steam the potatoes for an additional 10 minutes. 2. Place the romaine lettuce on a serving platter. Group the potatoes, green beans, tomatoes, radishes, olives, and tuna in different areas of the platter. If using the anchovies, place them around the platter.

Per Serving:

calories: 315 | fat: 9g | protein: 28g | carbs: 33g | fiber: 9g | sodium: 420mg

Warm Fennel, Cherry Tomato, and Spinach Salad

Prep time: 15 minutes | Cook time: 0 minutes | Serves 2

- 4 tablespoons chicken broth
- 4 cups baby spinach leaves
- 10 cherry tomatoes, halved
- Sea salt and freshly ground
- pepper, to taste
- 1 fennel bulb, sliced
- ¼ cup olive oil
- Juice of 2 lemons

1. In a large sauté pan, heat the chicken broth over medium heat. Add the spinach and tomatoes and cook until spinach is wilted. Season with sea salt and freshly ground pepper to taste. 2. Remove from heat and toss fennel slices in with the spinach and tomatoes. Let the fennel warm in the pan, then transfer to a large bowl. 3. Drizzle with the olive oil and lemon juice, and serve immediately.

Per Serving:

calories: 319 | fat: 28g | protein: 5g | carbs: 18g | fiber: 6g | sodium: 123mg

Grain-Free Kale Tabbouleh

Prep time: 15 minutes | Cook time: 0 minutes | Serves 8

- 2 plum tomatoes, seeded and chopped
- ½ cup finely chopped fresh parsley
- 4 scallions (green onions), finely chopped
- 1 head kale, finely chopped (about 2 cups)
- 1 cup finely chopped fresh
- mint
- 1 small Persian cucumber, peeled, seeded, and diced
- 3 tablespoons extra-virgin olive oil
- 2 tablespoons fresh lemon juice
- Coarsely ground black pepper (optional)

1. Place the tomatoes in a strainer set over a bowl and set aside to drain as much liquid as possible. 2. In a large bowl, stir to combine the parsley, scallions, kale, and mint. 3. Shake any remaining liquid from the tomatoes and add them to the kale mixture. Add the cucumber. 4. Add the olive oil and lemon juice and toss to combine. Season with pepper, if desired.

Per Serving:

1 cup: calories: 65 | fat: 5g | protein: 1g | carbs: 4g | fiber: 1g | sodium: 21mg

Arugula and Fennel Salad with Fresh Basil

Prep time: 5 minutes | Cook time: 0 minutes | Serves 4

- 3 tablespoons olive oil
- 3 tablespoons lemon juice
- 1 teaspoon honey
- ½ teaspoon salt
- 1 medium bulb fennel, very thinly sliced
- 1 small cucumber, very thinly
- sliced
- 2 cups arugula
- ¼ cup toasted pine nuts
- ½ cup crumbled feta cheese
- ¼ cup julienned fresh basil leaves

1. In a medium bowl, whisk together the olive oil, lemon juice, honey, and salt. Add the fennel and cucumber and toss to coat and let sit for 10 minutes or so. 2. Put the arugula in a large salad bowl. Add the marinated cucumber and fennel, along with the dressing, to the bowl and toss well. Serve immediately, sprinkled with pine nuts, feta cheese, and basil.

Per Serving:

calories: 237 | fat: 21g | protein: 6g | carbs: 11g | fiber: 3g | sodium: 537mg

Orange-Tarragon Chicken Salad Wrap

Prep time: 15 minutes | Cook time: 0 minutes | Serves 4

- ½ cup plain whole-milk Greek yogurt
- 2 tablespoons Dijon mustard
- 2 tablespoons extra-virgin olive oil
- 2 tablespoons chopped fresh tarragon or 1 teaspoon dried tarragon
- ½ teaspoon salt
- ¼ teaspoon freshly ground black pepper
- 2 cups cooked shredded chicken
- ½ cup slivered almonds
- 4 to 8 large Bibb lettuce leaves, tough stem removed
- 2 small ripe avocados, peeled and thinly sliced
- Zest of 1 clementine, or ½ small orange (about 1 tablespoon)

1. In a medium bowl, combine the yogurt, mustard, olive oil, tarragon, orange zest, salt, and pepper and whisk until creamy. 2. Add the shredded chicken and almonds and stir to coat. 3. To assemble the wraps, place about ½ cup chicken salad mixture in the center of each lettuce leaf and top with sliced avocados.

Per Serving:

calories: 491 | fat: 38g | protein: 28g | carbs: 14g | fiber: 9g | sodium: 454mg

Pear-Fennel Salad with Pomegranate

Prep time: 15 minutes | Cook time: 5 minutes | Serves 6

Dressing:
- 2 tablespoons red wine vinegar
- 1½ tablespoons pomegranate molasses
- 2 teaspoons finely chopped shallot

Salad:
- ¼ cup walnuts, coarsely chopped, or pine nuts
- 2 red pears, halved, cored, and very thinly sliced
- 1 bulb fennel, halved, cored, and very thinly sliced, fronds reserved

- ½ teaspoon Dijon mustard
- ½ teaspoon kosher salt
- ¼ teaspoon ground black pepper
- ¼ cup extra-virgin olive oil

- 1 tablespoon fresh lemon juice
- 4 cups baby arugula
- ½ cup pomegranate seeds
- ⅓ cup crumbled feta cheese or shaved Parmigiano-Reggiano cheese

1. Make the Dressing: In a small bowl or jar with a lid, combine the vinegar, pomegranate molasses, shallot, mustard, salt, and pepper. Add the oil and whisk until emulsified (or cap the jar and shake vigorously). Set aside. 2. Make the Salad: In a small skillet over medium heat, toast the nuts until golden and fragrant, 4 to 5 minutes. Remove from the skillet to cool. 3. In a large bowl, combine the pears and fennel. Sprinkle with the lemon juice and toss gently. 4. Add the arugula and toss again to evenly distribute. Pour over 3 to 4 tablespoons of the dressing, just enough to moisten the arugula, and toss. Add the pomegranate seeds, cheese, and nuts and toss again. Add more dressing, if necessary, or store remainder in the refrigerator for up to 1 week. Serve the salad topped with the reserved fennel fronds.

Per Serving:

calories: 165 | fat: 10g | protein:31g | carbs: 18g | fiber: 4g | sodium: 215mg

Panzanella (Tuscan Tomato and Bread Salad)

Prep time: 1 hour 5 minutes | Cook time: 0 minutes | Serves 2

- 3 tablespoons white wine vinegar, divided
- 1 small red onion, thinly sliced
- 4 ounces (113 g) stale, dense bread, such as French baguette or Italian (Vienna-style)
- 1 large tomato (any variety), chopped into bite-sized
- pieces
- 1 large Persian (or mini) cucumber, sliced
- ¼ cup chopped fresh basil
- 2 tablespoons extra virgin olive oil, divided
- Pinch of kosher salt
- ⅛ teaspoon freshly ground black pepper

1. Add 2 tablespoons of the vinegar to a small bowl filled with water. Add the onion and then set aside. 2. In a medium bowl, combine the remaining tablespoon of vinegar and 2 cups of water. Add the bread to the bowl and soak for 2–3 minutes (depending on how hard the bread is) until the bread has softened on the outside but is not falling apart. Place the bread in a colander and gently squeeze out any excess water and then chop into bite-sized pieces. Arrange the bread pieces on a large plate. 3. Drain the onion and add it to plate with the bread. Add the tomato, cucumber, basil, 1 tablespoon of the olive oil, kosher salt, and black pepper. Toss the ingredients carefully, then cover and transfer to the refrigerator to chill for a minimum of 1 hour. 4. When ready to serve, drizzle the remaining 1 tablespoon of olive oil over the top of the salad and serve promptly. This salad can be stored in the refrigerator for up to 5 hours, but should be consumed on the same day it is prepared.

Per Serving:

calories: 325 | fat: 16g | protein: 7g | carbs: 38g | fiber: 4g | sodium: 358mg

Valencia-Inspired Salad

Prep time: 5 minutes | Cook time: 0 minutes | Serves 4

- 2 small oranges, peeled, thinly sliced, and pitted
- 1 small blood orange, peeled, thinly sliced, and pitted
- 1 (7-ounce / 198-g) bag butter lettuce
- ½ English cucumber, thinly sliced into rounds
- 1 (6-ounce / 170-g) can pitted black olives, halved
- 1 small shallot, thinly sliced (optional)
- ¼ cup raw hulled pumpkin seeds
- 8 slices Manchego cheese, roughly broken
- 2 to 3 tablespoons extra-virgin olive oil
- Juice of 1 orange

1. In a large bowl, toss together the oranges, lettuce, cucumber, olives, shallot (if desired), pumpkin seeds, and cheese until well mixed. Evenly divide the mixture among four plates. 2. Drizzle the salads with the olive oil and orange juice. Serve.

Per Serving:

calories: 419 | fat: 31g | protein: 17g | carbs: 22g | fiber: 5g | sodium: 513mg

Superfood Salmon Salad Bowl

Prep time: 5 minutes | Cook time: 10 minutes | Serves 2

Salmon:
- 2 fillets wild salmon
- Salt and black pepper, to taste

Dressing:
- 1 tablespoon capers
- 1 teaspoon Dijon or whole-grain mustard
- 1 tablespoon apple cider vinegar or fresh lemon juice

Salad:
- ½ medium cucumber, diced
- 1 cup sugar snap peas, sliced into matchsticks
- ½ small red bell pepper, sliced
- ⅓ cup pitted Kalamata olives, halved
- 2 sun-dried tomatoes,

- 2 teaspoons extra-virgin avocado oil

- 3 tablespoons extra-virgin olive oil
- 1 teaspoon coconut aminos
- Salt and black pepper, to taste

  chopped
- 1 medium avocado, diced
- 3 tablespoons chopped fresh herbs, such as dill, chives, parsley, and/or basil
- 1 tablespoon pumpkin seeds
- 1 tablespoon sunflower seeds

1. Make the salmon: Season the salmon with salt and pepper. Heat a pan greased with the avocado oil over medium heat. Add the salmon, skin-side down, and cook for 4 to 5 minutes. Flip and cook

for 1 to 2 minutes or until cooked through. Remove from the heat and transfer to a plate to cool. Remove the skin from the salmon and flake into chunks. 2. Make the dressing: Mix all the dressing ingredients together in a small bowl. Set aside. 3. Make the salad: Place the cucumber, sugar snap peas, bell pepper, olives, sun-dried tomatoes, avocado, and herbs in a mixing bowl, and combine well. Add the flaked salmon. Dry-fry the seeds in a pan placed over medium-low heat until lightly golden. Allow to cool, then add to the bowl. Drizzle with the prepared dressing and serve. This salad can be stored in the fridge for up to 1 day.

Per Serving:

calories: 660 | fat: 54g | protein: 31g | carbs: 18g | fiber: 9g | sodium: 509mg

Wild Greens Salad with Fresh Herbs

Prep time: 10 minutes | Cook time: 20 minutes | Serves 6 to 8

- ¼ cup olive oil
- 2 pounds (907 g) dandelion greens, tough stems removed and coarsely chopped
- 1 small bunch chicory, trimmed and coarsely chopped
- 1 cup chopped fresh flat-leaf parsley, divided
- 1 cup chopped fresh mint, divided
- ½ cup water
- 2 tablespoons red wine

- vinegar or apple cider vinegar
- 1 tablespoon fresh thyme, chopped
- 2 cloves garlic, minced
- ½ teaspoon kosher salt
- ½ teaspoon ground black pepper
- ¼ cup almonds or walnuts, coarsely chopped
- 2 tablespoons chopped fresh chives or scallion greens
- 1 tablespoon chopped fresh dill

1. In a large pot over medium heat, warm the oil. Add the greens, half of the parsley, half of the mint, the water, vinegar, thyme, garlic, salt, and pepper. Reduce the heat to a simmer and cook until the greens are very tender, about 20 minutes. 2. Meanwhile, in a small skillet over medium heat, toast the nuts until golden and fragrant, 5 to 8 minutes. Remove from the heat. 3. If serving immediately, stir the chives or scallion greens, dill, and the remaining parsley and mint into the pot. If serving as a cool or cold salad, allow to come to room temperature or refrigerate until cold before stirring in the fresh herbs. Top with the toasted nuts before serving.

Per Serving:

calories: 190 | fat: 13g | protein: 6g | carbs: 17g | fiber: 7g | sodium: 279mg

Traditional Greek Salad

Prep time: 10 minutes | Cook time: 0 minutes | Serves 4

- 2 large English cucumbers
- 4 Roma tomatoes, quartered
- 1 green bell pepper, cut into 1- to 1½-inch chunks
- ¼ small red onion, thinly sliced
- 4 ounces (113 g) pitted Kalamata olives
- ¼ cup extra-virgin olive oil
- 2 tablespoons freshly

- squeezed lemon juice
- 1 tablespoon red wine vinegar
- 1 tablespoon chopped fresh oregano or 1 teaspoon dried oregano
- ¼ teaspoon freshly ground black pepper
- 4 ounces (113 g) crumbled traditional feta cheese

1. Cut the cucumbers in half lengthwise and then into ½-inch-thick half-moons. Place in a large bowl. 2. Add the quartered tomatoes, bell pepper, red onion, and olives. 3. In a small bowl, whisk together the olive oil, lemon juice, vinegar, oregano, and pepper. Drizzle over the vegetables and toss to coat. 4. Divide between salad plates and top each with 1 ounce (28 g) of feta.

Per Serving:

calories: 256 | fat: 22g | protein: 6g | carbs: 11g | fiber: 3g | sodium: 476mg

Marinated Greek Salad with Oregano and Goat Cheese

Prep time: 10 minutes | Cook time: 0 minutes | Serves 4

- ½ cup white wine vinegar
- 1 small garlic clove, minced
- 1 teaspoon crumbled dried Greek oregano
- ½ teaspoon salt
- ¼ teaspoon freshly ground black pepper
- 2 Persian cucumbers, sliced thinly

- 4 to 6 long, skinny red or yellow banana peppers or other mild peppers
- 1 medium red onion, cut into rings
- 1 pint mixed small heirloom tomatoes, halved
- 2 ounces (57 g) crumbled goat cheese or feta

1. In a large, nonreactive (glass, ceramic, or plastic) bowl, whisk together the vinegar, garlic, oregano, salt, and pepper. Add the cucumbers, peppers, and onion and toss to mix. Cover and refrigerate for at least 1 hour. 2. Add the tomatoes to the bowl and toss to coat. Serve topped with the cheese.

Per Serving:

calories: 98 | fat: 4g | protein: 4g | carbs: 13g | fiber: 3g | sodium: 460mg

Italian White Bean Salad with Bell Peppers

Prep time: 15 minutes | Cook time: 0 minutes | Serves 4

- 2 tablespoons extra-virgin olive oil
- 2 tablespoons white wine vinegar
- ½ shallot, minced
- ½ teaspoon kosher salt
- ¼ teaspoon freshly ground black pepper
- 3 cups cooked cannellini

- beans, or 2 (15-ounce / 425-g) cans no-salt-added or low-sodium cannellini beans, drained and rinsed
- 2 celery stalks, diced
- ½ red bell pepper, diced
- ¼ cup fresh parsley, chopped
- ¼ cup fresh mint, chopped

1. In a large bowl, whisk together the olive oil, vinegar, shallot, salt, and black pepper. 2. Add the beans, celery, red bell pepper, parsley, and mint; mix well.

Per Serving:

calories: 300 | fat: 8g | protein: 15g | carbs: 46g | fiber: 11g | sodium: 175mg

Flank Steak Spinach Salad

Prep time: 15 minutes | Cook time: 10 minutes | Serves 4

- 1 pound (454 g) flank steak
- 1 teaspoon extra-virgin olive oil
- 1 tablespoon garlic powder
- ½ teaspoon salt
- ½ teaspoon freshly ground black pepper
- 4 cups baby spinach leaves

- 10 cherry tomatoes, halved
- 10 cremini or white mushrooms, sliced
- 1 small red onion, thinly sliced
- ½ red bell pepper, thinly sliced

1. Preheat the broiler. Line a baking sheet with aluminum foil. 2. Rub the top of the flank steak with the olive oil, garlic powder, salt, and pepper and let sit for 10 minutes before placing under the broiler. Broil for 5 minutes on each side for medium rare. Allow the meat to rest on a cutting board for 10 minutes. 3. Meanwhile, in a large bowl, combine the spinach, tomatoes, mushrooms, onion, and bell pepper and toss well. 4. To serve, divide the salad among 4 dinner plates. Slice the steak on the diagonal and place 4 to 5 slices on top of each salad. Serve with your favorite vinaigrette.

Per Serving:

calories: 211 | fat: 7g | protein: 28g | carbs: 9g | fiber: 2g | sodium: 382mg

Peachy Tomato Salad

Prep time: 15 minutes | Cook time: 0 minutes | Serves 2

- 2 ripe peaches, pitted and sliced into wedges
- 2 ripe tomatoes, cut into wedges
- ½ red onion, thinly sliced
- Sea salt and freshly ground pepper, to taste
- 3 tablespoons olive oil
- 1 tablespoon lemon juice

1. Toss the peaches, tomatoes, and red onion in a large bowl. Season to taste. 2. Add the olive oil and lemon juice, and gently toss. Serve at room temperature.

Per Serving:

calories: 272 | fat: 21g | protein: 3g | carbs: 22g | fiber: 4g | sodium: 8mg

Arugula Salad with Grapes, Goat Cheese, and Za'atar Croutons

Prep time: 10 minutes | Cook time: 10 minutes | Serves 4

Croutons:
- 2 slices whole wheat bread, cubed

Vinaigrette:
- 2 tablespoons olive oil
- 1 tablespoon red wine vinegar
- ½ teaspoon chopped fresh rosemary

Salad:
- 4 cups baby arugula
- 1 cup grapes, halved
- ½ red onion, thinly sliced

- 2 teaspoons olive oil, divided
- 1 teaspoon za'atar

- ¼ teaspoon kosher salt
- ⅛ teaspoon ground black pepper

- 2 ounces (57 g) goat cheese, crumbled

1. Make the Croutons: Toss the bread cubes with 1 teaspoon of the oil and the za'atar. In a medium skillet over medium heat, warm the remaining 1 teaspoon oil. Cook the bread cubes, stirring frequently, until browned and crispy, 8 to 10 minutes. 2. Make the Vinaigrette: In a small bowl, whisk together the oil, vinegar, rosemary, salt, and pepper. 3. Make the Salad: In a large bowl, toss the arugula, grapes, and onion with the vinaigrette. Top with the cheese and croutons.

Per Serving:

calories: 204 | fat: 14g | protein: 6g | carbs: 15g | fiber: 2g | sodium: 283mg

No-Mayo Florence Tuna Salad

Prep time: 10 minutes | Cook time: 0 minutes | Serves 4

- 4 cups spring mix greens
- 1 (15-ounce / 425-g) can cannellini beans, drained
- 2 (5-ounce / 142-g) cans water-packed, white albacore tuna, drained (I prefer Wild Planet brand)
- ⅔ cup crumbled feta cheese
- ½ cup thinly sliced sun-dried tomatoes
- ¼ cup sliced pitted kalamata

- olives
- ¼ cup thinly sliced scallions, both green and white parts
- 3 tablespoons extra-virgin olive oil
- ½ teaspoon dried cilantro
- 2 or 3 leaves thinly chopped fresh sweet basil
- 1 lime, zested and juiced
- Kosher salt
- Freshly ground black pepper

1. In a large bowl, combine greens, beans, tuna, feta, tomatoes, olives, scallions, olive oil, cilantro, basil, and lime juice and zest. Season with salt and pepper, mix, and enjoy!

Per Serving:

1 cup: calories: 355 | fat: 19g | protein: 22g | carbs: 25g | fiber: 8g | sodium: 744mg

Chapter 12 Pizzas, Wraps, and Sandwiches

Dill Salmon Salad Wraps

**Prep time: 10 minutes |Cook time: 10 minutes|
Serves:6**

- 1 pound (454 g) salmon filet, cooked and flaked, or 3 (5-ounce / 142-g) cans salmon
- ½ cup diced carrots (about 1 carrot)
- ½ cup diced celery (about 1 celery stalk)
- 3 tablespoons chopped fresh dill
- 3 tablespoons diced red onion (a little less than ⅛ onion)
- 2 tablespoons capers
- 1½ tablespoons extra-virgin olive oil
- 1 tablespoon aged balsamic vinegar
- ½ teaspoon freshly ground black pepper
- ¼ teaspoon kosher or sea salt
- 4 whole-wheat flatbread wraps or soft whole-wheat tortillas

1. In a large bowl, mix together the salmon, carrots, celery, dill, red onion, capers, oil, vinegar, pepper, and salt. 2. Divide the salmon salad among the flatbreads. Fold up the bottom of the flatbread, then roll up the wrap and serve.

Per Serving:
calories: 185 | fat: 8g | protein: 17g | carbs: 12g | fiber: 2g | sodium: 237mg

Turkey Burgers with Feta and Dill

Prep time: 5 minutes | Cook time: 15 minutes | Serves 4

- 1 pound (454 g) ground turkey breast
- 1 small red onion, ½ finely chopped, ½ sliced
- ½ cup crumbled feta cheese
- ¼ cup chopped fresh dill
- 1 clove garlic, minced
- ½ teaspoon kosher salt
- ¼ teaspoon ground black pepper
- 4 whole grain hamburger rolls
- 4 thick slices tomato
- 4 leaves lettuce

1. Coat a grill rack or grill pan with olive oil and prepare to medium-high heat. 2. In a large bowl, use your hands to combine the turkey, chopped onion, cheese, dill, garlic, salt, and pepper. Do not overmix. Divide into 4 patties, 4' in diameter. 3. Grill the patties, covered, until a thermometer inserted in the center registers 165°F(74ºC), 5 to 6 minutes per side. 4. Serve each patty on a roll with the sliced onion, 1 slice of the tomato, and 1 leaf of the lettuce.

Per Serving:
calories: 305 | fat: 7g | protein: 35g | carbs: 26g | fiber: 3g | sodium: 708mg

Margherita Open-Face Sandwiches

Prep time: 10 minutes |Cook time: 5 minutes| Serves: 4

- 2 (6- to 7-inch) whole-wheat submarine or hoagie rolls, sliced open horizontally
- 1 tablespoon extra-virgin olive oil
- 1 garlic clove, halved
- 1 large ripe tomato, cut into 8 slices
- ¼ teaspoon dried oregano
- 1 cup fresh mozzarella (about 4 ounces / 113 g), patted dry and sliced
- ¼ cup lightly packed fresh basil leaves, torn into small pieces
- ¼ teaspoon freshly ground black pepper

1. Preheat the broiler to high with the rack 4 inches under the heating element. 2. Place the sliced bread on a large, rimmed baking sheet. Place under the broiler for 1 minute, until the bread is just lightly toasted. Remove from the oven. 3. Brush each piece of the toasted bread with the oil, and rub a garlic half over each piece. 4. Place the toasted bread back on the baking sheet. Evenly distribute the tomato slices on each piece, sprinkle with the oregano, and layer the cheese on top. 5. Place the baking sheet under the broiler. Set the timer for 1½ minutes, but check after 1 minute. When the cheese is melted and the edges are just starting to get dark brown, remove the sandwiches from the oven (this can take anywhere from 1½ to 2 minutes). 6. Top each sandwich with the fresh basil and pepper.

Per Serving:
calories: 176 | fat: 9g | protein: 10g | carbs: 14g | fiber: 2g | sodium: 119mg

Cucumber Basil Sandwiches

Prep time: 10 minutes | Cook time: 0 minutes | Serves 2

- Cucumber Basil Sandwiches
- 4 slices whole-grain bread
- ¼ cup hummus
- 1 large cucumber, thinly sliced
- 4 whole basil leaves

1. Spread the hummus on 2 slices of bread, and layer the cucumbers onto it. Top with the basil leaves and close the sandwiches. 2. Press down lightly and serve immediately.

Per Serving:

calories: 209 | fat: 5g | protein: 9g | carbs: 32g | fiber: 6g | sodium: 275mg

Flatbread Pizza with Roasted Cherry Tomatoes, Artichokes, and Feta

Prep time: 5 minutes | Cook time: 20 minutes | Serves 4

- 1½ pounds (680 g) cherry or grape tomatoes, halved
- 3 tablespoons olive oil, divided
- ½ teaspoon salt
- ½ teaspoon freshly ground black pepper
- 4 Middle Eastern–style
- flatbread rounds
- 1 can artichoke hearts, rinsed, well drained, and cut into thin wedges
- 8 ounces (227 g) crumbled feta cheese
- ¼ cup chopped fresh Greek oregano

1. Preheat the oven to 500°F(260°C). 2. In a medium bowl, toss the tomatoes with 1 tablespoon olive oil, the salt, and the pepper. Spread out on a large baking sheet. Roast in the preheated oven until the tomato skins begin to blister and crack, about 10 to 12 minutes. Remove the tomatoes from the oven and reduce the heat to 450°F(235°C). 3. Place the flatbreads on a large baking sheet (or two baking sheets if necessary) and brush the tops with the remaining 2 tablespoons of olive oil. Top with the artichoke hearts, roasted tomatoes, and cheese, dividing equally. 4. Bake the flatbreads in the oven for about 8 to 10 minutes, until the edges are lightly browned and the cheese is melted. Sprinkle the oregano over the top and serve immediately.

Per Serving:

calories: 436 | fat: 27g | protein: 16g | carbs: 34g | fiber: 6g | sodium: 649mg

Vegetable Pita Sandwiches

Prep time: 15 minutes | Cook time: 9 to 12 minutes | Serves 4

- 1 baby eggplant, peeled and chopped
- 1 red bell pepper, sliced
- ½ cup diced red onion
- ½ cup shredded carrot
- 1 teaspoon olive oil
- ⅓ cup low-fat Greek yogurt
- ½ teaspoon dried tarragon
- 2 low-sodium whole-wheat pita breads, halved crosswise

1. In a baking pan, stir together the eggplant, red bell pepper, red onion, carrot, and olive oil. Put the vegetable mixture into the air fryer basket and roast at 390ºF (199ºC) for 7 to 9 minutes, stirring once, until the vegetables are tender. Drain if necessary. 2. In a small bowl, thoroughly mix the yogurt and tarragon until well combined. 3. Stir the yogurt mixture into the vegetables. Stuff one-fourth of this mixture into each pita pocket. 4. Place the sandwiches in the air fryer and cook for 2 to 3 minutes, or until the bread is toasted. Serve immediately.

Per Serving:

calories: 115 | fat: 2g | protein: 4g | carbs: 22g | fiber: 6g | sodium: 90mg

Greek Salad Pita

Prep time: 15 minutes | Cook time: 0 minutes | Serves 4

- 1 cup chopped romaine lettuce
- 1 tomato, chopped and seeded
- ½ cup baby spinach leaves
- ½ small red onion, thinly sliced
- ½ small cucumber, chopped and deseeded
- 2 tablespoons olive oil
- 1 tablespoon crumbled feta cheese
- ½ tablespoon red wine vinegar
- 1 teaspoon Dijon mustard
- Sea salt and freshly ground pepper, to taste
- 1 whole-wheat pita

1. Combine everything except the sea salt, freshly ground pepper, and pita bread in a medium bowl. 2. Toss until the salad is well combined. 3. Season with sea salt and freshly ground pepper to taste. Fill the pita with the salad mixture, serve, and enjoy!

Per Serving:

calories: 123 | fat: 8g | protein: 3g | carbs: 12g | fiber: 2g | sodium: 125mg

Mediterranean Tuna Salad Sandwiches

Prep time: 10 minutes | Cook time: 5 minutes | Serves 2

- 1 can white tuna, packed in water or olive oil, drained
- 1 roasted red pepper, diced
- ½ small red onion, diced
- 10 low-salt olives, pitted and finely chopped
- ¼ cup plain Greek yogurt
- 1 tablespoon flat-leaf parsley, chopped
- Juice of 1 lemon
- Sea salt and freshly ground pepper, to taste
- 4 whole-grain pieces of bread

1. In a small bowl, combine all of the ingredients except the bread, and mix well. 2. Season with sea salt and freshly ground pepper to taste. Toast the bread or warm in a pan. 3. Make the sandwich and serve immediately.

Per Serving:

calories: 307 | fat: 7g | protein: 30g | carbs: 31g | fiber: 5g | sodium: 564mg

Herbed Focaccia Panini with Anchovies and Burrata

Prep time: 5 minutes | Cook time: 8 minutes | Serves 4

- 8 ounces (227 g) burrata cheese, chilled and sliced
- 1 pound (454 g) whole-wheat herbed focaccia, cut crosswise into 4 rectangles and split horizontally
- 1 can anchovy fillets packed in oil, drained
- 8 slices tomato, sliced
- 2 cups arugula
- 1 tablespoon olive oil

1. Divide the cheese evenly among the bottom halves of the focaccia rectangles. Top each with 3 or 4 anchovy fillets, 2 slices of tomato, and ½ cup arugula. Place the top halves of the focaccia on top of the sandwiches. 2. To make the panini, heat a skillet or grill pan over high heat and brush with the olive oil. 3. Place the sandwiches in the hot pan and place another heavy pan, such as a cast-iron skillet, on top to weigh them down. Cook for about 3 to 4 minutes, until crisp and golden on the bottom, and then flip over and repeat on the second side, cooking for an additional 3 to 4 minutes until golden and crisp. Slice each sandwich in half and serve hot.

Per Serving:

calories: 596 | fat: 30g | protein: 27g | carbs: 58g | fiber: 5g | sodium: 626mg

Mexican Pizza

Prep time: 10 minutes | Cook time: 7 to 9 minutes | Serves 4

- ¾ cup refried beans (from a 16-ounce / 454-g can)
- ½ cup salsa
- 10 frozen precooked beef meatballs, thawed and sliced
- 1 jalapeño pepper, sliced
- 4 whole-wheat pita breads
- 1 cup shredded pepper Jack cheese
- ½ cup shredded Colby cheese
- ⅓ cup sour cream

1. In a medium bowl, combine the refried beans, salsa, meatballs, and jalapeño pepper. 2. Preheat the air fryer for 3 to 4 minutes or until hot. 3. Top the pitas with the refried bean mixture and sprinkle with the cheeses. 4. Bake at 370ºF (188ºC) for 7 to 9 minutes or until the pizza is crisp and the cheese is melted and starts to brown. 5. Top each pizza with a dollop of sour cream and serve warm.

Per Serving:

calories: 484 | fat: 30g | protein: 24g | carbs: 32g | fiber: 7g | sodium: 612mg

Open-Faced Eggplant Parmesan Sandwich

Prep time: 10 minutes | Cook time: 10 minutes | Serves 2

- 1 small eggplant, sliced into ¼-inch rounds
- Pinch sea salt
- 2 tablespoons olive oil
- Sea salt and freshly ground pepper, to taste
- 2 slices whole-grain bread, thickly cut and toasted
- 1 cup marinara sauce (no added sugar)
- ¼ cup freshly grated, low-fat Parmesan cheese

1. Preheat broiler to high heat. 2. Salt both sides of the sliced eggplant, and let sit for 20 minutes to draw out the bitter juices. 3. Rinse the eggplant and pat dry with a paper towel. 4. Brush the eggplant with the olive oil, and season with sea salt and freshly ground pepper. 5. Lay the eggplant on a sheet pan, and broil until crisp, about 4 minutes. Flip over and crisp the other side. 6. Lay the toasted bread on a sheet pan. Spoon some marinara sauce on each slice of bread, and layer the eggplant on top. 7. Sprinkle half of the cheese on top of the eggplant and top with more marinara sauce. 8. Sprinkle with remaining cheese. 9. Put the sandwiches under the broiler until the cheese has melted, about 2 minutes. 10. Using a spatula, transfer the sandwiches to plates and serve.

Per Serving:

calories: 355 | fat: 19g | protein: 10g | carbs: 38g | fiber: 13g | sodium: 334mg

Classic Margherita Pizza

Prep time: 10 minutes | Cook time: 10 minutes | Serves 4

- All-purpose flour, for dusting
- 1 pound (454 g) premade pizza dough
- 1 (15-ounce / 425-g) can crushed San Marzano tomatoes, with their juices
- 2 garlic cloves
- 1 teaspoon Italian seasoning
- Pinch sea salt, plus more as needed
- 1½ teaspoons olive oil, for drizzling
- 10 slices mozzarella cheese
- 12 to 15 fresh basil leaves

1. Preheat the oven to 475°F (245°C). 2. On a floured surface, roll out the dough to a 12-inch round and place it on a lightly floured pizza pan or baking sheet. 3. In a food processor, combine the tomatoes with their juices, garlic, Italian seasoning, and salt and process until smooth. Taste and adjust the seasoning. 4. Drizzle the olive oil over the pizza dough, then spoon the pizza sauce over the dough and spread it out evenly with the back of the spoon, leaving a 1-inch border. Evenly distribute the mozzarella over the pizza. 5. Bake until the crust is cooked through and golden, 8 to 10 minutes. Remove from the oven and let sit for 1 to 2 minutes. Top with the basil right before serving.

Per Serving:
calories: 570 | fat: 21g | protein: 28g | carbs: 66g | fiber: 4g | sodium: 570mg

Sautéed Mushroom, Onion, and Pecorino Romano Panini

Prep time: 10 minutes | Cook time: 20 minutes | Serves 4

- 3 tablespoons olive oil, divided
- 1 small onion, diced
- 10 ounces (283 g) button or cremini mushrooms, sliced
- ½ teaspoon salt
- ¼ teaspoon freshly ground black pepper
- 4 crusty Italian sandwich rolls
- 4 ounces (113 g) freshly grated Pecorino Romano

1. Heat 1 tablespoon of the olive oil in a skillet over medium-high heat. Add the onion and cook, stirring, until it begins to soften, about 3 minutes. Add the mushrooms, season with salt and pepper, and cook, stirring, until they soften and the liquid they release evaporates, about 7 minutes. 2. To make the panini, heat a skillet or grill pan over high heat and brush with 1 tablespoon olive oil. Brush the inside of the rolls with the remaining 1 tablespoon olive oil. Divide the mushroom mixture evenly among the rolls and top each with ¼ of the grated cheese. 3. Place the sandwiches in the hot pan and place another heavy pan, such as a cast-iron skillet, on top to weigh them down. Cook for about 3 to 4 minutes, until crisp and golden on the bottom, and then flip over and repeat on the second side, cooking for an additional 3 to 4 minutes until golden and crisp. Slice each sandwich in half and serve hot.

Per Serving:
calories: 348 | fat: 20g | protein: 14g | carbs: 30g | fiber: 2g | sodium: 506mg

Roasted Vegetable Bocadillo with Romesco Sauce

Prep time: 10 minutes | Cook time: 20 minutes | Serves 4

- 2 small yellow squash, sliced lengthwise
- 2 small zucchini, sliced lengthwise
- 1 medium red onion, thinly sliced
- 4 large button mushrooms, sliced
- 2 tablespoons olive oil
- 1 teaspoon salt, divided
- ½ teaspoon freshly ground black pepper, divided
- 2 roasted red peppers from a jar, drained
- 2 tablespoons blanched almonds
- 1 tablespoon sherry vinegar
- 1 small clove garlic
- 4 crusty multigrain rolls
- 4 ounces (113 g) goat cheese, at room temperature
- 1 tablespoon chopped fresh basil

1. Preheat the oven to 400°F(205°C). 2. In a medium bowl, toss the yellow squash, zucchini, onion, and mushrooms with the olive oil, ½ teaspoon salt, and ¼ teaspoon pepper. Spread on a large baking sheet. Roast the vegetables in the oven for about 20 minutes, until softened. 3. Meanwhile, in a food processor, combine the roasted peppers, almonds, vinegar, garlic, the remaining ½ teaspoon salt, and the remaining ¼ teaspoon pepper and process until smooth. 4. Split the rolls and spread ¼ of the goat cheese on the bottom of each. Place the roasted vegetables on top of the cheese, dividing equally. Top with chopped basil. Spread the top halves of the rolls with the roasted red pepper sauce and serve immediately.

Per Serving:
calories: 379 | fat: 21g | protein: 17g | carbs: 32g | fiber: 4g | sodium: 592mg

Bocadillo with Herbed Tuna and Piquillo Peppers

Prep time: 5 minutes | Cook time: 20 minutes | Serves 4

- 2 tablespoons olive oil, plus more for brushing
- 1 medium onion, finely chopped
- 2 leeks, white and tender green parts only, finely chopped
- 1 teaspoon chopped thyme
- ½ teaspoon dried marjoram
- ½ teaspoon salt
- ¼ teaspoon freshly ground black pepper
- 3 tablespoons sherry vinegar
- 1 carrot, finely diced
- 2 (8-ounce / 227-g) jars Spanish tuna in olive oil
- 4 crusty whole-wheat sandwich rolls, split
- 1 ripe tomato, grated on the large holes of a box grater
- 4 piquillo peppers, cut into thin strips

1. Heat 2 tablespoons olive oil in a medium skillet over medium heat. Add the onion, leeks, thyme, marjoram, salt, and pepper. Stir frequently until the onions are softened, about 10 minutes. Stir in the vinegar and carrot and cook until the liquid has evaporated, 5 minutes. Transfer the mixture to a bowl and let cool to room temperature or refrigerate for 15 minutes or so. 2. In a medium bowl, combine the tuna, along with its oil, with the onion mixture, breaking the tuna chunks up with a fork. 3. Brush the rolls lightly with oil and toast under the broiler until lightly browned, about 2 minutes. Spoon the tomato pulp onto the bottom half of each roll, dividing equally and spreading it with the back of the spoon. Divide the tuna mixture among the rolls and top with the piquillo pepper slices. Serve immediately.

Per Serving:
calories: 416 | fat: 18g | protein: 35g | carbs: 30g | fiber: 5g | sodium: 520mg

Chapter 13 Pasta

Bowtie Pesto Pasta Salad

Prep time: 5 minutes | Cook time: 4 minutes | Serves 8

- 1 pound (454 g) whole-wheat bowtie pasta
- 4 cups water
- 1 tablespoon extra-virgin olive oil
- 2 cups halved cherry tomatoes
- 2 cups baby spinach
- ½ cup chopped fresh basil
- ½ cup prepared pesto
- ½ teaspoon ground black pepper
- ½ cup grated Parmesan cheese

1. Add pasta, water, and olive oil to the Instant Pot®. Close lid, set steam release to Sealing, press the Manual button, and set time to 4 minutes. 2. When the timer beeps, quick-release the pressure until the float valve drops and open lid. Drain off any excess liquid. Allow pasta to cool to room temperature, about 30 minutes. Stir in tomatoes, spinach, basil, pesto, pepper, and cheese. Refrigerate for 2 hours. Stir well before serving.

Per Serving:
calories: 360 | fat: 13g | protein: 16g | carbs: 44g | fiber: 7g | sodium: 372mg

Baked Ziti

Prep time: 10 minutes | Cook time: 55 minutes | Serves 8

For the Marinara Sauce:
- 2 tablespoons olive oil
- ¼ medium onion, diced (about 3 tablespoons)
- 3 cloves garlic, chopped
- 1 (28-ounce / 794-g) can whole, peeled tomatoes,

For the Ziti:
- 1 pound (454 g) whole-wheat ziti
- 3½ cups marinara sauce
- 1 cup low-fat cottage cheese

- roughly chopped
- Sprig of fresh thyme
- ½ bunch fresh basil
- Sea salt and freshly ground pepper, to taste

- 1 cup grated, low-fat mozzarella cheese, divided
- ¾ cup freshly grated, low-fat Parmesan cheese, divided

Make the marinara sauce: 1. Heat the olive oil in a medium saucepan over medium-high heat. 2. Sauté the onion and garlic, stirring until lightly browned, about 3 minutes. 3. Add the tomatoes and the herb sprigs, and bring to a boil. Lower the heat and simmer, covered, for 10 minutes. Remove and discard the herb sprigs. 4. Stir in sea salt and season with freshly ground pepper to taste. Make the ziti: 1. Preheat the oven to 375ºF (190ºC). 2. Prepare the pasta according to package directions. Drain pasta. Combine the pasta in a bowl with 2 cups marinara sauce, the cottage cheese, and half the mozzarella and Parmesan cheeses. 3. Spread the mixture in a baking dish, and top with the remaining marinara sauce and cheese. 4. Bake for 30–40 minutes, or until bubbly and golden brown.

Per Serving:
calories: 389 | fat: 12g | protein: 18g | carbs: 56g | fiber: 9g | sodium: 369mg

Couscous with Tomatoes and Olives

Prep time: 5 minutes | Cook time: 3 minutes | Serves 4

- 1 tablespoon tomato paste
- 2 cups vegetable broth
- 1 cup couscous
- 1 cup halved cherry tomatoes
- ½ cup halved mixed olives
- ¼ cup minced fresh flat-leaf parsley
- 2 tablespoons minced fresh
- oregano
- 2 tablespoons minced fresh chives
- 1 tablespoon extra-virgin olive oil
- 1 tablespoon red wine vinegar
- ½ teaspoon ground black pepper

1. Pour tomato paste and broth into the Instant Pot® and stir until completely dissolved. Stir in couscous. Close lid, set steam release to Sealing, press the Manual button, and set time to 3 minutes. When the timer beeps, let pressure release naturally for 10 minutes, then quick-release the remaining pressure and open lid. 2. Fluff couscous with a fork. Add tomatoes, olives, parsley, oregano, chives, oil, vinegar, and pepper, and stir until combined. Serve warm or at room temperature.

Per Serving:
calories: 232 | fat: 5g | protein: 7g | carbs: 37g | fiber: 2g | sodium: 513mg

Rotini with Spinach, Cherry Tomatoes, and Feta

Prep time: 5 minutes | Cook time: 30 minutes | Serves 2

- 6 ounces (170 g) uncooked rotini pasta (penne pasta will also work)
- 1 garlic clove, minced
- 3 tablespoons extra virgin olive oil, divided
- 1½ cups cherry tomatoes, halved and divided
- 9 ounces (255 g) baby leaf spinach, washed and chopped
- 1½ ounces (43 g) crumbled feta, divided
- Kosher salt, to taste
- Freshly ground black pepper, to taste

1. Cook the pasta according to the package instructions, reserving ½ cup of the cooking water. Drain and set aside. 2. While the pasta is cooking, combine the garlic with 2 tablespoons of the olive oil in a small bowl. Set aside. 3. Add the remaining tablespoon of olive oil to a medium pan placed over medium heat and then add 1 cup of the tomatoes. Cook for 2–3 minutes, then use a fork to mash lightly. 4. Add the spinach to the pan and continue cooking, stirring occasionally, until the spinach is wilted and the liquid is absorbed, about 4–5 minutes. 5. Transfer the cooked pasta to the pan with the spinach and tomatoes. Add 3 tablespoons of the pasta water, the garlic and olive oil mixture, and 1 ounce (28 g) of the crumbled feta. Increase the heat to high and cook for 1 minute. 6. Top with the remaining cherry tomatoes and feta, and season to taste with kosher salt and black pepper. Store covered in the refrigerator for up to 2 days.

Per Serving:
calories: 602 | fat: 27g | protein: 19g | carbs: 74g | fiber: 7g | sodium: 307mg

Neapolitan Pasta and Zucchini

Prep time: 5 minutes | Cook time: 28 minutes | Serves 3

- ⅓ cup extra virgin olive oil
- 1 large onion (any variety), diced
- 1 teaspoon fine sea salt, divided
- 2 large zucchini, quartered lengthwise and cut into ½-inch pieces
- 10 ounces (283 g) uncooked
- spaghetti, broken into 1-inch pieces
- 2 tablespoons grated Parmesan cheese
- 2 ounces (57 g) grated or shaved Parmesan cheese for serving
- ½ teaspoon freshly ground black pepper

1. Add the olive oil to a medium pot over medium heat. When the oil begins to shimmer, add the onions and ¼ teaspoon of the sea salt. Sauté for 3 minutes, add the zucchini, and continue sautéing for 3 more minutes. 2. Add 2 cups of hot water to the pot or enough to just cover the zucchini (the amount of water may vary depending on the size of the pot). Cover, reduce the heat to low, and simmer for 10 minutes. 3. Add the pasta to the pot, stir, then add 2 more cups of hot water. Continue simmering, stirring occasionally, until the pasta is cooked and the mixture has thickened, about 12 minutes. (If the pasta appears to be dry or undercooked, add small amounts of hot water to the pot to ensure the pasta is covered in the water.). When the pasta is cooked, remove the pot from the heat. Add 2 tablespoons of the grated Parmesan and stir. 4. Divide the pasta into three servings and then top each with 1 ounce (28 g) of the grated or shaved Parmesan. Sprinkle the remaining sea salt and black pepper over the top of each serving. Store covered in the refrigerator for up to 3 days.

Per Serving:
calories: 718 | fat: 33g | protein: 24g | carbs: 83g | fiber: 6g | sodium: 815mg

Yogurt and Dill Pasta Salad

Prep time: 10 minutes | Cook time: 4 minutes | Serves 8

- ½ cup low-fat plain Greek yogurt
- 1 tablespoon apple cider vinegar
- 2 tablespoons chopped fresh dill
- 1 teaspoon honey
- 1 pound (454 g) whole-wheat elbow macaroni
- 4 cups water
- 1 tablespoon extra-virgin olive oil
- 1 medium red bell pepper, seeded and chopped
- 1 medium sweet onion, peeled and diced
- 1 stalk celery, diced
- ½ teaspoon ground black pepper

1. In a small bowl, combine yogurt and vinegar. Add dill and honey, and mix well. Refrigerate until ready to use. 2. Place pasta, water, and olive oil to the Instant Pot®. Close lid, set steam release to Sealing, press the Manual button, and set time to 4 minutes. 3. When the timer beeps, quick-release the pressure until the float valve drops and open lid. Drain off any excess liquid. Cool pasta to room temperature, about 30 minutes. Add prepared dressing and toss until pasta is well coated. Add bell pepper, onion, celery, and black pepper, and toss to coat. Refrigerate for 2 hours. Stir well before serving.

Per Serving:
calories: 295 | fat: 5g | protein: 19g | carbs: 47g | fiber: 8g | sodium: 51mg

Shrimp with Angel Hair Pasta

Prep time: 10 minutes | Cook time: 5 minutes | Serves 4

- 1 pound (454 g) dried angel hair pasta
- 2 tablespoons olive oil
- 3 garlic cloves, minced
- 1 pound (454 g) large shrimp, peeled and deveined
- Zest of ½ lemon
- ¼ cup chopped fresh Italian parsley
- ¼ teaspoon red pepper flakes (optional)

1. Fill a large stockpot three-quarters full with water and bring to a boil over high heat. Add the pasta and cook according to the package instructions until al dente, about 5 minutes. Drain the pasta and set aside. 2. In the same pot, heat the olive oil over medium heat. Add the garlic and sauté until fragrant, about 3 minutes. Add the shrimp and cook for about 2 minutes on each side, until pink and fully cooked. 3. Turn off the heat and return the pasta to the pot. Add the lemon zest and mix well. 4. Serve garnished with the parsley and red pepper flakes, if desired.

Per Serving:

calories: 567 | fat: 10g | protein: 31g | carbs: 87g | fiber: 4g | sodium: 651mg

Simple Pesto Pasta

Prep time: 10 minutes | Cook time: 10 minutes | Serves 4 to 6

- 1 pound (454 g) spaghetti
- 4 cups fresh basil leaves, stems removed
- 3 cloves garlic
- 1 teaspoon salt
- ½ teaspoon freshly ground
- black pepper
- ¼ cup lemon juice
- ½ cup pine nuts, toasted
- ½ cup grated Parmesan cheese
- 1 cup extra-virgin olive oil

1. Bring a large pot of salted water to a boil. Add the spaghetti to the pot and cook for 8 minutes. 2. Put basil, garlic, salt, pepper, lemon juice, pine nuts, and Parmesan cheese in a food processor bowl with chopping blade and purée. 3. While the processor is running, slowly drizzle the olive oil through the top opening. Process until all the olive oil has been added. 4. Reserve ½ cup of the pasta water. Drain the pasta and put it into a bowl. Immediately add the pesto and pasta water to the pasta and toss everything together. Serve warm.

Per Serving:

calories: 1067 | fat: 72g | protein: 23g | carbs: 91g | fiber: 6g | sodium: 817mg

Whole-Wheat Capellini with Sardines, Olives, and Manchego

Prep time: 5 minutes | Cook time: 15 minutes | Serves 4

- 1 (7-ounce / 198-g) jar Spanish sardines in olive oil, chopped (reserve the oil)
- 1 medium onion, diced
- 4 cloves garlic, minced
- 2 medium tomatoes, sliced
- 1 pound (454 g) whole-wheat
- capellini pasta, cooked according to package instructions
- 1 cup pitted, chopped cured black olives, such as Kalamata
- 3 ounces (85 g) freshly grated manchego cheese

1. Heat the olive oil from the sardines in a large skillet over medium-high heat. Add the onion and garlic and cook, stirring frequently, until softened, about 5 minutes. Add the tomatoes and sardines and cook, stirring, 2 minutes more. 2. Add the cooked and drained pasta to the skillet with the sauce and toss to combine. 3. Stir in the olives and serve immediately, topped with the grated cheese.

Per Serving:

calories: 307 | fat: 11g | protein: 8g | carbs: 38g | fiber: 6g | sodium: 433mg

Penne with Broccoli and Anchovies

Prep time: 10 minutes | Cook time: 10 minutes | Serves 4

- ¼ cup olive oil
- 1 pound (454 g) whole-wheat pasta
- ½ pound (227 g) broccoli or broccoli rabe cut into 1-inch florets
- 3 to 4 anchovy fillets, packed
- in olive oil
- 2 cloves garlic, sliced
- Pinch red pepper flakes
- ¼ cup freshly grated, lowfat Parmesan
- Sea salt and freshly ground pepper, to taste

1. Heat the olive oil in a deep skillet on medium heat. 2. In the meantime, prepare the pasta al dente, according to the package directions. 3. Fry the broccoli, anchovies, and garlic in the oil until the broccoli is almost tender and the garlic is slightly browned, about 5 minutes or so. 4. Rinse and drain the pasta, and add it to the broccoli mixture. Stir to coat the pasta with the garlic oil. Transfer to a serving dish, toss with red pepper flakes and Parmesan, and season.

Per Serving:

calories: 568 | fat: 17g | protein: 21g | carbs: 89g | fiber: 11g | sodium: 203mg

Chapter 14 Snacks and Appetizers

Garlic Edamame

Prep time: 5 minutes | Cook time: 10 minutes | Serves 4

- Olive oil
- 1 (16-ounce / 454-g) bag frozen edamame in pods
- ½ teaspoon salt
- ½ teaspoon garlic salt
- ¼ teaspoon freshly ground black pepper
- ½ teaspoon red pepper flakes (optional)

1. Spray the air fryer basket lightly with olive oil. 2. In a medium bowl, add the frozen edamame and lightly spray with olive oil. Toss to coat. 3. In a small bowl, mix together the salt, garlic salt, black pepper, and red pepper flakes (if using). Add the mixture to the edamame and toss until evenly coated. 4. Place half the edamame in the air fryer basket. Do not overfill the basket. 5. Air fry at 375ºF (191ºC) for 5 minutes. Shake the basket and cook until the edamame is starting to brown and get crispy, 3 to 5 more minutes. 6. Repeat with the remaining edamame and serve immediately.

Per Serving:
calories: 125 | fat: 5g | protein: 12g | carbs: 10g | fiber: 5g | sodium: 443mg

Savory Mackerel & Goat'S Cheese "Paradox" Balls

Prep time: 10 minutes | Cook time: 0 minutes | Makes 10 fat bombs

- 2 smoked or cooked mackerel fillets, boneless, skin removed
- 4.4 ounces (125 g) soft goat's cheese
- 1 tablespoon fresh lemon juice
- 1 teaspoon Dijon or yellow mustard
- 1 small red onion, finely diced
- 2 tablespoons chopped fresh chives or herbs of choice
- ¾ cup pecans, crushed
- 10 leaves baby gem lettuce

1. In a food processor, combine the mackerel, goat's cheese, lemon juice, and mustard. Pulse until smooth. Transfer to a bowl, add the onion and herbs, and mix with a spoon. Refrigerate for 20 to 30 minutes, or until set. 2. Using a large spoon or an ice cream scoop, divide the mixture into 10 balls, about 40 g/1.4 ounces each. Roll each ball in the crushed pecans. Place each ball on a small lettuce leaf and serve. Keep the fat bombs refrigerated in a sealed container for up to 5 days.

Per Serving:
1 fat bomb: calories: 165 | fat: 12g | protein: 12g | carbs: 2g | fiber: 1g | sodium: 102mg

Mediterranean Mini Spinach Quiche

Prep time: 15 minutes | Cook time: 25 minutes | Serves 5

- 2 teaspoons extra virgin olive oil plus extra for greasing pan
- 3 eggs
- 3 ounces (85 g) crumbled feta
- 4 tablespoons grated Parmesan cheese, divided
- ¼ teaspoon freshly ground black pepper
- 6 ounces (170 g) frozen spinach, thawed and chopped
- 1 tablespoon chopped fresh mint
- 1 tablespoon chopped fresh dill

1. Preheat the oven to 375ºF (190ºC). Liberally grease a 10-cup muffin pan with olive oil. 2. In a medium bowl, combine the eggs, feta, 3 tablespoons of the Parmesan, black pepper, and 2 teaspoons of the olive oil. Mix well. Add the spinach, mint, and dill, and mix to combine. 3. Fill each muffin cup with 1 heaping tablespoon of the batter. Sprinkle the remaining Parmesan over the quiche. 4. Bake for 25 minutes or until the egg is set and the tops are golden. Set aside to cool for 3 minutes, then remove the quiche from the pan by running a knife around the edges of each muffin cup. Transfer the quiche to a wire rack to cool completely. 5. Store in the refrigerator for up to 3 days or freeze for up to 3 months. (If freezing, individually wrap each quiche in plastic wrap and then in foil.)

Per Serving:
calories: 129 | fat: 9g | protein: 8g | carbs: 4g | fiber: 1g | sodium: 291mg

Sfougato

Prep time: 10 minutes | Cook time: 8 minutes | Serves 4

- ½ cup crumbled feta cheese
- ¼ cup bread crumbs
- 1 medium onion, peeled and minced
- 4 tablespoons all-purpose flour
- 2 tablespoons minced fresh
- mint
- ½ teaspoon salt
- ½ teaspoon ground black pepper
- 1 tablespoon dried thyme
- 6 large eggs, beaten
- 1 cup water

1. In a medium bowl, mix cheese, bread crumbs, onion, flour, mint, salt, pepper, and thyme. Stir in eggs. 2. Spray an 8" round baking dish with nonstick cooking spray. Pour egg mixture into dish. 3. Place rack in the Instant Pot® and add water. Fold a long piece of foil in half lengthwise. Lay foil over rack to form a sling and top with dish. Cover loosely with foil. Close lid, set steam release to Sealing, press the Manual button, and set time to 8 minutes. 4. When the timer beeps, quick-release the pressure until the float valve drops. Open lid. Let stand 5 minutes, then remove dish from pot.

Per Serving:

calories: 226 | fat: 12g | protein: 14g | carbs: 15g | fiber: 1g | sodium: 621mg

Herbed Labneh Vegetable Parfaits

Prep time: 15 minutes | Cook time: 0 minutes | Serves 2

For the Labneh:
- 8 ounces (227 g) plain Greek yogurt (full-fat works best)
- Generous pinch salt
- 1 teaspoon za'atar seasoning

For the Parfaits:
- ½ cup peeled, chopped cucumber
- ½ cup grated carrots

- 1 teaspoon freshly squeezed lemon juice
- Pinch lemon zest

- ½ cup cherry tomatoes, halved

Make the Labneh: 1. Line a strainer with cheesecloth and place it over a bowl. 2. Stir together the Greek yogurt and salt and place in the cheesecloth. Wrap it up and let it sit for 24 hours in the refrigerator. 3. When ready, unwrap the labneh and place it into a clean bowl. Stir in the za'atar, lemon juice, and lemon zest. Make the Parfaits: 1. Divide the cucumber between two clear glasses. 2. Top each portion of cucumber with about 3 tablespoons of labneh.

3. Divide the carrots between the glasses. 4. Top with another 3 tablespoons of the labneh. 5. Top parfaits with the cherry tomatoes.

Per Serving:

calories: 143 | fat: 7g | protein: 5g | carbs: 16g | fiber: 2g | sodium: 187mg

Lemony Olives and Feta Medley

Prep time: 10 minutes | Cook time: 0 minutes | Serves 8

- 1 (1-pound / 454-g) block of Greek feta cheese
- 3 cups mixed olives (Kalamata and green), drained from brine; pitted preferred

- ¼ cup extra-virgin olive oil
- 3 tablespoons lemon juice
- 1 teaspoon grated lemon zest
- 1 teaspoon dried oregano
- Pita bread, for serving

1. Cut the feta cheese into ½-inch squares and put them into a large bowl. 2. Add the olives to the feta and set aside. 3. In a small bowl, whisk together the olive oil, lemon juice, lemon zest, and oregano. 4. Pour the dressing over the feta cheese and olives and gently toss together to evenly coat everything. 5. Serve with pita bread.

Per Serving:

calories: 269 | fat: 24g | protein: 9g | carbs: 6g | fiber: 2g | sodium: 891mg

Marinated Olives

Prep time: 5 minutes | Cook time: 5 minutes | Serves 8 to 10

- 3 tablespoons olive oil
- Zest and juice of 1 lemon
- ½ teaspoon Aleppo pepper or red pepper flakes
- ¼ teaspoon ground sumac

- 1 cup pitted Kalamata olives
- 1 cup pitted green olives, such as Castelvetrano
- 2 tablespoons finely chopped fresh parsley

1. In a medium skillet, heat the olive oil over medium heat. Add the lemon zest, Aleppo pepper, and sumac and cook for 1 to 2 minutes, occasionally stirring, until fragrant. Remove from the heat and stir in the olives, lemon juice, and parsley. 2. Transfer the olives to a bowl and serve immediately, or let cool, then transfer to an airtight container and store in the refrigerator for up to 1 week. The flavor will continue to develop and is best after 8 to 12 hours.

Per Serving:

1 cup: calories: 59 | fat: 6g | protein: 0g | carbs: 1g | fiber: 1g | sodium: 115mg

Roasted Stuffed Figs

Prep time: 5 minutes | Cook time: 10 minutes | Serves 5

- 10 medium fresh figs
- 1½ tablespoons finely chopped walnuts
- 1½ tablespoons finely chopped almonds
- ½ teaspoon ground cinnamon
- ½ teaspoon sesame seeds
- Pinch of salt
- 1½ teaspoons honey

1. Preheat the oven to 300°F (150°C). Line a large baking sheet with foil, and grease the foil with olive oil. 2. Using a sharp knife, make a small vertical cut into the side of each fig, making sure not to cut all the way through the fig. Set aside. 3. In a small bowl, combine the walnuts, almonds, cinnamon, sesame seeds, and salt. Mix well. 4. Stuff each fig with 1 teaspoon of the filling, gently pressing the filling into the figs. Place the figs on the prepared baking sheet, and bake for 10 minutes. 5. While the figs are baking, add the honey to a small saucepan over medium heat. Heat the honey for 30 seconds or until it becomes thin and watery. 6. Transfer the roasted figs to a plate. Drizzle a few drops of the warm honey over each fig before serving. Store in an airtight container in the refrigerator for up to 2 weeks.

Per Serving:

calories: 114 | fat: 3g | protein: 2g | carbs: 22g | fiber: 4g | sodium: 2mg

Spicy Roasted Potatoes

Prep time: 20 minutes | Cook time: 25 minutes | Serves 5

- 1½ pounds (680 g) red potatoes or gold potatoes
- 3 tablespoons garlic, minced
- 1½ teaspoons salt
- ¼ cup extra-virgin olive oil
- ½ cup fresh cilantro, chopped
- ½ teaspoon freshly ground black pepper
- ¼ teaspoon cayenne pepper
- 3 tablespoons lemon juice

1. Preheat the oven to 450°F(235°C). 2. Scrub the potatoes and pat dry. 3. Cut the potatoes into ½-inch pieces and put them into a bowl. 4. Add the garlic, salt, and olive oil and toss everything together to evenly coat. 5. Pour the potato mixture onto a baking sheet, spread the potatoes out evenly, and put them into the oven, roasting for 25 minutes. Halfway through roasting, turn the potatoes with a spatula; continue roasting for the remainder of time until the potato edges start to brown. 6. Remove the potatoes from the oven and let them cool on the baking sheet for 5 minutes. 7. Using a spatula, remove the potatoes from the pan and put them into a bowl. 8. Add the cilantro, black pepper, cayenne, and lemon juice to the potatoes and toss until well mixed. 9. Serve warm.

Per Serving:

calories: 203 | fat: 11g | protein: 3g | carbs: 24g | fiber: 3g | sodium: 728mg

Roasted Za'atar Chickpeas

Prep time: 5 minutes | Cook time: 1 hour | Serves 8

- 3 tablespoons za'atar
- 2 tablespoons extra-virgin olive oil
- ½ teaspoon kosher salt
- ¼ teaspoon freshly ground
- black pepper
- 4 cups cooked chickpeas, or 2 (15-ounce / 425-g) cans, drained and rinsed

1. Preheat the oven to 400ºF (205ºC). Line a baking sheet with foil or parchment paper. 2. In a large bowl, combine the za'atar, olive oil, salt, and black pepper. Add the chickpeas and mix thoroughly. 3. Spread the chickpeas in a single layer on the prepared baking sheet. Bake for 45 to 60 minutes, or until golden brown and crispy. Cool and store in an airtight container at room temperature for up to 1 week.

Per Serving:

calories: 150 | fat: 6g | protein: 6g | carbs: 17g | fiber: 6g | sodium: 230mg

Sweet Potato Hummus

Prep time: 10 minutes | Cook time: 1 hour | Serves 8 to 10

- 1 pound (454 g) sweet potatoes (about 2)
- 1 (15-ounce / 425-g) can chickpeas, drained
- 4 garlic cloves, minced
- 2 tablespoons olive oil
- 2 tablespoons fresh lemon
- juice
- 2 teaspoons ground cumin
- 1 teaspoon Aleppo pepper or red pepper flakes
- Pita chips, pita bread, or fresh vegetables, for serving

1. Preheat the oven to 400ºF (205ºC). 2. Prick the sweet potatoes in a few places with a small, sharp knife and place them on a baking sheet. Roast until cooked through, about 1 hour, then set aside to cool. Peel the sweet potatoes and put the flesh in a blender or food processor. 3. Add the chickpeas, garlic, olive oil, lemon juice, cumin, and ⅓ cup water. Blend until smooth. Add the Aleppo pepper. 4. Serve with pita chips, pita bread, or as a dip for fresh vegetables.

Per Serving:

calories: 178 | fat: 5g | protein: 7g | carbs: 30g | fiber: 9g | sodium: 149mg

Baked Eggplant Baba Ganoush

Prep time: 10 minutes | Cook time: 1 hour | Makes about 4 cups

- ♦ 2 pounds (907 g, about 2 medium to large) eggplant
- ♦ 3 tablespoons tahini
- ♦ Zest of 1 lemon
- ♦ 2 tablespoons lemon juice
- ♦ ¾ teaspoon kosher salt
- ♦ ½ teaspoon ground sumac, plus more for sprinkling (optional)
- ♦ ⅓ cup fresh parsley, chopped
- ♦ 1 tablespoon extra-virgin olive oil

1. Preheat the oven to 350°F (180°C). Place the eggplants directly on the rack and bake for 60 minutes, or until the skin is wrinkly. 2. In a food processor add the tahini, lemon zest, lemon juice, salt, and sumac. Carefully cut open the baked eggplant and scoop the flesh into the food processor. Process until the ingredients are well blended. 3. Place in a serving dish and mix in the parsley. Drizzle with the olive oil and sprinkle with sumac, if desired.

Per Serving:

calories: 50 | fat: 16g | protein: 4g | carbs: 2g | fiber: 1g | sodium: 110mg

Bravas-Style Potatoes

Prep time: 15 minutes | Cook time: 50 minutes | Serves 8

- ♦ 4 large russet potatoes (about 2½ pounds / 1.1 kg), scrubbed and cut into 1' cubes
- ♦ 1 teaspoon kosher salt, divided
- ♦ ½ teaspoon ground black pepper
- ♦ ¼ teaspoon red-pepper flakes
- ♦ ½ small yellow onion, chopped
- ♦ 1 large tomato, chopped
- ♦ 1 tablespoon sherry vinegar
- ♦ 1 teaspoon hot paprika
- ♦ 1 tablespoon chopped fresh flat-leaf parsley Hot sauce (optional)

1. Preheat the oven to 450°F(235°C). Bring a large pot of well-salted water to a boil. 2. Boil the potatoes until just barely tender, 5 to 8 minutes. Drain and transfer the potatoes to a large rimmed baking sheet. Add 1 tablespoon of the oil, ½ teaspoon of the salt, the black pepper, and pepper flakes. With 2 large spoons, toss very well to coat the potatoes in the oil. Spread the potatoes out on the baking sheet. Roast until the bottoms are starting to brown and crisp, 20 minutes. Carefully flip the potatoes and roast until the other side is golden and crisp, 15 to 20 minutes. 3. Meanwhile, in a small skillet over medium heat, warm the remaining 1 teaspoon oil. Cook the onion until softened, 3 to 4 minutes. Add the tomato and cook until it's broken down and saucy, 5 minutes. Stir in the vinegar, paprika, and the remaining ½ teaspoon salt. Cook for 30

seconds, remove from the heat, and cover to keep warm. 4. Transfer the potatoes to a large serving bowl. Drizzle the tomato mixture over the potatoes. Sprinkle with the parsley. Serve with hot sauce, if using.

Per Serving:

calories: 173 | fat: 2g | protein: 4g | carbs: 35g | fiber: 3g | sodium: 251mg

Salted Almonds

Prep time: 5 minutes | Cook time: 25 minutes | Makes 1 cup

- ♦ 1 cup raw almonds
- ♦ 1 egg white, beaten
- ♦ ½ teaspoon coarse sea salt

1. Preheat oven to 350°F (180°C). 2. Spread the almonds in an even layer on a baking sheet. Bake for 20 minutes until lightly browned and fragrant. 3. Coat the almonds with the egg white and sprinkle with the salt. Put back in the oven for about 5 minutes until they have dried. Cool completely before serving.

Per Serving:

calories: 211 | fat: 18g | protein: 8g | carbs: 8g | fiber: 5g | sodium: 305mg

Burrata Caprese Stack

Prep time: 5 minutes | Cook time: 0 minutes | Serves 4

- ♦ 1 large organic tomato, preferably heirloom
- ♦ ½ teaspoon salt
- ♦ ¼ teaspoon freshly ground black pepper
- ♦ 1 (4 ounces / 113 g) ball burrata cheese
- ♦ 8 fresh basil leaves, thinly sliced
- ♦ 2 tablespoons extra-virgin olive oil
- ♦ 1 tablespoon red wine or balsamic vinegar

1. Slice the tomato into 4 thick slices, removing any tough center core and sprinkle with salt and pepper. Place the tomatoes, seasoned-side up, on a plate. 2. On a separate rimmed plate, slice the burrata into 4 thick slices and place one slice on top of each tomato slice. Top each with one-quarter of the basil and pour any reserved burrata cream from the rimmed plate over top. 3. Drizzle with olive oil and vinegar and serve with a fork and knife.

Per Serving:

calories: 109 | fat: 7g | protein: 9g | carbs: 3g | fiber: 1g | sodium: 504mg

Eggplant Fries

Prep time: 10 minutes | Cook time: 7 to 8 minutes per batch | Serves 4

- 1 medium eggplant
- 1 teaspoon ground coriander
- 1 teaspoon cumin
- 1 teaspoon garlic powder
- ½ teaspoon salt
- 1 cup crushed panko bread crumbs
- 1 large egg
- 2 tablespoons water
- Oil for misting or cooking spray

1. Peel and cut the eggplant into fat fries, ⅜- to ½-inch thick. 2. Preheat the air fryer to 390ºF (199ºC). 3. In a small cup, mix together the coriander, cumin, garlic, and salt. 4. Combine 1 teaspoon of the seasoning mix and panko crumbs in a shallow dish. 5. Place eggplant fries in a large bowl, sprinkle with remaining seasoning, and stir well to combine. 6. Beat eggs and water together and pour over eggplant fries. Stir to coat. 7. Remove eggplant from egg wash, shaking off excess, and roll in panko crumbs. 8. Spray with oil. 9. Place half of the fries in air fryer basket. You should have only a single layer, but it's fine if they overlap a little. 10. Cook for 5 minutes. Shake basket, mist lightly with oil, and cook 2 to 3 minutes longer, until browned and crispy. 11. Repeat step 10 to cook remaining eggplant.

Per Serving:

calories: 163 | fat: 3g | protein: 7g | carbs: 28g | fiber: 6g | sodium: 510mg

Fig-Pecan Energy Bites

Prep time: 20 minutes |Cook time: 0 minutes| Serves: 6

- ¾ cup diced dried figs (6 to 8)
- ½ cup chopped pecans
- ¼ cup rolled oats (old-fashioned or quick oats)
- 2 tablespoons ground flaxseed
- or wheat germ (flaxseed for gluten-free)
- 2 tablespoons powdered or regular peanut butter
- 2 tablespoons honey

1. In a medium bowl, mix together the figs, pecans, oats, flaxseed, and peanut butter. Drizzle with the honey, and mix everything together. A wooden spoon works well to press the figs and nuts into the honey and powdery ingredients. (If you're using regular peanut butter instead of powdered, the dough will be stickier to handle, so freeze the dough for 5 minutes before making the bites.) 2. Divide the dough evenly into four sections in the bowl. Dampen your hands with water—but don't get them too wet or the dough will stick to them. Using your hands, roll three bites out of each of the four sections of dough, making 12 total energy bites. 3. Enjoy immediately or chill in the freezer for 5 minutes to firm up the bites

before serving. The bites can be stored in a sealed container in the refrigerator for up to 1 week.

Per Serving:

calories: 196 | fat: 10g | protein: 4g | carbs: 26g | fiber: 4g | sodium: 13mg

Cheese-Stuffed Dates

Prep time: 10 minutes | Cook time: 10 minutes | Serves 4

- 2 ounces (57 g) low-fat cream cheese, at room temperature
- 2 tablespoons sweet pickle relish
- 1 tablespoon low-fat plain Greek yogurt
- 1 teaspoon finely chopped fresh chives
- ¼ teaspoon kosher salt
- ⅛ teaspoon ground black pepper
- Dash of hot sauce
- 2 tablespoons pistachios, chopped
- 8 Medjool dates, pitted and halved

1. In a small bowl, stir together the cream cheese, relish, yogurt, chives, salt, pepper, and hot sauce. 2. Put the pistachios on a clean plate. Put the cream cheese mixture into a resealable plastic bag, and snip off 1 corner of the bag. Pipe the cream cheese mixture into the date halves and press the tops into the pistachios to coat.

Per Serving:

calories: 196 | fat: 4g | protein: 3g | carbs: 41g | fiber: 4g | sodium: 294mg

Roasted Rosemary Olives

Prep time: 5 minutes | Cook time: 25 minutes | Serves 4

- 1 cup mixed variety olives, pitted and rinsed
- 2 tablespoons lemon juice
- 1 tablespoon extra-virgin
- olive oil
- 6 garlic cloves, peeled
- 4 rosemary sprigs

1. Preheat the oven to 400ºF (205ºC). Line the baking sheet with parchment paper or foil. 2. Combine the olives, lemon juice, olive oil, and garlic in a medium bowl and mix together. Spread in a single layer on the prepared baking sheet. Sprinkle on the rosemary. Roast for 25 minutes, tossing halfway through. 3. Remove the rosemary leaves from the stem and place in a serving bowl. Add the olives and mix before serving.

Per Serving:

calories: 100 | fat: 9g | protein: 0g | carbs: 4g | fiber: 0g | sodium: 260mg

Cream Cheese Wontons

Prep time: 15 minutes | Cook time: 6 minutes | Makes 20 wontons

- Oil, for spraying
- 20 wonton wrappers
- 4 ounces (113 g) cream cheese

1. Line the air fryer basket with parchment and spray lightly with oil. 2. Pour some water in a small bowl. 3. Lay out a wonton wrapper and place 1 teaspoon of cream cheese in the center. 4. Dip your finger in the water and moisten the edge of the wonton wrapper. Fold over the opposite corners to make a triangle and press the edges together. 5. Pinch the corners of the triangle together to form a classic wonton shape. Place the wonton in the prepared basket. Repeat with the remaining wrappers and cream cheese. You may need to work in batches, depending on the size of your air fryer. 6. Air fry at 400ºF (204ºC) for 6 minutes, or until golden brown around the edges.

Per Serving:

1 wonton: calories: 43 | fat: 2g | protein: 1g | carbs: 5g | fiber: 0g | sodium: 66mg

Baked Italian Spinach and Ricotta Balls

Prep time: 15 minutes | Cook time: 2 minutes | Serves 4

- 1½ tablespoons extra virgin olive oil
- 1 garlic clove
- 9 ounces (255 g) fresh baby leaf spinach, washed
- 3 spring onions (white parts only), thinly sliced
- 9 ounces (255 g) ricotta, drained
- 1¾ ounces (50 g) grated Parmesan cheese
- 2 tablespoons chopped fresh basil
- ¾ teaspoon salt, divided
- ¼ teaspoon plus a pinch of freshly ground black pepper, divided
- 4½ tablespoons plus ⅓ cup unseasoned breadcrumbs, divided
- 1 egg

1. Preheat the oven to 400°F (205ºC). Line a large baking pan with parchment paper. 2. Add the olive oil and garlic clove to a large pan over medium heat. When the oil begins to shimmer, add the spinach and sauté, tossing continuously, until the spinach starts to wilt, then add the spring onions. Continue tossing and sautéing until most of the liquid has evaporated, about 6 minutes, then transfer the spinach and onion mixture to a colander to drain and cool for 10 minutes. 3. When the spinach mixture has cooled, discard the garlic clove and squeeze the spinach to remove as much of the liquid as possible. Transfer the spinach mixture to a cutting board and finely chop. 4. Combine the ricotta, Parmesan, basil, ½ teaspoon of the salt, and ¼ teaspoon of the black pepper in a large bowl. Use a fork to mash the ingredients together, then add the spinach and continue mixing until the ingredients are combined. Add 4½ tablespoons of the breadcrumbs and mix until all ingredients are well combined. 5. In a small bowl, whisk the egg with the remaining ¼ teaspoon salt and a pinch of the black pepper. Place the remaining ⅓ cup of breadcrumbs on a small plate. Scoop out 1 tablespoon of the spinach mixture and roll it into a smooth ball, then dip it in the egg mixture and then roll it in the breadcrumbs. Place the ball on the prepared baking pan and continue the process with the remaining spinach mixture. 6. Bake for 16–20 minutes or until the balls turn a light golden brown. Remove the balls from the oven and serve promptly. Store covered in the refrigerator for up to 1 day. (Reheat before serving.)

Per Serving:

calories: 311 | fat: 19g | protein: 18g | carbs: 18g | fiber: 3g | sodium: 684mg

Sweet Potato Fries

Prep time: 15 minutes | Cook time: 40 minutes | Serves 4

- 4 large sweet potatoes, peeled and cut into finger-like strips
- 2 tablespoons extra-virgin
- olive oil
- ½ teaspoon salt
- ½ teaspoon freshly ground black pepper

1. Preheat the oven to 350°F (180ºC). Line a baking sheet with aluminum foil. Toss the potatoes in a large bowl with the olive oil, salt, and pepper. 2. Arrange the potatoes in a single layer on the baking sheet and bake until brown at the edges, about 40 minutes. Serve piping hot.

Per Serving:

calories: 171 | fat: 7g | protein: 2g | carbs: 26g | fiber: 4g | sodium: 362mg

Chapter 15 Staples, Sauces, Dips, and Dressings

Spicy Cucumber Dressing

Prep time: 5 minutes | Cook time: 0 minutes | Serves 2

- 1½ cups plain, unsweetened, full-fat Greek yogurt
- 1 cucumber, seeded and peeled
- ½ lemon, juiced and zested
- 1 tablespoon dried, minced garlic
- ½ tablespoon dried dill
- 2 teaspoons dried oregano
- Salt

1. In a food processor, combine the yogurt, cucumber, lemon juice, garlic, dill, oregano, and a pinch of salt and process until smooth. Adjust the seasonings as needed and transfer to a serving bowl.

Per Serving:

calories: 209 | fat: 10g | protein: 18g | carbs: 14g | fiber: 2g | sodium: 69mg

Basic Brown-Onion Masala

Prep time: 20 minutes | Cook time: 6½ hours | Makes 4 cups

- 2 tablespoons rapeseed oil
- 6 onions, finely diced
- 8 garlic cloves, finely chopped
- 1¾ pounds (794 g) canned plum tomatoes
- 3-inch piece fresh ginger, grated
- 1 teaspoon salt
- 1½ teaspoons turmeric
- Handful fresh coriander stalks, finely chopped
- 3 fresh green chiles, finely chopped
- 1 teaspoon chili powder
- 1 teaspoon ground cumin seeds
- 1 cup hot water
- 2 teaspoons garam masala

1. Preheat the slow cooker on high (or to the sauté setting, if you have it). Then add the oil and let it heat. Add the onions and cook for a few minutes until they start to brown. Make sure you brown the onions well so you get a deep, flavorsome base. 2. Add the garlic and continue to cook on high for about 10 minutes. 3. Add the tomatoes, ginger, salt, turmeric, coriander stalks, chopped chiles, chili powder, cumin seeds, and water. 4. Cover the slow cooker and cook on low for 6 hours. 5. Remove the lid and stir. Let the masala cook for another 30 minutes uncovered to reduce a little. 6. Add the garam masala after the masala has cooked. 7. Use right away, or freeze it in small tubs or freezer bags. Just defrost what you need, when you need it.

Per Serving:

calories: 286 | fat: 8g | protein: 7g | carbs: 52g | fiber: 8g | sodium: 656mg

Tabil (Tunisian Five-Spice Blend)

Prep time: 2 minutes | Cook time: 0 minutes | Makes 2 tablespoons

- 1 tablespoon ground coriander
- 1 teaspoon caraway seeds
- ¼ teaspoon garlic powder
- ¼ teaspoon cayenne pepper
- ¼ teaspoon ground cumin

1. Combine all the ingredients in a small bowl. 2. It may be stored in an airtight container for up to 2 weeks.

Per Serving:

calories: 13 | fat: 1g | protein: 1g | carbs: 2g | fiber: 1g | sodium: 2mg

Skinny Cider Dressing

Prep time: 5 minutes | Cook time: 0 minutes | Serves 2

- 2 tablespoons apple cider vinegar
- ⅓ lemon, juiced
- ⅓ lemon, zested
- Salt
- Freshly ground black pepper

1. In a jar, combine the vinegar, lemon juice, and zest. Season with salt and pepper, cover, and shake well.

Per Serving:

calories: 2 | fat: 0g | protein: 0g | carbs: 1g | fiber: 0g | sodium: 0mg

Tahini Sauce

Prep time: 5 minutes | Cook time: 0 minutes | Makes about 1 cup

- ½ cup tahini
- ½ cup water
- ¼ cup lemon juice (2 lemons)
- 2 garlic cloves, minced

1. Whisk all ingredients in bowl until smooth (mixture will appear broken at first). Season with salt and pepper to taste. Let sit at room temperature for at least 30 minutes to allow flavors to meld. (Sauce can be refrigerated for up to 4 days; bring to room temperature before serving.)

Per Serving:

¼ cup: calories: 184 | fat: 16g | protein: 5g | carbs: 8g | fiber: 3g | sodium: 36mg

Parsley-Mint Sauce

Prep time: 5 minutes | Cook time: 0 minutes | Serves 6

- ½ cup fresh flat-leaf parsley
- 1 cup fresh mint leaves
- 2 garlic cloves, minced
- 2 scallions (green onions), chopped
- 2 tablespoons pomegranate molasses
- ¼ cup olive oil
- 1 tablespoon fresh lemon juice

1. Combine all the ingredients in a blender and blend until smooth. Transfer to an airtight container and refrigerate until ready to use. Can be refrigerated for 1 day.

Per Serving:

calories: 90 | fat: 9g | protein: 1g | carbs: 2g | fiber: 0g | sodium: 5mg

Lemon Tahini Dressing

Prep time: 5 minutes | Cook time: 0 minutes | Makes ½ cup

- ¼ cup tahini
- 3 tablespoons lemon juice
- 3 tablespoons warm water
- ¼ teaspoon kosher salt
- ¼ teaspoon pure maple syrup
- ¼ teaspoon ground cumin
- ⅛ teaspoon cayenne pepper

1. In a medium bowl, whisk together the tahini, lemon juice, water, salt, maple syrup, cumin, and cayenne pepper until smooth. Place in the refrigerator until ready to serve. Store any leftovers in the refrigerator in an airtight container up to 5 days.

Per Serving:

2 tablespoons: calories: 90 | fat: 7g | protein: 3g | carbs: 5g | fiber: 1g | sodium: 80mg

Orange Dijon Dressing

Prep time: 5 minutes | Cook time: 0 minutes | Serves 2

- ¼ cup extra-virgin olive oil
- 2 tablespoons freshly squeezed orange juice
- 1 orange, zested
- 1 teaspoon garlic powder
- ¾ teaspoon za'atar seasoning
- ½ teaspoon salt
- ¼ teaspoon Dijon mustard
- Freshly ground black pepper, to taste

1. In a jar, combine the olive oil, orange juice and zest, garlic powder, za'atar, salt, and mustard. Season with pepper and shake vigorously until completely mixed.

Per Serving:

calories: 284 | fat: 27g | protein: 1g | carbs: 11g | fiber: 2g | sodium: 590mg

Red Pepper Hummus

Prep time: 5 minutes | Cook time: 30 minutes | Makes 2 cups

- 1 cup dried chickpeas
- 4 cups water
- 1 tablespoon plus ¼ cup extra-virgin olive oil, divided
- ½ cup chopped roasted red pepper, divided
- ⅓ cup tahini
- 1 teaspoon ground cumin
- ¾ teaspoon salt
- ½ teaspoon ground black pepper
- ¼ teaspoon smoked paprika
- ⅓ cup lemon juice
- ½ teaspoon minced garlic

1. Place chickpeas, water, and 1 tablespoon oil in the Instant Pot®. Close the lid, set steam release to Sealing, press the Manual button, and set time to 30 minutes. 2. When the timer beeps, quick-release the pressure until the float valve drops. Press the Cancel button and open lid. Drain, reserving the cooking liquid. 3. Place chickpeas, ⅓ cup roasted red pepper, remaining ¼ cup oil, tahini, cumin, salt, black pepper, paprika, lemon juice, and garlic in a food processor and process until creamy. If hummus is too thick, add reserved cooking liquid 1 tablespoon at a time until it reaches desired consistency. Serve at room temperature, garnished with reserved roasted red pepper on top.

Per Serving:

2 tablespoons: calories: 96 | fat: 8g | protein: 2g | carbs: 10g | fiber: 4g | sodium: 122mg

Riced Cauliflower

Prep time: 5 minutes | Cook time: 10 minutes | Serves 6 to 8

- 1 small head cauliflower, broken into florets
- ¼ cup extra-virgin olive oil
- 2 garlic cloves, finely minced
- 1½ teaspoons salt
- ½ teaspoon freshly ground black pepper

1. Place the florets in a food processor and pulse several times, until the cauliflower is the consistency of rice or couscous. 2. In a large skillet, heat the olive oil over medium-high heat. Add the cauliflower, garlic, salt, and pepper and sauté for 5 minutes, just to take the crunch out but not enough to let the cauliflower become soggy. 3. Remove the cauliflower from the skillet and place in a bowl until ready to use. Toss with chopped herbs and additional olive oil for a simple side, top with sautéed veggies and protein, or use in your favorite recipe.

Per Serving:

calories: 69 | fat: 7g | protein: 1g | carbs: 2g | fiber: 1g | sodium: 446mg

Kidney Bean Dip with Cilantro, Cumin, and Lime

Prep time: 10 minutes | Cook time: 30 minutes | Serves 16

- 1 cup dried kidney beans, soaked overnight and drained
- 4 cups water
- 3 cloves garlic, peeled and crushed
- ¼ cup roughly chopped
- cilantro, divided
- ¼ cup extra-virgin olive oil
- 1 tablespoon lime juice
- 2 teaspoons grated lime zest
- 1 teaspoon ground cumin
- ½ teaspoon salt

1. Place beans, water, garlic, and 2 tablespoons cilantro in the Instant Pot®. Close the lid, set steam release to Sealing, press the Bean button, and cook for the default time of 30 minutes. 2. When the timer beeps, let pressure release naturally, about 20 minutes. Press the Cancel button, open lid, and check that beans are tender. Drain off excess water and transfer beans to a medium bowl. Gently mash beans with potato masher or fork until beans are mashed but chunky. Add oil, lime juice, lime zest, cumin, salt, and remaining 2 tablespoons cilantro and stir to combine. Serve warm or at room temperature.

Per Serving:

calories: 65 | fat: 3g | protein: 2g | carbs: 7g | fiber: 2g | sodium: 75mg

Creamy Grapefruit-Tarragon Dressing

Prep time: 5 minutes | Cook time: 0 minutes | Serves 4to 6

- ½ cup avocado oil mayonnaise
- 2 tablespoons Dijon mustard
- 1 teaspoon dried tarragon or 1 tablespoon chopped fresh tarragon
- Zest and juice of ½ grapefruit
- (about 2 tablespoons juice)
- ½ teaspoon salt
- ¼ teaspoon freshly ground black pepper
- 1 to 2 tablespoons water (optional)

1. In a large mason jar or glass measuring cup, combine the mayonnaise, Dijon, tarragon, grapefruit zest and juice, salt, and pepper and whisk well with a fork until smooth and creamy. If a thinner dressing is preferred, thin out with water.

Per Serving:

calories: 49 | fat: 4g | protein: 0g | carbs: 4g | fiber: 0g | sodium: 272mg

Piri Piri Sauce

Prep time: 5 minutes | Cook time: 0 minutes | Makes about 1 cup

- 4 to 8 fresh hot, red chiles, stemmed and coarsely chopped
- 2 cloves garlic, minced
- Juice of 1 lemon
- Pinch of salt
- ½ to 1 cup olive oil

1. In a food processor, combine the chiles (with their seeds), garlic, lemon juice, salt, and ½ cup of olive oil. Process to a smooth purée. Add additional oil as needed to reach the desired consistency. 2. Pour the mixture into a glass jar or non-reactive bowl, cover, and refrigerate for at least 3 days before using. Store in the refrigerator for up to a month.

Per Serving:

calories:84 | fat: 10g | protein: 0g | carbs: 0g | fiber: 0g | sodium: 13mg

Sofrito

Prep time: 10 minutes | Cook time: 10 minutes | Serves 8 to 10

- 4 tablespoons olive oil
- 1 small onion, chopped
- 1 medium green bell pepper, seeded and chopped
- ¼ teaspoon salt
- 6 garlic cloves, minced
- ½ teaspoon red pepper flakes
- ¼ teaspoon freshly ground black pepper
- 1 cup finely chopped fresh cilantro
- 2 tablespoons red wine vinegar or sherry vinegar

1. In a 10-inch skillet, heat 2 tablespoons of the olive oil over medium-high heat. Add the onion, bell pepper, and salt. Cook, stirring occasionally, for 6 to 8 minutes, until softened. 2. Add the garlic, red pepper flakes, and black pepper; cook for 1 minute. 3. Transfer the vegetables to a blender or food processor and add the remaining 2 tablespoons olive oil, the cilantro, and the vinegar. Blend until smooth.

Per Serving:

calories: 63 | fat: 6g | protein: 0g | carbs: 2g | fiber: 0g | sodium: 67mg

Appendix 1:

MEASUREMENT CONVERSION CHART

VOLUME EQUIVALENTS(DRY)

US STANDARD	METRIC (APPROXIMATE)
1/8 teaspoon	0.5 mL
1/4 teaspoon	1 mL
1/2 teaspoon	2 mL
3/4 teaspoon	4 mL
1 teaspoon	5 mL
1 tablespoon	15 mL
1/4 cup	59 mL
1/2 cup	118 mL
3/4 cup	177 mL
1 cup	235 mL
2 cups	475 mL
3 cups	700 mL
4 cups	1 L

VOLUME EQUIVALENTS(LIQUID)

US STANDARD	US STANDARD (OUNCES)	METRIC (APPROXIMATE)
2 tablespoons	1 fl.oz.	30 mL
1/4 cup	2 fl.oz.	60 mL
1/2 cup	4 fl.oz.	120 mL
1 cup	8 fl.oz.	240 mL
1 1/2 cup	12 fl.oz.	355 mL
2 cups or 1 pint	16 fl.oz.	475 mL
4 cups or 1 quart	32 fl.oz.	1 L
1 gallon	128 fl.oz.	4 L

TEMPERATURES EQUIVALENTS

FAHRENHEIT(F)	CELSIUS(C) (APPROXIMATE)
225 °F	107 °C
250 °F	120 °C
275 °F	135 °C
300 °F	150 °C
325 °F	160 °C
350 °F	180 °C
375 °F	190 °C
400 °F	205 °C
425 °F	220 °C
450 °F	235 °C
475 °F	245 °C
500 °F	260 °C

WEIGHT EQUIVALENTS

US STANDARD	METRIC (APPROXIMATE)
1 ounce	28 g
2 ounces	57 g
5 ounces	142 g
10 ounces	284 g
15 ounces	425 g
16 ounces (1 pound)	455 g
1.5 pounds	680 g
2 pounds	907 g

Appendix 2:

The Dirty Dozen and Clean Fifteen

The Environmental Working Group (EWG) is a nonprofit, nonpartisan organization dedicated to protecting human health and the environment Its mission is to empower people to live healthier lives in a healthier environment. This organization publishes an annual list of the twelve kinds of produce, in sequence, that have the highest amount of pesticide residue-the Dirty Dozen-as well as a list of the fifteen kinds ofproduce that have the least amount of pesticide residue-the Clean Fifteen.

THE DIRTY DOZEN	THE CLEAN FIFTEEN
• The 2016 Dirty Dozen includes the following produce. These are considered among the year's most important produce to buy organic:	• The least critical to buy organically are the Clean Fifteen list. The following are on the 2016 list:

THE DIRTY DOZEN

Strawberries	Spinach
Apples	Tomatoes
Nectarines	Bell peppers
Peaches	Cherry tomatoes
Celery	Cucumbers
Grapes	Kale/collard greens
Cherries	Hot peppers

• *The Dirty Dozen list contains two additional items kale/collard greens and hot peppers-because they tend to contain trace levels of highly hazardous pesticides.*

THE CLEAN FIFTEEN

Avocados	Papayas
Corn	Kiw
Pineapples	Eggplant
Cabbage	Honeydew
Sweet peas	Grapefruit
Onions	Cantaloupe
Asparagus	Cauliflower
Mangos	

• *Some of the sweet corn sold in the United States are made from genetically engineered (GE) seedstock. Buy organic varieties of these crops to avoid GE produce.*

Appendix 3: Recipes Index

Made in the USA
Coppell, TX
25 November 2024

41050857R00059